# THE FIVE-HUNDRED-WORD THEME

**Lee J. Martin**

*Revised by*

**Harry P. Kroitor**
*Texas A&M University*

**Prentice-Hall, Inc., Englewood Cliffs, New Jersey**

605

*Library of Congress Cataloging in Publication Data*

MARTIN, LEE J.
    The five-hundred-word theme.

    1. English language—Rhetoric.   I. Kroitor,
Harry P., 1924–   II. Title.
PE1408.M3866   1974        808'.042        73-16481
ISBN 0–13–321505–9 (pbk.)

10 9 8 7 6 5 4 3


Printed in the United States of America

Prentice-Hall International, Inc., *London*
Prentice-Hall of Australia, Pty. Ltd., *Sydney*
Prentice-Hall of Canada, Ltd., *Toronto*
Prentice-Hall of India Private Limited, *New Delhi*
Prentice-Hall of Japan, Inc., *Tokyo*

# Contents

# Preface

This book offers the freshman composition student the basic knowledge necessary to write a short theme of the type most often required in beginning composition courses. I have made two assumptions: that most students will profit little in college by further formal study of "mechanics" of the language, and that students need above all an orderly approach to the problem of organizing and writing a short paper that makes a logical point and supports it. Such an orderly approach is the subject of this book. The student is not burdened with the trivia of mechanics.

I have used the five-hundred-word theme because in this length a student can best learn and practice basic principles that apply to all writing. *Never do I intend to imply, however, that themes assigned should be exactly five hundred words.* I do intend that they should be close to this length. A shorter paper gives the student little opportunity to develop his subject; a longer one becomes burdensome for both student and teacher without offering any particular advantage to the beginning writer.

I have stressed organization. Indeed, the diagrams in the book present a pattern for organizing the short theme—a pattern for the beginning student to follow one step at a time until he has learned and practiced the basic principles of composition. I have purposely forced the student into a mold to minimize the mysteries of writing expository prose and to teach him to support his ideas as logically as possible. *I would not expect him to stay in the mold after his first semester of college composition, but I would expect him to apply the principles taught here to all his writing.*

I am deeply indebted to my wife Harriet, who supplied a number of the exercises and offered invaluable editorial help. My thanks also go to Sterling Swift, Jim Campbell, and Paul O'Connell of Prentice-Hall; and to Professor Gary Tate, The University of Tulsa; Professor Donald J. Tighe, St. Petersburg Junior College; and Professor John R. Willingham, The University of Kansas, who read the manuscript and offered helpful criticism.

The student essays included for analysis were contributed by former students of mine. I express my appreciation to Maxine Batts, Eleanor Bostick, Gerald Ellison, Jerry Griffiths, Dorthea Robinson, William Swindle, Doris Thompson, Carey Lee White, and Louise Ward.

L. J. M.

# Preface to
# the Revised Edition

## To the Student

Everyone needs practice in writing papers that make one logical point clearly and support it adequately. Everyone, even professionals writing for money. By stressing a preplanned picture-outline, this book presents one way to tackle this problem successfully. Throughout, the revised edition reminds you that the basic pattern it describes is a highly successful way to *begin*, that writing according to a clear plan doesn't necessarily destroy creativity, and that writing involves both organized thought and a specific attitude. It also reminds you that there are other ways to write papers and that you should eventually try to build beyond basic patterns. But if your papers seem to be ineffective even if you follow the pattern closely, it may be because you haven't assumed a definite attitude—toward your subject, toward your reader. In fact, many of us never think of the audience we are writing for, and the result is a kind of "writing in a vacuum" that keeps us from sounding like human beings. Your writing should take on strength and life if you practice the two basic skills this book emphasizes—clearly explaining a main point with supporting evidence, and honestly projecting a convincing attitude with self-confidence. The first part of this book (Focus, Discovery, Organization) stresses primarily the first skill; the second part (Revision and Style) shows you that there's more to writing than merely following a formula.

## To the Teacher

This book presents a method, not a theory. Without any major changes in approach or method, the revision emphasizes and expands some of the material often overlooked in the first edition. The method is a starting point, not a rigid pattern to be followed slavishly or indefinitely; the definition of exposition used includes writing with an argumentative bias; writing with conviction means honestly convincing yourself first and extending this tone of conviction to include a specific audience. The result is, I think, a book with greater flexibility and greater rhetorical depth, *without* any loss in instructional value to the student.

Still aimed at the freshman composition student, the book gives him explicit thinking and writing instructions to follow. Its assumptions and methods are basically those of rhetoric as it has been known for over two thousand years: Discovery and invention, arrangement and organization, and, through revision, an introduction to some of the problems of tone and style.

I am pleased to have this opportunity to continue work begun with Dr. Martin some years ago and to reaffirm my confidence in a book whose conciseness, directness, and clarity have won for it the support and respect of hard-working teachers at many schools.

H. P. K.
1973

# FOCUS, DISCOVERY, ORGANIZATION

**one**

# 1

# Seeing
# the Whole Paper

## Introduction

Like most skills, writing can be taught in principle and improved by practice. The first part of this book (Focus, Discovery, Organization) teaches you the basic principles you need to write a simple five-hundred-word paper—principles involved in any kind of writing—and you can practice these principles when you do the exercises in each chapter. It introduces the parts of the five-hundred-word paper one at a time and lets you practice each before going to the next. It also shows you how to put these parts together as a whole paper focused on a single point. The second part (Revision and Style) provides practical guides to revision, including some ways to make your paper more convincing, since successful communication requires not only the controlled presentation of ideas but the projection of attitudes as well.

### What Learning to Write Better Can Do for You

The most obvious advantage of improving your writing is that you can put your ideas into an understandable and valid form. Many students have good ideas, but they don't know how to express them, either in writing or speaking. Composing a paper is one way you can learn to state your ideas specifically and to show the evidence you have to support those ideas. Unless you write down the ideas, however, they are likely to remain half-formed, and when you try to express them, you may find you are not successful in communicating exactly what you mean. Suppose, for example, that your best friend has decided to run for a class office and you think he or she would make an outstanding class officer. Suppose that he asks you, as his close friend, to present these qualities to the student body by writing a letter to the college newspaper. How would you go about explaining these qualities so that the readers of the newspaper would believe in your friend as you do? Practicing the techniques of expository writing as we shall define it will make it much easier for you to express and support your ideas clearly and concisely in any situation. And by carefully revising your diction and sentence structure to fit the attitude you have in mind, you will add strength and conviction to your paper.

Having communication skills at your command will help you gain confidence in your own ability to function as an individual—a person who can carry his own weight in any social or business situation. Suppose, again, you have decided to try to get a job next summer in one of the national parks or in a summer camp as a counselor. You would have to write a letter outlining all your qualifications for this job, and you would have to sell yourself to the person doing the hiring. You would actually be doing two things: (1) *Describing your qualifications with supporting evidence,* and (2) *projecting a convincing attitude of self-confidence.* To do those things well on paper you must be confident of your presentation of yourself to your prospective employer. Similarly, in your school work a knowledge of the techniques of expository writing will greatly increase your chances for a better grade in any writing course. Writing an essay examination or a paper requires more than a clear grasp of the facts; it also requires an organization of those facts and an application of the techniques of revision that strengthen your presentation and make it convincing. The more effectively you present your ideas and the knowledge you have, the more your writing will improve and the better your grade will be on that piece of writing.

Perhaps most important to you, however, as a citizen of our democracy, is the ability to write logically and to recognize logical thought when you read or hear it. The techniques of expository writing require you to use all the evidence you can collect to support the ideas you want your reader to understand or accept. As you collect evidence, you should be able to judge the logic of your ideas. If the evidence disproves your ideas, then you should discard or alter them. But if your evidence shows that you are probably right, you are then justified in presenting and supporting your ideas in your paper. Knowing this, you should also become more cautious about accepting generalizations *others* make, unless they support them with valid evidence. This cautious approach to ideas is necessary for the survival of democracy as we know it: For no one person or group can lead an entire nation down an undesired or wrong path as long as people demand proof in support of ideas. Open debate, the critical examination of ideas and their proof, has always been fundamental to the growth of our country, as the Vietnam war and antipollution battles have recently demonstrated.

### What You Must Bring to Writing

But good writing isn't easy; it demands patience and discipline. Don't expect to sit down and produce a successful paper in the time it takes you to write down five hundred words. Maybe a few experienced writers can do this, for their very experience enables them to choose the proper word and to frame sentences exactly; but even established writers find writing hard work and know the value of revision. Beginning writers should realize that if they are to produce work that they can be proud of and that will communicate their intentions precisely, they must work hard and revise thoroughly. Good writing also requires self-discipline. You must learn to write paragraphs that convey your intention and that are unified and coherent. You'll need to learn economy and effectiveness in wording and, most important, how to stick to a single, limited subject so that you finish the paper with a definite, preplanned point that you have developed and supported. Before you write the first word, you must discipline yourself to think through your subject thoroughly and to decide on a definite attitude toward that subject. And even though the act of writing itself will generate new ideas as your paper grows—ideas you will want to add if they fit your purposes— your starting point will be those ideas you discover before you begin writing.

The thought you bring to writing is most important; without it you cannot write at all, for writing *is* the communication of thought. You must think through your subject *before* you start to write, selecting or rejecting ideas that occur to you. And you must write logically. For instance, you may have to discard some of your prejudices—those ideas and opinions you hold without logic and evidence to back them up—because they are based in emotion rather than in fact. Have you, for example, ever really examined the *facts* about your college, town, or state, and compared them to the facts about other schools, towns, or states in order to develop a mature attitude toward "home"? Or do you automatically defend your views emotionally without looking at the facts? Although everyone thinks emotionally at times, the emotional has only a limited place in most writing. You must have an open and inquiring mind, as free from prejudice and unsupported opinion as you can make it, so that you can accept fact where you find it and can develop the habit of using only fact to support generalizations.

What you must bring to writing, then, is the desire to become educated. You must want to develop the ability to face fact without coloring or slanting it to fit a set of prejudices, to communicate soundly supported ideas to others either in speech or writing, to lose any narrow provincialism, and to consider *all* ideas, particularly those that go beyond restricted interests. This ability will help you become mature and objective; learning the techniques of effective communication in writing will hasten the process.

### What You Are Expected to Do

Since this book is about expository writing, we should define it. *Exposition* is one of the four principal types of prose, the other three being *argumentation, description,* and *narration.* Expository writing is the simple explanation of an idea, an object, or a process. For example, if you want to establish the idea that the organization of political clubs on your campus would in some ways benefit the students, you would be writing *exposition;* that is, you would be explaining and supporting an idea. Or if you want to explain some of the difficulties involved in following a road map or making a cake or rebuilding a motor, again you would be using *exposition.* The basic aim of exposition is to get your reader to say, "I understand." If, however, you try to *prove* that political clubs should be outlawed on your campus, you would be using *argumentation.* The basic aim of argumentation is to take the reader beyond understanding, to get him to say, "I agree," or "I will act." If you want to describe how something looks, feels, tastes, smells, or what it sounds like, you would be using *description;* you would be concerned with selective, ordered observation. And if you want to give an account of an event or how something happened, you would be using *narration* and would be concerned mostly with the actions of people. You would be telling a story. You could, of course, also narrate the actions of animals or of the forces of nature—tornadoes or thunderstorms, for example. In ordinary writing these four types are not always used separately; two or more of the types are often combined in a single paper. Argumentation is often used to reenforce exposition; or description may be blended with narration. Any writing—no matter what combination of types is used—that has as its *primary* purpose *to make a subject clear*, to get the reader to say "I understand," we will consider expository writing.

For the purposes of this book, your writing will consist chiefly of papers of approximately five hundred words and, in addition, single paragraphs of more than one hundred words. You need to write single paragraphs to practice the discipline and skill of using the various means of developing paragraphs clearly. They should not be written as ends in themselves but as parts of clearly organized and well-developed papers. If you follow the principles set down in this book, carefully examining the illustrations and the exercises, you should be able to compose a clearly organized and well-developed paper of five hundred words. And because the principles of good expository writing apply to any writing situation, whether it is a scientific report or a letter to a friend, these principles will help you in all that you write.

## Organizing the Paper

Assuming you have discovered that you have something to say, you cannot begin to write it down effectively until you have a fairly specific idea of the product you are supposed to create. Your product, a five-hundred-word paper, can be schematically diagrammed to show it as a whole and to indicate the relationship of each part of the paper to the other parts. Such a diagram follows; look at it closely. Each block in the diagram represents one paragraph of the paper, which to begin with will be arbitrarily limited to four very functional paragraphs.

The first block shows the *introductory paragraph*. The line across the bottom is used to suggest that the final sentence of the paragraph is the *thesis statement* of your paper, the one main point that you will develop and support. This end-position for the thesis statement is quite arbitrary, since you can place it at the end of the whole paper. Or you may omit the statement entirely; you can imply it in a way that makes the reader determine for himself the logical point the evidence supports. For the first papers you write, however, put the thesis statement at the end of the introductory paragraph and save more difficult types of organization until you become more experienced. This end-position for the thesis in the introductory paragraph has several advantages: It lets you use the first sentences of the paragraph to set the general tone

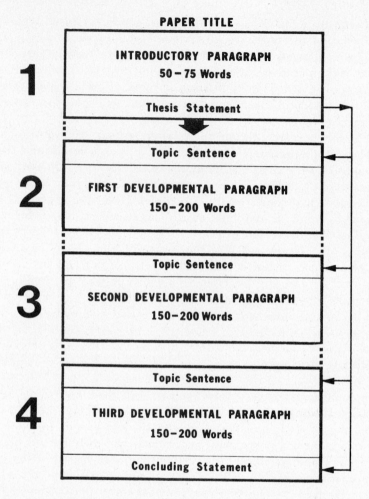

**PAPER TITLE**

**1**

**INTRODUCTORY PARAGRAPH**
50 – 75 Words

**Thesis Statement**

**2**

**Topic Sentence**

**FIRST DEVELOPMENTAL PARAGRAPH**
150 – 200 Words

**3**

**Topic Sentence**

**SECOND DEVELOPMENTAL PARAGRAPH**
150 – 200 Words

**4**

**Topic Sentence**

**THIRD DEVELOPMENTAL PARAGRAPH**
150 – 200 Words

**Concluding Statement**

of communication between your reader and yourself, to establish a kind of common ground; it does not give you a chance to confuse or mislead your reader with information placed between a first-sentence thesis statement and the first paragraph of the body; and it facilitates coherence because it positions the thesis close to the body of the paper, creating a link with the topic sentence of the first developmental paragraph.

The relation of the thesis statement to the rest of the paper influences the organization of the paper. If, for example, you withhold the thesis statement until you reach the end of the paper, you would be presenting details or *particulars* first, building toward the *general* idea represented by the thesis at the end of the paper. This technique of presenting facts or evidence first, of reasoning from individual instances to a general or universal statement, is the *inductive* method. It makes the introductory paragraph almost unnecessary or forces it to serve only the more traditional purposes of getting the reader's attention and establishing tone or common ground. However, if you give the thesis statement in the introductory paragraph at the beginning of the paper, as recommended for your first attempts, and then follow it with supporting evidence, you will be reasoning from a *general* statement to *particulars* that explain or illustrate it. In some ways similar to a *deductive* method of reasoning, it is this technique that you should begin with. Once you become more skilled and creative, you can try the inductive method and other ways of organizing your ideas. Careful analysis of professional writing will show you that the method presented here of handling the thesis statement in the introductory paragraph is only one of many.

You will learn more about the introductory paragraph later. Right now you need to consider one more function this paragraph can have: It can serve as a kind of "map" or "blueprint" for the rest of the paper by suggesting the order of presentation for the ideas in the rest of the paper. This order may be suggested by the thesis sentence itself, or it may be implied elsewhere in the introductory paragraph. Either way the "blueprint" can be a valuable guide to the reader as he moves through the developmental paragraphs that follow. Your first paragraph, therefore, is very important: It contains a thesis statement, it establishes tone and common ground, and it can provide a "blueprint" for the following ideas.

In the block representing the paper's second paragraph and labeled First Developmental Paragraph, the first sentence is the *topic sentence*. Again, this position is arbitrary. The topic sentence can come in the middle or at the end of the paragraph, or it can be implied. But for the first few papers you write, place all topic sentences, specifically stated, at the beginning of developmental paragraphs. The topic sentence is to the paragraph what the thesis statement is to the whole paper, that is, it is the one point the paragraph makes. But it is even more closely related to the thesis statement; it is one reason the thesis statement is valid. The remainder of the paragraph, about 150 to 200 words, is evidence presented to establish the soundness of the topic sentence. So when this paragraph is written, there will be one tightly reasoned unit supporting the main point of the paper. In the first papers you write, you will include two more such units; however, there's no reason why a paper shouldn't have more than three developmental paragraphs, or only two.

The topic sentence in the Second Developmental Paragraph is the second "proof" of the thesis and the material presented in the paragraph supports this second topic sentence. When you have completed this paragraph, support of the thesis statement becomes much stronger. You have given two reasons to show that the thesis statement is valid, and you have supported each of those reasons with logical evidence.

The final paragraph, the Third Developmental Paragraph, should be the strongest in support of the thesis statement. Make the most important reason—the one you think will clinch the point—the topic sentence of this paragraph. Give it strong support in the remainder of the paragraph, and you will leave the reader with the understanding you want him to have. Once you have him at this point, hit him with the concluding statement as the last sentence in the whole paper. The *concluding statement* simply restates the thesis statement so that you finish by reminding the reader that this is the point you have made in the paper. It is better not to make the point in the exact words used at the beginning of the paper, so change the wording enough to serve as an "echo," to have a greater effect on the reader as it concludes your strongest paragraph.

Don't tell the reader you are ending your paper. Such statements as "In conclusion it can be seen that . . ." or "To sum up . . ." are trite and unnecessary. Neither is a formal concluding paragraph necessary. In a much longer paper, summing up is often desirable; but in a five-hundred-word paper, the concluding statement does the necessary summing up, and you and the reader are spared the tediousness and triteness of a bloated concluding paragraph that adds nothing to the paper.

This basic diagram is a kind of picture-outline, and it represents only *one* convenient pattern for writing a five-hundred-word paper. But it is just that—a formula, a recipe. If your subject requires variation, then alter the formula; add or delete a paragraph. You will know how because you will have learned the basic pattern and will be able to see the whole paper. But until you do learn the basic pattern, follow the diagram we have just examined.

The writer of the paper, "Dogs on the Loose," followed the basic diagram exactly, without dullness and without letting the "formula" shout too loudly at the reader. To help you follow the pattern, the thesis statement, topic sentences, and concluding statement are italicized.

### Dogs on the Loose

If you are a dog lover don't read this. Tend to your dogs instead: Train them, restrain them, kennel them. But don't let them run loose in my neighborhood or backyard—unless you don't mind a beaten dog with fear in his heart and a permanent whimper in his voice. Not that I dislike dogs. Not at all. Any of my friends will tell you that I have been known to pat even big dogs quite affectionately and pet puppies of all kinds. What I dislike is what unleashed dogs do. Their habit of marking their romping trails and leaving a mess for bare feet on a lawn is bad enough. Even worse, they can be a menace. For *dogs on the loose are a serious nuisance* because they terrorize people, create traffic hazards, and damage gardens.

Although barking dogs may not bite, *they can scare you half to death.* I don't know which is worse, the little yappers or the big barkers. If you're riding a bicycle the yappers are mostly a nuisance, though they are threatening enough to force you to zig-zag dangerously on the street. It is a brave cyclist who can ignore the barker whose flashing teeth are nipping at the handle bars. I have seen school children panic on their bicycles when a barker leaps out at them, forcing them to turn wildly to avoid the beast and sometimes even causing a youngster to fall onto the road. Or suppose you are walking at night and one of the yappers rushes out, snapping and snarling only inches away from your heels. I tend to freeze in my steps, cuss quite a bit, and wish I had a big stick. I don't think I'd actually beat the creature, but I sure would like to.

Both *yappers and barkers are traffic hazards* because motorists and cyclists and pedestrians, conditioned by dog-lovers to think of these brutes as people, automatically react to protect them. Just watch a jaywalking dog saunter across a busy highway in some suburban town. Cars swerve, brakes screech, accidents occur. The unsuspecting driver thinks the dog is patiently waiting for a break in the traffic, or for a light to turn green, perhaps. Then without warning man's best friend heads across. The sickening thud of flesh against metal is a sound that will haunt any driver for weeks—if he escapes traffic in the adjoining lane as he tries unthinkingly to avoid the dog. Equally hazardous are those dogs that dart onto the road they think they own, barking at everything rolling by. Once a little yapper so worried me that I ran my bicycle into a parked car. Throw together one dog, two cyclists, and several cars and the results can be treacherous. Or watch a young pedestrian trying to coax his reluctant mutt across a car-filled street. Frightening. And dangerous.

If you are a gardener then you probably react as I do after *some night-marauding barker with size thirteen feet has stomped through your flower bed or tomato patch.* The first time I saw a three-inch-deep depression in the soft soil I reached for my shotgun, certain some wild beast had chosen my yard for a den. Just as irritating is the systematic territory marker who has chosen a corner of the front hedge and the base of the yard lamp as routine targets—with Master only feet away, half-sharply calling, "No, no Spot! You mustn't!" But what really makes me irate is when I'm crossing the lawn barefooted on a Sunday morning to get the newspaper and I step into some marker's calling card. I don't think I'd actually shoot the nuisance if I caught him, but I'm sure I would like to. *Yappers, barkers, markers are fine as puppies, or firmly on a leash, or in a kennel; on the loose they're definitely a menace.*

Note that this paper makes just one main point, dogs on the loose are a serious nuisance, stated at the end of the introductory paragraph and followed by a kind of "blueprint" of supporting reasons. These reasons are then presented in the order mentioned in the introduction, one in each topic sentence, to convince the reader of the validity of the main point. The first topic sentence, italicized in the second paragraph, makes the point that dogs on the loose are a nuisance because they can scare a person half to death. The remainder of the paragraph establishes this topic sentence as valid by suggesting some serious consequences of being scared. It mentions that cyclists are forced to zig-zag on the road, that school children panic and turn wildly, and that a person walking at night will freeze in his steps. The second topic sentence, italicized in the third paragraph, directly states that barking dogs on the loose are traffic hazards. To support this statement the writer says that people automatically protect dogs by swerving to miss them, which can be dangerous; to avoid dogs cyclists may run into things; and on busy streets youngsters trying to get their dogs across become a frightening hazard. The third topic sentence, italicized at the beginning of the fourth paragraph, presents the writer's strongest feelings—that dogs damage gardens, destroying flowers and vegetables by making deep depressions in the soil, marring hedges and yard objects by spotting them, and messing on lawns. This paragraph is the most personal and probably the most emotional one in the theme, suggesting that the writer's chief gripe is a personal one. The concluding statement, italicized at the end of the fourth paragraph, restates the thesis statement and echoes the paper's title.

Although this paper could be strengthened in many ways, the writer has made his point and supported it with evidence based on his own experience and observation. One criticism that could be made of this paper is that it overuses "I" in attempting to sound personal and to keep the reader interested. But even very serious papers sometimes use "I," as you can see immediately if you check the introductory paragraphs on pages 78, 80, 159-60. However, your instructor may ask you to avoid using "I" in your first papers (it's not easy to do well). This doesn't mean you have to be impersonal and dull, as the freshman introductory paragraph on page 157 shows. A more straightforward approach that boldly asserts the subject (without using "I") can be seen in the more formal introductory paragraphs on pages 77,

79, and 160. There are additional examples of papers that present their subject directly without using "I" in the exercises at the end of this chapter.

The organization of the five-hundred-word paper can be shown in another type of diagram. This one inserts the supporting points for each topic sentence. The result is a picture-outline that clearly shows the paper's main points and their relation to each other and to the support given for each point. It is a diagram that can be used to test the validity of either a preliminary outline or a first draft of a paper.

**PAPER TITLE: DOGS ON THE LOOSE**

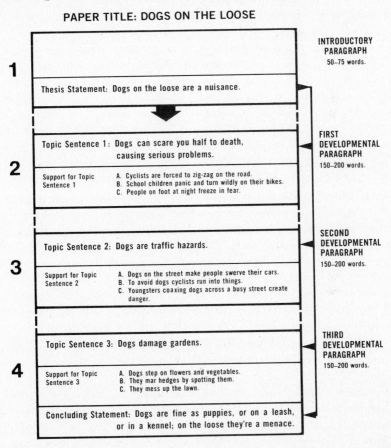

With this framework of thesis statement, three reasons to uphold the thesis statement, support for the reasons, and a concluding statement, you could have written the five-hundred-word paper on the nuisances of dogs on the loose. Now study the paper below and decide whether it is better than the one about dogs.

### The Practical College Marriage

Two really can live as cheaply as one, but as any struggling coed and her haunted husband can testify, those two had better prepare for a painful existence, but *practical*. The money that the folks were glad to send their young one must now serve two. The lessons this pair learns are the most practical in the world, though. They know before the honeymoon is over that, although they'll cry a lot, they'll learn to slice their output and savor their income. They learn to be practical about entertainment, about the care and mending of garments, and about the nourishing qualities of peanut butter.

Entertainment is not what it used to be. In the old days, Mary took for granted two or three movies a week and dancing at least on Saturday night. Mom and Dad didn't mind paying that little bit, as long as their college daughter kept up her grades. Now in their room-with-kitchen-privileges apartment Mary and Jim get along fine—but movies are out, and they wouldn't dream of trying to squeeze a dancing cover charge out of what little Dad sends and they can earn. For entertainment, Jim can help with the dishes, and they can walk together, hand in hand, to the library for a blissful evening of research. It's a terribly *practical* pursuit, actually.

The clothing situation gets serious. Neither Mary nor her Jim would dare gain weight, even if their home-cooked meals were that tempting. They dressed well in their single days, and they still do, but alas, in the very same garments that looked so much better last semester. Shoes get resoled now, instead of replaced, and the shine on Jim's "good" suit is more noticeable. It isn't as though he had to keep up with his fraternity brothers any longer. Camaraderie with that carefree group is nice to remember, but meeting with the boys is no longer practical. Mary watches fashions, but she does not buy the fads. She found out in a hurry that it is not the *practical* way to dress.

Their menu does not vary much, and there is no longer the balanced touch of the dormitory dietician. They watch out for yellow and green vegetables, of course, and a potato a day with some kind of protein. But the old zip is gone, and with it went between-class cokes and Sunday at the Garden Steakhouse with the rest of the English majors. They are grateful, naturally, to the famous scientist who developed peanut butter. Even if it does stick to the palate and begin to grow old too soon, Mary and Jim buy more peanut butter, because it's very *practical*. But when it's all over and the children are grown, Jim and Mary will look back on these days as some of the best in their lives, because look at the great lessons they learned.

Compare this paper with the diagram for the five-hundred-word paper, and you will see that this paper follows the diagram exactly but is not a slavish, mechanical, line-by-line copy of it. *Nor should it be. Translating the basic diagram into a paper truly your own requires decisions in tone, in diction, in sentence structure, in organization of ideas.* Note how this writer establishes a friendly, informal tone in the first few sentences by choosing words to fit his friendly attitude: *really, coed, haunted, folks,* and *they'll* are good examples. This writer, however, decides not to use "I," creating a somewhat less personal tone than that created by the writer of the paper on dogs. You don't have to write a stiff, formal paper just because you are following a preplanned picture-outline. A little creative thinking will help you write a fresh, personal paper. Eventually you'll want to experiment with patterns of organization quite unlike the basic diagram you are studying here and with papers considerably longer than five hundred words.

## EXERCISES

I. Analyze the following papers for organization. Answer the questions at the end of each paper to aid your analysis.

### A. Misplaced Goals in Education Stifle the Inquiring Mind

1. Lack of encouragement of creativity in the present school system discourages a real search for knowledge. Importance continually placed on following a certain form has given the student a misplaced set of values.

2. Even though following directions is important, too often a pupil is graded solely on how well he does this. In spite of his original thought, his grade may be low because he left too small a margin, he wrote on the bottom line, or he numbered the pages in the wrong corner. Following a rigid form of Roman numerals, the student loses sight of the content of the material. If he has researched the subject, he might lose all credit because he has not tagged his sources properly. Emphasis should be placed on the thought shown in his work rather than on rigid adherence to a given form.

3. Thinking things through for himself, the student might come up with an idea other than his professor's. Grade school and high school have taught him that this is not advisable. The student who can most nearly duplicate the teacher's instruction is regarded most highly. If the teacher will "lay it on the line," then it can be easily duplicated. Such narrow goals restrict the student, making him conform to the ideas already set out for him. Stepping outside the expected way of working a problem, finding a different meaning to a passage in literature, or bringing some original idea to class is penalized.

4. Memorization of details clutters the mind with facts that are never assimilated. World geography consists of a detailed compilation of

isolated facts on individual countries. "How many square miles is Uruguay?" and "What is its population?" are asked rather than "How has its location in South America affected its economic growth?" The value of associating the past with the future is lost in history classes where twenty dates are given—the student is asked to write who was president and vice-president.

5. With elementary and secondary education goals set on teaching students to follow strict forms or to reproduce an instructor's or text's words and memorize details without connecting them, it is easily understandable that students today apparently lack an inquiring mind. Any deviation from the usual they wish to do must be done outside their classwork.

6. To encourage original thought educational goals must be realigned. Importance must be placed on the entire content of the material and its broad implications. Reslanting history to increase the value, using geography in studies of modern economics and politics, looking into physics proofs rather than just formulas will help stimulate thought. A broadening of teachers' views will broaden the scope and responsibility of the student. More scholastic freedom and more creative goals will reawaken the inquiring mind.

## QUESTIONS FOR ANALYSIS OF PAPER *A*

This exercise answers its own questions so that you can understand what you are expected to do in analyzing the organization of the paragraphs.

1. What is the thesis statement of Paper *A?*

Answer: The thesis statement is the first sentence: *Lack of encouragement of creativity in the present school system discourages a real search for knowledge.*

2. How does the second paragraph support this thesis statement?

Answer: It gives and supports one reason for the validity of the thesis statement. It makes the point that the student is frequently graded on how well he follows form rather than on how deeply he thinks.

3. What is the function of the second sentence in the introductory paragraph?

Answer: This sentence does not belong in the introductory paragraph. It should be the first sentence of the second paragraph, because it is really the topic sentence of that paragraph. All the second paragraph is a discussion of the subject given in the second sentence of the introductory paragraph. Nowhere else in the paper is *following a certain form* discussed. The introductory paragraph should be revised so that it is a paragraph of about fifty to seventy-five words and not just a single sentence. The thesis statement should come at the end of the revised introductory paragraph.

4. How does the third paragraph support the thesis statement?

Answer: It gives and supports a second reason for the validity of the thesis statement. It makes the point that too frequently the student is rewarded for simply parroting the teacher's ideas and is penalized if he puts forward the result of his own thinking.

5. Which sentence is the topic sentence of the third paragraph?

Answer: The last sentence in the paragraph is the topic sentence. It would be better placed as the first sentence.

6. a. Which sentence is the topic sentence of the fourth paragraph?

   b. What is the function of this paragraph in the paper?

Answer: a: The first sentence in the fourth paragraph is the topic sentence.

   b. The fourth paragraph gives and supports a third reason for the validity of the thesis statement. It deplores the emphasis on insignificant details.

7. What is the function of the fifth paragraph?

Answer: The fifth paragraph sums up the points that have been made in support of the thesis statement. The paper would be more effectively organized if most of the material in the fifth paragraph were part of the revised introductory paragraph and if a concluding statement were placed at the end of the fourth paragraph. (This weakness in organization, especially demonstrated by the inadequacy of the introductory paragraph, is probably caused by the writer's failure to think through his subject before starting to write. He probably devised his support for the thesis statement as he wrote from paragraph to paragraph. Then when he got to the end he could see what his support was and summed it up there. It takes a skillful student to succeed at the organize-as-you-write plan. This student was not quite skillful enough.)

8. Does the sixth paragraph support the thesis statement? Does it belong in the paper? Why or why not?

Answer: The sixth paragraph does not support the thesis statement because it does not give and support a reason for the validity of the thesis. In fact, this paragraph does not belong in the paper because it introduces a second subject by attempting to explain what should be done about the situation. The subject of this paragraph could be explored and supported in another paper, not here.

9. Where should this paper end?

Answer: The paper should end with the fourth paragraph.

### B. Educators That Discourage Thinking

1. There is no doubt that today's public school student is lacking in creative thinking. He finds it far less trouble to develop a sort of mnemonic memorizing mind that follows but never leads. Therefore, most students prefer to memorize and leave tiresome thinking for later.

2. Classroom discussion is different. There students are often willing to shine forth orally, but never, never in writing. They would rather be asked to respond with a *T* for True and *F* for False on a simple and clear-

cut objective exam than be asked to think an issue through and discuss it in writing.

3. Students are inclined to drag their feet when it comes to showing their teacher, via clear and thorough essay-type discussions, that they have a full understanding of course content. But this is hardly the fault of the student, at least not in the high school that I attended. In fact, from the elementary level up to Grade 12, we were trained to memorize, and we soon learned that perfecting the practice of spouting out the outlined truths, with no time out for understanding and tying together of isolated facts, was the way to the best grades. We worked out the formula for success and we learned to like it, in the way any child learns to adapt to the security of a system.

4. If the nation is to continue to survive and even to progress, then such trends as this must be halted. Such lazy testing is developed for lazy grading, and the obvious answer is that teachers must begin to care enough to improve their methods. Teachers must be taught before they can teach; otherwise, the inquiring minds of our potential leaders will never be freed from the regimented, "fill-in-the-blank" type of nonthinking. It could even be that there is more truth in the ancient admonition: If you can't do it, teach it; if you can't teach it, teach others to teach it.

## QUESTIONS FOR ANALYSIS OF PAPER *B*

1. The thesis statement of this paper is the last sentence of the first paragraph: *Most students prefer to . . . leave tiresome thinking for later.* The writer makes only one point in the remainder of the paper to support this thesis. What is it?

2. The second paragraph consists of only two sentences and does not give or support an idea. Could these two sentences be integrated into any other paragraph in the paper? If so, which one? If not, why not?

3. The third paragraph is the only one that can be called a developmental paragraph. What topic sentence does it develop?

4. What is the purpose of the fourth paragraph? Does it contain material that might be used in the third paragraph? Is there another subject here that might be used as a topic sentence in support of the thesis statement? What is it?

5. Since the paper gives only one reason for the validity of the thesis statement, make up two more reasons that might be supported in developmental paragraphs. (The writer of this paper can handle the language fairly well. From all indications, however, he wrote this paper without much planning. The result is that the paper does not fully support its thesis, that some ideas and paragraphs are left undeveloped, and that the whole ends with a vague *such trends as this must be halted.*)

### C. Why Students No Longer Inquire

1. Today's high school students are not interested in "why." They prefer to be led to simple answers already set down for them, as they have always been led. They do not seek out solutions to problems of economics or geography or literature. In fact, one of the standard slogans at testing time at my high school was always: "We don't know the questions, just the answers." All we knew was what our teachers told us: just the facts. These we memorized, because memorizing is all that was ever required of us.

2. It seems to be a workbook world, and such a teaching method teaches nobody anything. In chemistry labs across the country, the student is handed tubes and burners and a problem to "solve." But he is shackled by the workbook at his elbow. Mix so-and-so much of *A* with this-and-that amounts of *B*. You get *C*. Here's what happened, and why. The student reacts with a yawn. The experiment got him nowhere. He discovered nothing, and he arrived at no conclusion but that one concluded for him.

3. When the same student is given something tangible to work toward, he shows his mettle. What did the word *slave* mean to Ancient Sparta? What was the real relationship between Philip and Alexander, and how do you know? Where's the proof of romanticism in Wordsworth's ode? How can that teacher call a triangle *beautiful?* Such questions stir a student to think and to research. He is challenged. He wants to know, and he will find out.

4. When a student is introduced to an unanswered problem, he cannot help working up an interest in finding an answer. He wants to assume responsibility. Even if he arrives at only a half-right conclusion, at least he has had the freedom of investigating. He might, in his struggles, hit upon an original idea. How nice to have understood the question, to have cared enough to try for an answer, to have contributed to the world's knowledge.

### QUESTIONS FOR ANALYSIS OF PAPER *C*

1. What is the thesis statement of Paper *C?*

2. What is the purpose of the rest of the introductory paragraph? Does this paragraph indicate any reason for the validity of the thesis statement? If so, are these reasons developed and supported in the remainder of the paper?

3. The first sentence of the second paragraph is the topic sentence. What did the writer do in the remainder of the paragraph to establish his point as a valid one? Has he offered enough evidence to establish his point? What might be done to make the topic sentence valid?

4. Does the third paragraph support the topic sentence? Look at it

closely. Does it give and support a second reason for the validity of the thesis statement? If so, is the evidence offered in support of the topic sentence enough to establish it as valid? If not, what is the purpose of the third paragraph?

5. In what way is the fourth paragraph related to the thesis statement? What is its purpose in the paper?

### D. The Case Against Football

1. High school football is an outrageous waste. The game is too expensive: in dollars and cents, in hours and minutes, in morale, and in physical well-being. When gym equipment and coaching salaries grow more important than academic progress and class work waits upon athletes, when the student's sense of values is distorted and fine young bodies are deliberately exposed to physical violence, then football does indeed cost too much.

2. Seldom does the total gate receipt for the season, even with the added dimes and quarters from concession stands, smooth out the balance. The school administrator and his staff pay top prices for dummies, pads, cleated shoes, and face guards; their boys need and deserve the best possible protection out there on the field of danger. Turfs, sturdy bleachers, and weather-conditioned gymnasiums are theirs to maintain (with a giant slice of the school board's carefully balanced budget). And the hiring of the go-gettingest coach available is one of the greatest expenses the school faces. But all that is the simple, red-and-black side of the ledger. Other problems growing out of football are far more important, though they may not be quite so obvious to the outsider.

3. The existing situation makes it almost shameful for a student to neglect his team in favor of class work. When there are posters to put out, tickets to sell, or athletic banquets to be arranged, the student is often expected to make the time, even during a class period, if the heat is on, to back the team. He can hardly be expected to pay more attention to his Biology III notebook than he pays to the Homecoming Game; why, it's practically a breach of faith! So he sets aside the biology assignment and the Latin translation, and the three chapters in the Hardy novel due tomorrow, so he won't be late for the pep rally. After all, Miss Hopkins and those other teachers must realize (they've heard it all week over the intercom) that Coach Jamison and his boys need all the spirit that can be whipped up if they're to ring up another victory for Consolidated High. And therein lies another serious failure of the football-centered school.

4. The song that resounds across the campus for the week is not an echo of that old softie that insists "It is not that we win or lose, but how we play the game!" None of that mush for the up-to-date pigskin elevens. It's no more who we play, but who we beat. The coach shouts out his determined promises, then the bugles blare for the captain Himself, the biggest imaginable Man on Campus. So long to the fellow with the A average and to all the other wearers of the letter sweater, the mark of the scholar. And often the school's reputation is built on its team's success, not on the

number of serious students who go on to excel in their college studies. Still, all this is to say nothing of the deliberate exposure to physical dangers, even death, to which public schools subject their students in the glorious name of football. We'd rather not dwell on the number of boys who either don't make it at all or who are carried out between quarters to a life of lameness, of back or brain. Besides those caught in the crossfire on the gridiron, too, are those who suffer (or die) in automobile or school bus collisions en route to the Big Game.

5. There's no winner in high school football. When the count is taken of money, time, energy, and suffering spent on "the game," both teams have lost, no matter how many times the boys first downed, touched down, touched back, or kicked goal. The real score (obscured by the glaring numbers on the great electric scoreboard) reads NOTHING to NOTH-ING.

(Note that this paper has five paragraphs instead of the four pre-scribed in the diagram of the five-hundred-word paper. The writer developed his fourth paragraph so fully that he felt the need for a con-cluding paragraph. The paper is stronger for it.)


## QUESTIONS FOR ANALYSIS OF PAPER *D*

1. Outline Paper *D* so that it fits the diagram for a five-hundred-word paper. Arrange the outline in this way:
> Thesis Statement: . . . . . . . . . . . . . . . . . . . . . . . . . . . . . . . . . . . . . . . . . . .
> Topic Sentence 1: . . . . . . . . . . . . . . . . . . . . . . . . . . . . . . . . . . . . . . . .
> Topic Sentence 2: . . . . . . . . . . . . . . . . . . . . . . . . . . . . . . . . . . . . . . . .
> Topic Sentence 3: . . . . . . . . . . . . . . . . . . . . . . . . . . . . . . . . . . . . . . . .

2. Is Paper *D* well organized? Why or why not?

### E. Law and Order

1. Often we are subjected to a cry for "law and order." U.S. Presidents have made that one of the major issues in their campaigns for the White House. In their speeches, governors and mayors and congressmen also call for "law and order." Newspaper editorials remind us that we are becoming a lawless nation. Certainly, we know that our country is undergoing radical changes. New philosophies are being presented; fresh ideas claim our attention. And if we are to continue as a repre-sentative democracy, we must maintain an orderly system for granting change.

2. No honest American is opposed to "law and order." We all understand that the democratic processes require calm evaluation of new proposals. I would, for example, be the last person to advocate civil disobedience as a laudable method of gaining just ends. Our nation, although it grew out of an act of civil disobedience, has established orderly chan-nels that effectively preclude the need for lawlessness.

3. But many Americans are worried that our country can devolve into anarchy. They are worried about militant minorities. They are bothered by student unrest. They fear corruption in government. They feel that certain Supreme Court rulings have unfairly tied the hands of the police in their attempts to protect society from organized crime. And those Americans, too, are sincere.

4. Yet I feel the issue of "law and order" is spurious. Those who have adopted this cry are motivated by fear and influenced by propaganda. In effect, I am arguing that sincere people are worried, and politicians are trading upon that fear.

5. There are those who say that crime in America has increased in direct proportion to the increase in the budget of the FBI. This view, although an exaggeration, does contain an element of truth. For today we have much better methods of reporting crimes. Furthermore, some actions now are considered crimes that in recent years were dismissed as "youthful folly." Finally, we know that an increasing urbanization *must* result in increasing crime.

6. I believe, however, that the new emphasis on "law and order" masks the innate prejudice of white Americans against increasing cries for justice by oppressed minority groups: blacks, Indians, Chicanos, the poor, college students. In other words, when some southern politicians scream for "law and order" what they really mean is "keep the niggers down." When some traditional Republicans say "law and order" what they really mean is "preserve the conservative establishment."

7. Propaganda helps produce the image of lawlessness. Lurid stories about murder and rape sell newspapers and keep viewers watching television. And the mass media may not really understand how they contribute toward increasing the fears of the "average American." Reporters insist on reporting the news, whether it is an armed robbery or a student demonstration or a riot in a ghetto. What they sometimes overlook are the causes behind the events they are reporting.

8. Two things are obvious: America must maintain its established institutions of democracy and freedom. But America must also maintain its traditional open-mindedness. We must not be misled by those who would use our concern to further their own ends.

9. It is probably true that disorders have increased in America. As more people become educated, they recognize that America still has plenty of unsolved problems. Sociologists have theorized that a new generation, faced with the prospect of instant atomic-missile destruction, believe that our nation can no longer afford leisurely evolution. "Freedom Now" is their rallying cry.

10. Let us, then, beware those who would use "Freedom Now" as an excuse for destruction. But let us also beware those who would use "law and order" as a barrier to legitimate cries for help.

## QUESTIONS FOR ANALYSIS OF PAPER *E*

Paper *E* has been included because it departs in many ways from the basic diagram you have been studying. The purpose of this exercise is to help you discover some of these differences and to compare them with the pattern you already know.

1. a. What is the chief difference between the title of this paper and the titles of the other papers used as illustrations in this chapter?

b. Without omitting the words *law* and *order,* can you phrase a better title? Why do you consider yours better?

2. a. What is the purpose of the fourth paragraph of this paper?

b. Could the basic idea of this paragraph be stated earlier in the paper without a loss of effect? What *is* this effect?

c. What is the relation of this paragraph to those preceding and to those following it? To the title?

3. a. What purposes do the first three paragraphs serve? To what part of the basic diagram you have been studying do they compare? Could they be combined into one paragraph? What effect would this have?

b. Why has this student writer chosen to devote so much space to the first three paragraphs? Does his decision strengthen or weaken the paper?

c. Which general references in these paragraphs could be made more specific? Explain how.

4. Is this paper *expository* or *argumentative?* Or both? Why?

5. a. What ties together paragraphs four, eight, and ten?

b. Would it be possible to combine eight and ten? Try writing one version.

6. a. Which of the paragraphs would you call developmental? Why?

b. What kind of support and evidence does the writer present? Explain.

c. Do you consider this paper convincing? Why?

d. In what ways does the writer try to make his paper convincing? Does he seem to have a specific audience in mind? How would you characterize the general feeling (tone) of the paper: Formal? Informal? Serious? Quiet? Judicious? Argumentative? What is the basis for your opinion?

7. Try to draw a diagram to represent the relation of this paper's parts to one another. Could this diagram be made to fit the four-paragraph diagram you've been studying? Do you think a closer adherence to the basic pattern would improve the paper? Explain why.

II. So you can discover how well you manage a five-hundred-word paper, write one to fit the basic pattern studied in this chapter. Choose as the starting point for your thinking one of the following statements.

A. The paper titled "Law and Order" is convincing.

B. When I'm with a group of students, I'm not myself.

C. In the "Law and Order" paper the thesis statement is in the wrong place.

D. Without laws or rules of behavior community living would be impossible.

E. College life demands that students play many roles.

F. Dogs on the loose are (are not) a nuisance.

G. Writing exams bothers me.

H. The dating game is a nuisance.

I. Television commercials (or programs) are deceptive.

J. Death and sleep are similar.

K. I couldn't get along without paper clips.

L. Today's seventeen-year-old has too much (not enough) freedom.

M. Wives belong (do not belong) at home.

N. Trial marriages are (are not) desirable.

O. Women should (should not) have equal rights with men.

# 2

# Getting Started

## Discovery

Writing is *discovery*—of feeling, of thought, of the means of communicating real messages to real people. For good writers the process of writing *is* an act of discovery. As they put down words—playing the game of selecting, enjoying, rejecting—they *discover* words that fit exactly the thoughts and feelings they are trying to communicate. If you have trouble getting started, it is probably because you aren't letting this discovery process work for you. Or you may not be allowing enough time to play with your feelings and thoughts and the words that fit them. Last-minute, one-shot writing lacks this sense of play, of discovery; it carries with it, instead, a feeling of fumbling, of false starts hastily covered up with uncomfortable words, of fuzzy thought in worn-out language. If you are a fumbler or a last-minute writer, learn to discover your exact thoughts and feelings before you try to set them down—that's what getting started is all about. Then continue this discovery process as you write your paper.

As you write, new ideas will come to you. Like the more experienced writer, you should discover that the writing process itself generates ideas, adding to those you've already decided on. Don't hesitate to include these new thoughts, for they are an important part of the creative process of writing. Equally important, however, is an additional discovery you should make—that your in-class papers must somehow become those "real messages" and that you and your teacher are the "real people" involved.

Some of the exercises you will be asked to do in a later section of this book are designed to make you more aware of this person-to-person relationship in writing and to help you overcome the artificiality which often creeps into classroom themes. For example, you may be asked to write for a specific audience (a close friend, your parents, your teacher in a friendly mood, someone younger than you, an old person, someone in Congress). Or you may be asked to play a role, writing as if you were someone very specific (yourself in a disguised mood, your mother, a city official, a sports writer, a television newscaster). You should discover new things to say and new ways of saying the things you already know; you should discover that language and thoughts and people are always part of the writing equation.

How much time you take to think and write will depend on the difficulty of the subject, your knowledge of the subject, and your experience with it. The good writer always takes the prewriting time he needs—hours, days, perhaps weeks—before choosing a specific idea and the writing strategy to go with it. You may not have as much time, but you probably have more thinking time available than you are aware of— while eating, showering, or shaving, combing your hair, brushing your teeth, or walking to class. And you must set aside some thinking or reading time specifically for this discovery process, for jotting down ideas that occur to you. Because the aim of this chapter is to get you started quickly and efficiently, you will be asked to think about and to practice solving the following problems: (1) the specific, limited subject you are going to write about; (2) the precise main point (or thesis) you are going to establish; and (3) the exact purpose of your paper.

## Choosing a Subject

At the beginning of a writing course, your instructor may assign a specific subject for each five-hundred-word paper and clearly define each paper's purpose. But sometimes you will simply be given a broad subject or be sent to the library to find your own. To cut down on false starts and unnecessary fumbling, you need to practice selecting and limiting subjects you can discuss adequately in five hundred words.

You already have enough subjects to write about—you have been places, seen things. You've had experiences, some of them unique to you. These you can write about and use as evidence to support your assertions. Even if you have never left home, you have used your five senses: You have observed people, places, and things; you have formed opinions and impressions; you know smells and sounds and colors and textures. You have been in school for a dozen years, storing information. You have read billboards, newspapers, and books; you know television and the movies. Most important, you have formed some definite and strongly held opinions that you can support in writing. Of course, you may find (as we all do) that you have some opinions and ideas you cannot justify logically when you try to write them down. But you do have a vast supply of material; all you have to do is to discover it by putting your memory to work.

Suppose you have selected four possible subjects for your paper:

1. The Life of Abraham Lincoln

2. Dates I Have Had

3. My College

4. The Battles of the Civil War

Any of these subjects could be used for a paper, depending on its length. For the first and fourth subjects you would probably use material you had learned in school or from your reading, or possibly from research in the library. The second and third would come from your own experience and observation; you would discover the material by giving your mind time to think.

But none of the four subjects is suitable for development in a five-hundred-word paper. Since many volumes have been written about Lincoln's life, you could not possibly write five hundred significant words about Lincoln's whole life. Similarly, the second subject, as it stands, can't be used as the subject of a five-hundred-word paper, since you probably can say nothing meaningful about *all* your dates in so short a paper. You will do better if you choose one date, or part of one date, and then say something significant about it. The third subject presents the same problem. Any college has numerous "parts"—faculty, students, dormitories, courses, sports, student union, and so on—but you can't possibly write about all of these within one broad subject. Not in five hundred words. If you select a subject such as the third, you are obligated to do so. Obviously the last subject is unsatisfactory too. No one can say anything meaningful about all the battles of the Civil War in a short paper. You will need to think further and more exactly before you start to write.

## Limiting Your Subject

If you are to explain an idea, object, or process, you must confine your explanation to a *single* subject rather than try to discuss a broad subject area. You must examine one specific subject or establish one main point. Limiting yourself to a single subject is like focusing a camera sharply; it is called *giving your paper direction* or *unity*. Sharp focus and single direction are easier when you choose a limited subject.

Suppose, for example, your instructor asks you to write a paper about your high school. This is a broad subject area, for it contains many possibilities for more limited subjects—the teachers, the courses, the school's academic standing, the amount of homework assigned, the physical plant, the PTA, the students' social life, the governing body, athletics, or any number of other even more limited subjects. Since you can't even touch on all these subjects in five hundred words, pick *one* of them to write about and be sure you cover your one point adequately. If you don't limit your subject in this way, you will write a paper without focus, without single direction, and you will be making no point at all.

How do you go about limiting a subject? First, reject any notions that you have nothing to write about. You *do* have material for writing good papers. You have accumulated some knowledge in your lifetime (or else what have you been doing all this time?). You have had a variety of experiences; you have made observations of all sorts; and you have formed opinions.

Think about this list of broad subjects:

| | | | |
|---|---|---|---|
| Advertising | Dating | Jobs | Reading |
| Aggression | Dogs | Laws | Recreation |
| Ambitions | Drinking | Liquids | School |
| Animals | Education | Movies | Solids |
| Birds | Family | Music | Space |
| Boys | Fear | Neighborhood | Sports |
| Buildings | Flight | Newspapers | Television |
| Cars | Freedom | People | Travel |
| Clothes | Friends | Pets | Trials |
| Clubs | Girls | Planes | Voting |
| College | Guns | Pollution | |
| Community | Hobbies | Population | |
| Congress | Hostility | Prejudices | |

With proper limitation, you could easily write a five-hundred-word paper on any of these subjects, and if you put your mind to work, you could discover many more. None of these, for instance, would let you use much of the knowledge you've picked up in your study of literature or history or science. A quick mental tour of these studies should suggest many possible broad subjects—wars, battles, great men, novels, plays, poems, chemicals, animals, air, gas, and geese are a few. Discovery is a game; play it with a positive attitude and you will find getting started much easier than you think.

Once you have selected a general subject, or it has been assigned to you, the job is barely begun. Although you *can* write a short paper on a broad subject, the odds are overwhelming that it will be a poor one because you will not have planned carefully enough or limited your subject to one that can be covered in relatively few words.

*Limiting* is the process of dividing a general subject into its parts, selecting one of these parts, and then further limiting it. Suppose that from the list of general subjects above you decided to write on *sports*. You must now begin to think of possible *divisions* of this subject, as suggested in the following diagram:

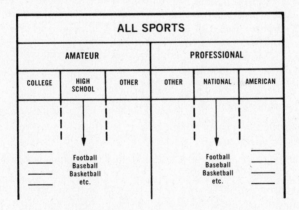

The kind of systematic division suggested by this diagram will help you discover subjects that might not otherwise occur to you. For example, all professional sports are not part of the National and American leagues, and an examination of the division "other" should suggest professional sports like golf, bowling, or tennis. Some of the divisions suggested by the subject *sports* would include the following:

| | |
|---|---|
| Amateur Sports | Professional Football |
| Professional Sports | Professional Baseball |
| College Sports | Professional Golf |
| High School Sports | Amateur Golf |

The next step is to select one division you know enough about, or can find enough information on, to be certain of your ground. From that division, list more specific subjects you might be able to discuss adequately in five hundred words. Suppose, since you would likely know more about high school sports than the others, you select that subject. But "High School Sports" is still far too general, for you would have to give an account of *all* the sports in your school—football, basketball, golf, tennis, volleyball, baseball, swimming, track, and perhaps others. So you must limit the subject more severely; choose *football* as the specific subject you want to discuss. Now, play the game of discovery, rack your brain for specific subjects *about* high school football and write them down. You might come up with a list like the one below.

### Football as a High School Sport

1. The Value of Football to My High School
2. The Value of High School Football to the Player
3. The Value of High School Football to the Nonplaying Student
4. The Effect of High School Football on My Community
5. Expense of High School Football
6. An Adequate Football Stadium for My High School
7. The Emphasis on Football in My High School
8. Safety Equipment for the High School Football Player
9. The Treatment of Football Players by the Teachers
10. The Academic Standing of Football Players
11. The Treatment of Football Players by Other Students
12. Student Support of Football
13. The Football Hero
14. The Experience of Playing on a High School Football Team

First, delete those subjects that least appeal to you; then select the one you best understand, and you are under way. You are not ready to start writing yet, however, until you do more planning and thinking.

## Framing Your Thesis Statement

A good thesis statement is vital to your paper. It is the main point you are going to make and support in your paper. This statement will shape your paper's direction more than anything else you do. Without it the paper can have no structure; with it the paper has a foundation for development. It gives you the main point and it gives you a purpose

—to establish this point in the remainder of the paper. Where you put the thesis statement is important. You already know that the recommended position is at the end of the introductory paragraph. If you put it there, and if it is a good statement, you will be headed in the right direction for the remainder of the paper.

Writing a thesis statement is no different from writing any other sentence, except for the care you must take in framing the thesis as the main point of your paper. It has, as do other sentences, a subject area and a predicate area. The subject area of the thesis statement, as in all sentences, announces what is being written about (the subject of the sentence). The predicate area, as in all sentences, says something about the subject. Here is a diagram of a thesis statement.

**Complete Thesis Statement**

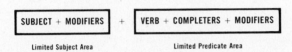

| SUBJECT + MODIFIERS | + | VERB + COMPLETERS + MODIFIERS |
| :---: | :---: | :---: |
| Limited Subject Area | | Limited Predicate Area |

You have just studied the process of limiting a subject so that it can be handled in five hundred words, and you have read through a list of fourteen specific subjects derived from the broader subject "High School Football." Any one of these fourteen will serve in the limited subject area of a thesis statement. For instance, take the first one listed, "The Value of Football to My High School." This phrase could easily become the subject area of a thesis statement if you simply add a predicate area to it, but you would probably not want to use this exact phrase. Decide, instead, what you think the value of football is to your high school. You might decide that it has no value at all when the matter is closely examined. In fact, you might believe that it would be better if there were no football at your high school. In this case, you might frame a thesis statement such as this one (we will call your school Consolidated High):

| Varsity football | should be discontinued at Consolidated High. |

*Varsity football* constitutes the limited subject area of this thesis statement, and *should be discontinued at Consolidated High* makes up the limited predicate area. Unless you limit the predicate area in this way, your thesis statement will still probably lack specific direction. For another example, suppose you want to write about the fifth subject on the list, "Expense of High School Football." By limiting the predicate area, you might decide that football is too expensive for what it gives the school. You might then frame this thesis statement:

**Varsity football at Consolidated High is an outrageous waste.**

Here *Varsity football at Consolidated High* is the subject area of the statement, and *is an outrageous waste* is the predicate area.

What this discussion emphasizes is that to frame a thesis statement you must do two things: (1) select a single, limited subject (subject area), and (2) say something specific *about* the subject (predicate area). There is a little more to it than this, however, as you might suspect. Look, then, a little more closely at each of these directions for writing a thesis statement.

### 1. Select a Single, Limited Subject

If your paper is to have a single direction, it must develop a single subject. If your thesis statement contains more than one subject, it is not a good one because you are obligated to develop each subject. Consider this statement:

**Our student election is not being run properly and we must do something about it.**

Here are two thesis statements. The first condemns existing procedures and the second urges action to revise the faulty procedures; it is not clear to the reader which of these is the real point of the paper. This sentence is composed of two sentences (actually independent clauses) joined by the conjunction *and*. The two parts of this sentence have equal importance because both have exactly the same construction. But both parts can be included in an acceptable thesis statement, if one part is changed to become less important than the other. Thus, the thesis statement can become this:

**Since our student election is not being run properly, we must do something about it.**

Now, with the addition of the subordinating conjunction *since*, the first part of the sentence has been cast in a dependent clause, and it becomes subordinate to the second part of the sentence, which now contains the single subject and predicate areas for the thesis statement. However, this thesis statement would be much better if the dependent clause *Since our student election is not being run properly* were reduced even further to a phrase:

**We must correct improper procedures in our student election.**

or

**Improper procedures in our student election must be corrected.**

Each of these last two thesis statements has one specific, limited subject area and one specific, limited predicate area. For either, the remainder of a five-hundred-word paper would answer the question, *Why must we correct election procedures?*

### 2. Say Something about the Subject

What you say about the subject in the predicate area is the most important part of the thesis statement, for it is here that you give expression to your own point of view that is going to be explored and supported in the rest of the paper. This point of view will be the key to the content of your paper. Consequently, you must take considerable care to be certain that your point of view can be supported and that it is clear to the reader. To make it so, learn the following guidelines for the predicate area of the thesis statement.

a. *The predicate area must also be limited.* Even though you've gone through the process of limiting the subject of the thesis statement, you may find when you write your statement that it's still too broad to deal with. It probably needs limiting in the predicate area. Consider this thesis statement:

**The United States is the best of all countries.**

Proving this thesis would be easy if you were planning to write several volumes, but you cannot do it in a short paper. The predicate area of this thesis, *is the best of all countries,* obligates the writer to prove that the United States is better than *any* other country. To fulfill this obligation, he would have to consider the economic, moral, religious, political, and social conditions in every country of the world and then contrast them to those in the United States. This is not possible in five hundred words. Similarly, a statement such as

**Lee was a greater general than Grant.**

cannot be established without considering the campaigns of each general and then comparing them. Neither is this a job for a short paper.

b. *The predicate area of the thesis statement should present an argumentative point of view toward the subject.* If you are to establish a main point, or prove a thesis, your paper must be partially argumentative. After all, you are trying to explain to the reader that your point is a sound one. Your paper will have no other purpose than to support the validity of this main point, which you will argue by presenting all the logical reasons and sound evidence you can muster. Your thesis statement must be the trumpet's call that sounds the challenge—you on one side, your reader on the other. You will try to get your reader to say, "I understand" *and* "I agree," giving your paper an argumentative edge. So be bold about it; issue your challenge clearly and forcefully, as if you were engaging in debate. Use no weak phrases such as "to me" or "in my opinion" in your thesis, nor anywhere else in your paper, for they leave with your reader the impression that you are merely stating an opinion and that you are apologetic about attempting to prove it. Step from the crowd and write something like these thesis statements:

> The high school student needs more responsibility.
> Lady Macbeth is more masculine than feminine.
> Watching television encourages violence.
> Freshman English is a farce.
> Charles Dickens found American life bewildering.
> The mind must be exercised.

Only if your thesis statement reflects a specific attitude toward a specific subject, phrased with directness and conviction, will you grab your reader's interest. And even if the instructor is your only reader, he will like your paper better simply because you caught his attention and challenged his thought.

But a striking thesis statement alone will not win you a good grade; the thesis still has to be properly developed and logically supported. Select a thesis you can believe in and support. If you do not believe what you say, neither will the reader, and *you are writing to convince your reader.*

c. *The predicate area must say something meaningful.* A thesis statement about which there can be no controversy, about which everyone agrees, can hardly result in a paper that anyone will want to read. If, for instance, you try to write a paper using a thesis like

**Travel by plane saves time.**

or

**Good conservation practices help the farmer.**

you are not going to get much of a reaction from your reader except "Ho-hum. So what?" And justifiably, for these statements are trite and meaningless.

d. *The predicate area must say something exact about the subject.* Look at this thesis statement:

**Football is an exciting game.**

The predicate area is made up of the phrase *is an exciting game.* If you are to write a paper on this thesis, its content must be controlled by the key word *exciting,* because it gives your paper its single direction. There is no other emotion or feeling you can write about in your paper. What exactly does *exciting* mean? It is hard to define and does not *lead* the reader sufficiently. What might be exciting to one person might leave another cold. And there is the problem with such a predicate area—it does not get to a precise point. It is not exact. It allows the writer to say almost anything as long as it is in any way associated with football. Consequently, the writer can ramble and come to no specific point in his paper. To improve this statement, make an exact point about one variety of football:

**Even touch football is dangerous.**

You can see that the same difficulty exists in this thesis statement:

**Macbeth makes fascinating reading.**

If you are assigned a paper on *Macbeth,* make an exact point about the play:

**Macbeth's early recognition of guilt increases his conflict.**

The two diagrams below review the process of framing a thesis statement as it has been presented so far. The first represents the process in general terms; the second uses a specific example to illustrate the process.

In the first diagram, the broad topic might be one already suggested, "My School." For illustration, assume that your school is Glory University. To restrict this broad topic to a more manageable subject, you must then list the divisions of that broad topic that you will be able to write about from your observation and experience. Would you choose sports, professors, dormitory life, registration day, academic work, or the

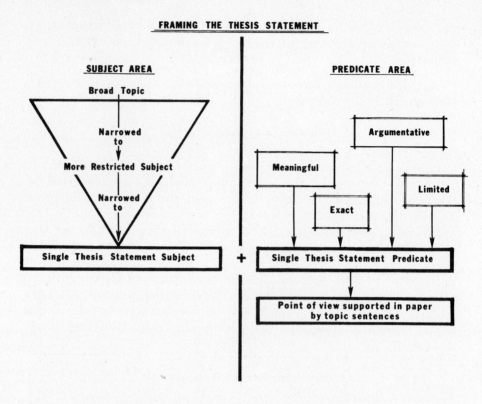

## FRAMING THE THESIS STATEMENT

student union? Because you have been through it recently, you might pick *registration day*. You now have a subject for the specific thesis statement of your five-hundred-word paper. To complete the statement, you must form the predicate area by saying something about the subject. What you say, of course, will depend on your own experience. You might say that you found registration day frustrating or tiring or confusing or inefficient or pleasant or efficient or none of these. To illustrate, let's say that you found it confusing. You now have a thesis statement in its barest form:

### Registration day was confusing.

In reaching a specific thesis statement you have gone through the process of selection shown by this second diagram.

The large block on the left indicates the broad topic, "Glory University." The smaller blocks in the middle of the page represent six of the many restricted subjects that are a part of the broad topic. The shading of the fourth block shows that only one part, *registration day*, has been selected as the subject of the paper. The blocks on the right of the

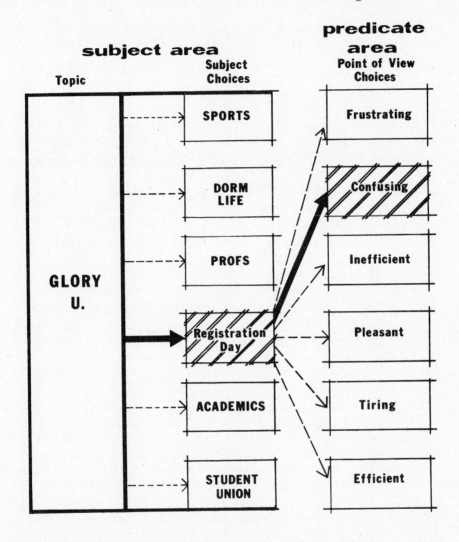

page show some of the many attitudes that might have been formed about the limited subject, *registration day*. The shading of the block labeled *confusing* indicates the selection of a point of view toward the subject. Now, the content of the paper is restricted to the subject matter represented by the two shaded blocks. Material from no other block can be used in writing the paper. The paper may be concerned only with demonstrating that registration day was confusing. The key word that controls the content of the paper is *confusing*. Any material that does not establish the validity of that key word does not belong in the paper.

Now you have a thesis statement: *Registration day was confusing.*

This statement, however, is not a particularly good expression of the thesis. First, because the paper is to concern Glory University as its broad topic, mention it in your thesis statement:

**Registration day at Glory University was confusing.**

Everything being equal, a complex sentence, one that contains a dependent clause, will probably be best as a thesis statement, depending on the context of the introductory paragraph. So try a complex sentence:

**Although I had memorized every step I was to take, registration day at Glory University was confusing.**

This sentence can be improved by making the verb active. Revise it to this version:

**Although I had memorized every step I was to take, registration day at Glory University confused me.**

## EXERCISES

A. Here are some thesis statements. Below each is a criticism based on the characteristics of a good thesis statement.

1. Water skiing is more fun than any other sport I have tried.
   (The word *fun* in the predicate area is not exact. It is so vague that anything associated with water skiing could be brought into the paper. What might be fun to one person might not be fun at all to another. In addition, the predicate is not sufficiently limited. Many sports would have to be compared to water skiing. A better thesis is *The water-skier has to be foolhardy.*)

2. Intercollegiate sports benefit the university and they build spirit in the student body.
   (This thesis statement has two subjects, each of them in a separate independent clause. One or the other of these must be chosen as the thesis. The first clause about benefit to the university is too unlimited in the predicate area to be treated in five hundred words. One benefit might be appropriate: *The chief function of intercollegiate football is to advertise the university.* Both subjects can be included in the thesis statement, depending on the context in which the statement appears, if one is made into a less important dependent clause: *Although intercollegiate football builds spirit in the student body, its chief function is to advertise the university.* Now, the thesis statement is the independent clause of the sentence.)

3. College sports offer many advantages to the student.

(Neither the subject area nor the predicate area of this thesis statement is sufficiently limited. *College sports* can be divided into at least two parts—intramural and intercollegiate. As the thesis stands, which of these two parts would the paper discuss? *Many advantages* in the predicate is likewise too broad for five hundred words; so one advantage is enough to explore in the paper. A more limited thesis on this subject is: *Collegiate intramural sports shape the character of participating students.*)

B. Considering the characteristics of a good thesis statement, write a criticism of each of the following thesis statements. Some of these may be acceptable for development in five hundred words.

1. The politician's speech was very interesting and inspiring.
2. Basketball intrigues me.
3. Social fraternities encourage scholarship.
4. My vacation in Europe was the most educational trip I have taken.
5. Women drive as well as men do.
6. People should consider all aspects of medicare.

## Stating Your Purpose

Once you have written a good thesis statement, the next step is to add a *because* to it, and then jot down all the reasons you can think of for your point of view toward your subject. Suppose, for instance, you decided to use this thesis statement:

**Interschool football should be discontinued at Consolidated High.**

If you actually believe this statement, you should have little difficulty in listing a number of reasons for your belief. Your list might be something like the following:

Interschool football should be discontinued at Consolidated High because:

1. The school loses money on interschool football.
2. The average student is unable to participate in the game.
3. Players are seriously injured each year.
4. Students lose class time in activities supporting the team.
5. Students' attention is taken away from academic subjects.

6. Students lose study time attending pep rallies.
7. Trips to neighboring cities are dangerous.
8. The importance of the football player is overrated.
9. Football is likely to teach players the wrong set of values.
10. Too much attention is given to football at the expense of scholarship.
11. The coach seems more important than other teachers.
12. The cost of building and maintaining the stadium is high.
13. The value of the school is likely to be judged by the success of its football team.
14. The winning coach is paid a premium salary.
15. Winning at all costs becomes too important.

If you inspect this list, you can see that certain reasons may be grouped together because they are closely related. This process of grouping is called *classification,* a key to sorting and managing information. It is the reverse process of logical *division,* which you used early in this chapter to discover limited, manageable "parts" of broad subject areas. Now that you are at the other end of the process, you use classification to sort your ideas systematically. You will soon discover that some of the reasons you have listed at random may have to be left out and others may have to be modified so that you can get the grouping that best points to your thesis statement. Also, after you begin the actual writing of the paper, new reasons probably will occur to you and some of your attitudes may change. Don't hesitate to add the reasons to your list or to make other changes you feel are needed. The following *sentence outline* is one way to arrange your reasons:

I. The cost of interschool football is prohibitive.
   A. The school loses money on interschool football.
   B. The cost of building and maintaining a stadium is high.
   C. The winning coach is paid a premium salary.

II. Scholarship is forced to take second place to football.
   A. Students lose class time in activities that support the team.
   B. Students' attention is taken away from academic study.
   C. Students lose study time attending pep rallies.
   D. Coaches seem more important than other teachers.

III. The effect of interschool football on the student body is deleterious.
   A. It builds the wrong set of values.
      1. Winning at any cost becomes too important.
      2. The importance of the star football player is magnified out of proportion.
      3. The school is judged by the success of its football team.

B. Students are placed in unnecessary danger.
  1. Players are seriously injured each year.
  2. Students driving to out-of-town games invite tragedy.

You now have ample material to write your paper—so much, in fact, you may not want to use it all. But you can use it all by writing it up in three developmental paragraphs preceded by a brief introductory statement.

Now that the material to be used has been arranged in a logical order (but by no means the only one), you are ready to write a *purpose statement*. In the purpose statement, you tell exactly what your paper will cover and how you are going about it. It will not become a part of your paper, but it is important to you in giving direction and organization to your paper. Your instructor may ask you to turn in a purpose statement for each paper you write. A purpose statement for a paper using the material arranged from the thesis on football might turn out like this:

In this paper, I intend to support the main point that interschool football should be discontinued at Consolidated High because (1) the cost of interschool football is prohibitive, (2) scholarship is forced to take second place to football, and (3) the effect of interschool football on the student body is deleterious.

With the writing of this purpose statement, you have completed all the important thinking for your paper. This type of planning will make the actual writing of the paper much easier: The writing will go smoothly if your thesis statement has a specific purpose, if you have clearly thought out the focus and direction, and if you know how to present logical support in well-ordered paragraphs.

### EXERCISES

A. The *sentence outline* on page 40 could easily be written as a *topic outline* if the key terms were taken from each sentence and simply listed. A slight change in wording sometimes helps; for example, II, A, B, and C of the outline might appear as "lost class time," "diverted attention," and "lost study time." Practice spotting key terms by rewriting the sentence outline as a topic outline.

B. Here are some broad subject areas taken from the list on page 28. Choose three of these, and for each discover and list the parts into which each can be divided. (You may find your job easier if you check again the diagrams on pages 29 and 37.) Each list should contain at least six or seven parts.

| | | |
|---|---|---|
| Advertising | Dating | People |
| Ambitions | Dogs | Pets |
| Animals | Education | Planes |
| Birds | Family | Prejudices |
| Clothes | Guns | Reading |
| College | Liquids | Solids |
| Community | Movies | Television |
| Congress | Music | |

C. From the lists you composed in Exercise B, select five parts (at least one part from each list) and write a good thesis statement for each of the five parts.

D. Finding ideas is a matter of *getting started*—"inside," as well as "outside" on paper. But all of us get stuck—often early in the discovery process. The following exercises should suggest many *ways* of getting your "inside" moving.

1. Bring to class a full-page, color ad from a magazine. Study the ad closely and then answer the following questions (your instructor may want you to make notes).

   a. Disregarding the *words* of the ad, describe what is left. What are *all* the other things you see?

   b. Disregarding the "meaning," what can you still say about the *whole* ad?

   c. How many different *kinds* of information are you receiving from the ad? Are they equally important? Why?

   d. Do you *like* the ad? Can you say why (or why not)? Does it appeal to your thinking? To your emotions? Or to both? Explain.

   e. What does the ad want you to *assume* that is not actually stated? How can you tell?

   f. In what ways is this ad *similar* to other ads? (You could look at your neighbors' ads.) How is yours *different* from the others?

   g. Does the ad remind you of other things you've experienced or observed? For example?

   h. What are the main "parts" of the ad? How do these parts work together?

   i. To what line of thinking is the "statement" of the ad apparently a conclusion? Explain.

   j. Can the "statement" in the ad be proven? Is the "statement" supported? How?

   k. Is there a play on words in the ad? What is the purpose? Can you take the words literally?

   l. Disregarding the overall meaning, what *kinds* of objects and people are pictured? What are you supposed to assume about them? (Look closely.)

2. Which of the questions asked above in part one of this exercise are included in the following *general* questions:

   a. Can you *define* the object and its parts?

b. What kind of *structure* does it have?
c. To what is it *similar?*
d. How is it *different from* other objects like it?
e. What *cause-effect relationships* does it suggest?
f. What other *relationships* does it suggest?
g. What does it suggest about the *possible?* The *impossible?*
h. Who *needs* it? Who *uses* it? Who ought to use it?
i. What can be affected by it? In what ways?
j. Do you *react to it favorably? Unfavorably?* Why?

3. Answer the general questions given in the second part of this exercise in relation to each of the following:
   a. an automobile
   b. a science teacher
   c. love (or fear)
   d. power (or law)
   e. milk (or water)
   f. a television set (or stereo)
   g. aspirin (or morphine)
   h. a paper clip (or an oak tree)
   i. death (or sleep)
   j. Choose anything suggested by the list given in Exercise B, or on page 28.

4. On the basis of your experience in the first three parts of this exercise list five *basic* questions you think you can ask about *any* subject.

5. Be prepared to discuss what you have learned about the discovery process.

E. Once you have discovered a subject and a thesis statement and have jotted down some details to use in support, you will find classification an effective way to sort and organize thoughts. Here are some exercises in classification.

   1. Examine the following foods carefully, then arrange them into groups so that the items within each group all have something in common (label each group clearly): ice cream sundaes, iced tea, green beans, beef stew, french fries, cakes, milk, pies, beef steak, coffee, peas, fried chicken, cokes, carrots, meat loaf, roast beef, hot chocolate, pudding, hamburger steak.

   2. Suppose you have been asked to write a simple expository paper titled "Major Causes of Automobile Accidents." Quickly jot down at least a dozen causes. Now examine this list of causes and arrange them into two or three major groups, each clearly labeled. When you have done this classification, you should be able to complete the following statement:

**The major causes of automobile accidents are**

**(a) _____, (b) _____, and (c) _____.**

3. Choose one of the five thesis statements you wrote for Exercise C (above) and quickly jot down all the supporting details you can think of. Now arrange these details into major groups (each labeled) that might serve as the main points presented by a paper on the chosen thesis statement. (If you have trouble with this exercise, recheck the exercises on page 39 and the outline on page 40.)

F. You may not have agreed with the paper about football in the last chapter, so copy the following diagram and fill it in, taking the opposite view. Start with a thesis statement that says something like *Football is the best thing that ever happened to our high school,* and give your reasons. Make your reasons and your support for the reasons as strong as you possibly can. Don't forget to put your most persuasive reason last.

Thesis Statement: ...............................................................
                        (The thesis statement is valid because....)
    Reason 1: ...............................................................
                        (Reason 1 is valid because....)
      Reason A: ...............................................................
      Reason B: ...............................................................
      Reason C: ...............................................................
                        (The thesis statement is valid because....)
    Reason 2: ...............................................................
                        (Reason 2 is valid because....)
      Reason A: ...............................................................
      Reason B: ...............................................................
      Reason C: ...............................................................
                        (The thesis statement is valid because....)
    Reason 3: ...............................................................
                        (Reason 3 is valid because....)
      Reason A: ...............................................................
      Reason B: ...............................................................
      Reason C: ...............................................................
Concluding Statement: ...............................................................

G. Write a purpose statement from the outline you composed in Exercise F.

H. Write a five-hundred-word paper from the outline for Exercise D, 3, or from the outline for Exercise E.

I. Rewrite the outline used in question F so that it is (a) a topic outline, or (b) a good sentence outline.

# 3

# Maintaining
# Unity and Coherence

Each five-hundred-word paper works toward clarifying a single point, and every statement in the paper focuses toward a single objective: convincing the reader that the thesis statement is valid. Thus the paper needs unity—singleness of tone and purpose. And, although every paragraph and every sentence furthers that sole intent, each of the paper's parts must hold together to keep the reader's attention. Coherence devices hold paragraph to paragraph and sentence to sentence to allow the reader passage from thought to thought in support of the thesis statement. Unity is the "togetherness" of the whole paper, whereas coherence is the means we use to insure that the individual parts flow naturally and easily from one to another.

## Unity

Unity means oneness. In all the writing you do, whether it is a sentence or a book, you will have to be concerned with this oneness. Unity works much as a compass does. A compass gives direction. You can, by following a specific compass direction, move steadily south or east or north or west or in any direction between these main points. But if you do not follow one point on the compass, you will never reach your destination. Say, for instance, you wanted to arrive at a spot east of your present position. You go toward that spot as long as you follow east on your compass, but if you veer south and then west, you obviously will never arrive. The same is true of writing. Start in a single direction and stick to it. Unity in writing is a matter of direction, that is, of maintaining the *single* direction you began with.

When you write a paper, the thesis statement gives you a single direction to be followed throughout the paper. The whole paper must consist of support for the one point of your thesis statement. Within the paragraph, the topic sentence gives you that direction. If you deviate from directly supporting either a thesis statement or a topic sentence, you violate the principle of unity. This is why it is so important to use care in framing the thesis statement and the topic sentences of your papers.

Look, for instance, at the following paragraph.

European castles still standing prove that life in those great damp structures was far from comfortable. Cold, wet drafts blew through the long corridors, and heating such a barn was difficult and expensive. Although many bedrooms had fireplaces in them, the beds still had to be heavily curtained in winter before the occupants could keep from freezing to death. Walls were draped with tapestries and curtains to keep the cold winds out of other rooms. Five hundred years ago, it might have been easy for a lord to retain a hundred carpenters to build enough heavy oak pieces to furnish his manor, but today such an undertaking would cost thousands of dollars. For instance, just installing wall-to-wall carpeting in one of the gigantic rooms would make a dent in a multimillionaire's bank roll. And think of the staff that would have to be maintained if a castle were to be lived in today. There would be the kitchen help, a whole battalion of housekeepers, several moat cleaners, and an army of grounds keepers.

This paragraph may, at first reading, seem to be fairly good; but look at it again, and you will see that it does not move in a single direction even if it is concerned only with castles. The paragraph actually moves in three different directions. First, it tells how uncomfortable castles were and how their inhabitants met this discomfort. Second, it mentions how much money it would cost to furnish such castles today, and finally, it veers to the subject of domestic help. So the paragraph contains three subjects and moves in three directions. Consequently, it makes no point because none of the three subjects is adequately developed, and certainly the principle of unity is violated. A unified paragraph could be written on any one of the three subjects.

The following paragraph, although written tongue-in-cheek, discusses the cost of castlekeeping:

At today's prices, maintaining a castle in the way the feudal lords of the middle ages did would be impossible even for the Really Rich. Any castle worth mentioning needed a big enough staff of domestics to at least keep the chewed-on bones shoveled up off the mead hall floor while the fulltime silversmith hammered out the amulets for next week's dragon slayers. Then there would have to be thatch put on the gardener's hut while he replanted the rosemary and thyme, and scullery jacks and jills to turn the pig on the spit in the galley. Menservants stood by in platoons to weld the knights into their armor and to let down the drawbridge and grind it up again if the Danes tried sneaking through. Add knights and embroidered squires waiting permission to Crusade, and pink and pretty ladies-in-waiting standing by to deliver the next sonnet to Milady's courtly lover. Add the cost for all this to the expense of feeding the Poor Porters, the cellarful of emaciated unknowns, and the fishes in the moat. The monthly expense of the noble family's entourage would be enough to eat the heart out of any modern multimillionaire's paycheck.

This paragraph develops only one subject—a multimillionaire today could not afford the upkeep of a medieval castle—and it sticks to that subject from start to finish. It has unity of *purpose*. But the paragraph also has a singleness of *tone* throughout, established mainly by the use of exaggeration and some special effects: *chewed-on bones, dragon slayers, scullery jacks and jills, embroidered squires, pink and pretty ladies-in-waiting, Poor Porters, emaciated unknowns*. The writer's *attitude* toward his subject remains consistent; he never loses the tongue-in-cheek, humorous feeling he wants to communicate to his reader. Together, this oneness of subject and oneness of attitude give the paragraph a strong sense of unity. You must also strive for unity of purpose *and* tone in your writing.

Here is another paragraph for analysis. Read through it to see if you think it maintains unity.

Egypt was civilized long before there was any written history of the country. Egypt has an area of 386,000 square miles. Ancient Egyptians knew so much about embalming that some of their mummies are preserved for us to view in museums. The people of the world are concerned about saving these treasures, and others, now that the course of the Nile River is to be altered in the next decade. The Egyptians carried on commerce with neighboring nations. They studied and were successful with military strategy. For a time they lived under a system of government-controlled production. There is a wide area of fertile farmland along the Nile River. The early Egyptians built great halls and temples whose ruins still stand. Without modern machinery, they built the great pyramids near Cairo. Tourists come in great numbers each year to visit them. Today Cairo is the country's hurried and noisy commercial capital. Long before the birth of Christ, Egyptians knew how to turn wastelands into arable fields. They encouraged the arts and held great meetings where learned men gathered. They were always a religious people, holding to their beliefs in many gods until about 1400 B.C. when Aton, the single god who represented the life-giving power of the sun, was established as the Egyptian deity. In 1945, Egypt gained charter membership in the United Nations.

You should see quickly that this paragraph does not maintain unity but races from subject to subject, each loosely associated with Egypt. To analyze this paragraph, look first at the opening sentence. According to the organizational diagram for the five-hundred-word paper in the last chapter, this sentence is the topic sentence for the paragraph. That is, it specifically announces the subject the paragraph is going to be concerned with. This sentence gives the paragraph its single direction.

The opening sentence of the paragraph is: *Egypt was civilized long before there was any written history of the country.* If the remainder of the paragraph is to support this topic sentence and to be concerned with no other subject, the sentence must contain a word or phrase that can be called the *pointer.* It points to the single direction the remainder of the paragraph must follow to be unified. The topic sentence about Egypt has such a pointer. The word *civilized* controls the direction the paragraph will follow. If any sentence does not prove that Egypt was civilized, it does not belong in the paragraph, and it must be deleted.

For purposes of analysis, here are the sentences of the paragraph listed and numbered.

1. Egypt has an area of 386,000 square miles.
2. Ancient Egyptians knew so much about embalming that some of their mummies are preserved for us to view in museums.

3. It is these treasures that the world is concerned about saving.

4. Early Egyptians carried on commerce with neighboring nations.

5. They studied and were successful with military strategy.

6. They lived under a system of government-controlled production.

7. A wide area of fertile farmland edges the Nile.

8. The Egyptians built great halls and temples whose ruins still stand.

9. Without modern machinery, they built the great pyramids near Cairo.

10. Tourists come in great numbers each year to view Egypt's ruins.

11. Long before the birth of Christ, Egyptians knew how to turn wastelands into arable fields.

12. They encouraged the arts and held great meetings where learned men gathered.

13. They were always a religious people.

14. In 1945, Egypt gained charter membership in the United Nations.

These sentences need to be analyzed one at a time to see if they give support to the pointer word, *civilized,* in the topic sentence. Sentence 1, since it tells about the land area of Egypt, has nothing to do with Egypt's being civilized. It does not support the topic sentence. Delete it. Sentence 2, which tells about the Egyptians' knowledge of embalming, does support the idea that Egypt was civilized, so it may remain a part of the paragraph. Sentence 3 says that the world is concerned about saving Egyptian treasures, but because it discusses the present world's concern and not Egypt's past, it must be eliminated if the paragraph is to follow a single direction. Sentence 4, about Egypt's commerce with neighboring nations, can be retained because it does explain Egypt's past civilization, as can 5 and 6, about the early Egyptians' knowledge of military strategy and control of production. Sentence 7 must be left out; the fact that there is fertile farmland in Egypt does not prove that Egypt was civilized. But that the Egyptians built great halls, temples, and pyramids—Sentences 8 and 9—does prove their civilization, so they stay. The number of tourists who visit Egypt does not prove that Egypt was civilized because tourists often visit places that have not been civilized. So Sentence 10 must go. Sentence 11, which tells about the Egyptians' farming abilities, does indicate that ancient Egyptians were civilized, and this sentence can be retained. Any nation that cultivates the arts and holds conferences of learned men would be said to have a fairly high level of civilization. Sentence 12, then, should stay in the paragraph. Sentence 13, about the Egyptians' religious feelings, does not necessarily establish their civilization, for uncivilized peoples also have deep religious inclinations, and the sentence must be deleted. That Egypt gained charter membership in the United Nations has nothing to do with Egypt's past civilization. It is concerned with the present only, and so sentence 14 will have to be left out.

Eliminating those sentences not supporting the topic sentence with its pointer leaves these:

2. The ancient Egyptians knew so much about embalming that some of their mummies are preserved for us to view in museums.
4. Early Egyptians carried on commerce with neighboring nations.
5. They studied, and were successful with, military strategy.
6. They lived under a system of government-controlled production.
8. The Egyptians built great halls and temples whose ruins still stand.
9. Without modern machinery they built the great pyramids near Cairo.
11. Long before the birth of Christ, Egyptians knew how to turn wastelands into arable fields.
12. They encouraged the arts and held great meetings where learned men gathered.

The remaining sentences can be put together into a unified paragraph, but it is neither well-developed nor readable.

Egypt was civilized long before there was any written history of the country. These ancient people knew so much about embalming that some of their mummies are preserved for us to view in museums. These people carried on commerce with neighboring nations. They studied, and were successful with, military strategy. They lived under a system of government-controlled production. The Egyptians built great halls and temples whose ruins still stand. Without modern machinery, they built the great pyramids near Cairo. Long before the birth of Christ, Egyptians knew how to turn wastelands into arable fields. They encouraged the arts and held great meetings where learned men gathered.

Now, with all the material that does not directly support the topic sentence deleted, the paragraph is at least unified. All the remaining sentences support the idea that ancient Egypt was civilized.

Here is one more paragraph for analysis of its unity.

The composition student, in one year alone, sees enough waste to permanently destroy his sense of well-being. He sacrifices fifty minutes a day, five days a week, thirty-six weeks of the otherwise useful year. If his scooter is missing or if Mary Lou wasn't home when he called last night or if breakfast was burned, it's hard for him to keep his mind on paper writing. No matter how full of vitality he is when he marches into the classroom, the essay writer droops away, physically exhausted, when the final bell rings.

One of those "dedicated" teachers can turn a potential writer into a nervous, quaking mouse with her constant shoulder-tapping, headshaking, and advice-giving. Even the most enthusiastic student is ready to give up when he has to be listening always to reprimands about spelling and where to put the semicolon. Writing is bad enough, but writing under such a dictator who denies the classroom citizen his basic freedoms is unbearable. Writing materials are wasted, too. High school students have to buy ball point pens for one class, cartridge pens for another, and compasses and drawing pencils for others. It's sometimes pretty difficult to figure out how the Public Education System can call itself "free." Some of the less expensive notebooks fall apart when one semester is about half through, which means probably the notebook was not a wise choice after all.

The topic sentence of this paragraph is, as expected, the first sentence in the paragraph: *The composition student, in one year alone, sees enough waste to permanently destroy his sense of well-being.* The pointer here is the word *waste.* Any sentence that does not show the waste a composition student sees does not belong in this paragraph. This paragraph can also be analyzed by considering each sentence separately to determine if it is following the direction the pointer indicates. This time the sentences that do not follow this direction, that is, that do not support the idea of waste in composition, are marked through.

1. He sacrifices fifty minutes a day, five days a week, thirty-six weeks of the otherwise useful year.
2. ~~If his scooter is missing, or if Mary Lou wasn't at home when he called last night, or if breakfast was burned, it's hard for him to keep his mind on paper writing.~~
3. No matter how full of vitality he is when he marches into the classroom, the essay writer droops away, physically exhausted, when the final bell rings.
4. ~~One of these "dedicated" teachers can turn a potential writer into a nervous, quaking mouse with her constant shoulder-tapping, headshaking, and advice giving.~~
5. ~~Even the most enthusiastic student is ready to give up when he has to be listening always to reprimands about spelling and where to put semicolons.~~
6. ~~Writing is bad enough, but writing under such a dictator who denies the classroom citizen his basic freedoms is unbearable.~~
7. Writing materials are wasted, too.
8. ~~High school students have to buy ball point pens for one class, cartridge pens for another, and compasses and drawing pencils for others.~~
9. ~~It's sometimes pretty difficult to figure out how the Public Education System can call itself "free."~~

This analysis indicates that only three sentences out of the whole paragraph follow the direction indicated by the pointer.

1. He sacrifices fifty minutes a day, five days a week, thirty-six weeks of the otherwise useful year.
2. No matter how full of vitality he is when he marches into the classroom, the essay writer droops away, physically exhausted, when the final bell rings.
3. Writing materials are wasted, too.

Put in their simplest form, these three sentences say that the composition student who writes in class wastes his time, his vitality, and his materials.

At this point, you are no doubt concluding that a paragraph is simply a short paper, as indeed it is. The methods of development are the same for both. Both have a single, central thought that is to be explored and developed. For the paper, that central thought is contained in the thesis statement; in the paragraph, it is contained in the topic sentence. As in the thesis statement, the predicate area of the topic sentence contains the pointer word, or phrase, that is the key to the content of the paragraph, and consequently to the single direction of the paragraph.

Look again, for instance, at the paragraph about the composition student and waste. It leads off with a topic sentence: *The composition student, in one year alone, sees enough waste to permanently destroy his sense of well-being.* In its predicate area, the single word *waste* is the pointer. The rest of the paragraph answers the question, *Why does the student see waste?* It gives three reasons: The student sees waste because he wastes (1) his time, (2) his vitality, and (3) his writing materials. The paragraph will be unified as long as it sticks to developing these three reasons.

A unified paragraph can be illustrated by a diagram.

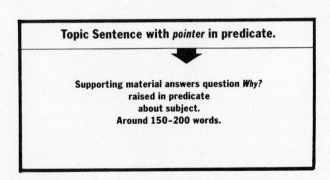

**Topic Sentence with *pointer* in predicate.**

**Supporting material answers question *Why?*
raised in predicate
about subject.
Around 150–200 words.**

## EXERCISES

A. Pick out the pointer in each of the following topic sentences.
   1. We are a frustrated generation.
   2. Vague words can be useful.
   3. History has indicated that these rulers were unduly optimistic.
   4. Reasoning from analogy is dangerous.
   5. The small car has suffered an astounding decline in popularity.
   6. Reason is opposed to dogmatism.
   7. Marriage demands cooperation between husband and wife.
   8. Chaos reigned everywhere.
   9. The good cook needs only a few simple rules.
   10. The computer has changed management procedures.

B. For each of the following paragraphs, first write down the pointer in the topic sentence, and then list by number the sentences that support the pointer.

**1.**

(1) The family predicted that Jodie would some day make a fine veterinarian. (2) He had always shown a real tenderness toward animals. (3) Stray dogs and cats seemed to collect around the farm. (4) Once a beautiful trained Collie showed up and never left again, but that wasn't as surprising as the pair of sleek Siamese cats that moved in. (5) Those cats killed every rat in the barn inside of a week. (6) Animals all loved Jodie, too. (7) Folks used to drive out from town on Sundays to look at the whole families of painted buntings that ate with Jodie's chickens. (8) He kept Rhode Island Reds, mostly. (9) They say the bunting is rare in this part of the state. (10) Jodie was the quickest kid for learning things. (11) His teachers every one had nothing but praise for him. (12) He was never content to play until he had all of his homework done. (13) And he never missed a Sunday but once, going to church all through grammar school.

**2.**

(1) Elmer Dugan studied the coffee table. (2) There was something embarrassing about it, he realized. (3) The bowl of slightly melted Christmas candy should have been cleaned and refilled weeks ago. (4) Beside the candy jar sat an ashtray running over with bobby pins, bits of rick rack, and three spools of yellow thread. (5) Next to the ashtray was the current issue of *Wild and Free* magazine, the trashy literature his wife and her good friend next door read and traded constantly. (6) John Thompson was getting a little nervous. (7) Elmer hoped that John and his loud-mouthed wife would get bored enough to leave soon. (8) But they didn't, and

Elmer's gaze wandered to the second tier of the coffee table. (9) Adele Thompson was raving on about her eight-year-old's ballet accomplishments. (10) She could go on forever, and Mary kept encouraging the chatter. (11) Elmer counted eight magazines on the second shelf of the coffee table, and one darning egg. (12) He supposed the darning egg had its rights, but why couldn't Mary keep it on the thirty-nine-dollar, three-legged, Early American rock maple sewing stand she had insisted he buy for her last Christmas? (13) What he saw next, and couldn't believe, was a small, dead, and dried scorpion that Mary had reported killing three weeks ago. (14) The phone rang, a wrong number, and Adele Thompson started in on one of her favorite and most boring of all topics, the community and its telephone manners.

### 3.

(1) It was plain to the doctor that his day was going to be dreary. (2) Already twelve patients waited in the outer office. (3) The happy Tiller teenager giggled over a comic book as she rolled up her sleeve for her shot. (4) It was a joy to chat for a moment now and then with a happy, healthy, and well-adjusted kid. (5) It didn't improve the day, either, to be haunted by the difficult tonsillectomy facing him Monday morning. (6) By mid-afternoon poor old Mrs. Clark would come begging for another bottle of sugar pills to pull her through another half-dozen "heart attacks." (7) The Everson infant needed surgery, but there was no convincing his backward parents, and the telephone jangled constantly. (8) Both the Mumford twins were down with a dangerous relapse. (9) Not that he had really hoped to fish tomorrow, but already a cold mist was falling. (10) By morning his little world would be iced over. (11) At least Nurse Hearne wouldn't be around to annoy him. (12) Never again. (13) He had gladly let her go when she demanded a sizeable pay raise and an extra half-day off. (14) He meditated for the length of one cigarette, coughed, and studied the frayed edge of his office carpet. (15) Craig Adams' test had come back positive, of course, and young Mrs. Adams would go into hysterics. (16) It would take until closing time to calm her. (17) And the town drunk, in for another Cure, was at this moment passing out in the waiting room.

C. Read this paragraph by E. B. White.

It is a miracle that New York works at all. The whole thing is implausible. Every time the residents brush their teeth, millions of gallons of water must be drawn from the Catskills and the hills of Westchester. When a young man in Manhattan writes a letter to his girl in Brooklyn, the love message gets blown to her through pneumatic tube—*pfft*—just like that. The subterranean system of telephone cables, power lines, steam pipes, gas mains and sewer pipes is reason enough to abandon the island to the gods and the weevils. Every time an incision is made in the pavement, the noisy surgeons expose ganglia that are tangled beyond belief. By rights New York should have destroyed itself long ago, from panic or fire or rioting or failure of some vital supply line in its circulatory system or from some deep labyrinthine short circuit. Long ago the city should have experienced an insoluble traffic-snarl at some impossible bottleneck. It should have perished of hunger when food lines failed for a few days. It should have been wiped out by a plague starting in its slums or carried in by ships' rats. It should have been overwelmed by the sea that licks at it on every side. The workers in its myriad cells should have succumbed to nerves, from the fearful pall of smoke-fog that drifts over every few days from Jersey, blotting out all light at noon, and leaving the high offices suspended, men groping and depressed, and the sense of world's end. It should have been touched in the head by the August heat and gone off its rocker.[1]

This paragraph maintains unity through its tight organization. To determine its organization, answer the following questions.

1. What is the topic sentence of the paragraph? What is the pointer?

2. Two principal reasons are given in support of the topic sentence and its pointer. What are they?

3. These two reasons also have supporting details to establish their validity. Write down the two principal reasons supporting the topic sentence, one at the head of one column and one at the head of another. Then, making two columns, list the supporting details for each of the two reasons.

4. a. List some of the words or phrases that seem to give the paragraph a relaxed, half-serious feeling.
   b. Does the writer maintain this feeling throughout the paragraph? How?
   c. On the basis of your answer to Question 2, what would you conclude about the author's attitude toward New York?
   d. On the basis of the pointer you found in the topic sentence and the feeling you examined in *a* and *b*, what else could you conclude about the author's attitude toward New York?

5. On the basis of your answers to Question 4, is unity of subject matter and support the only kind of unity in this paragraph? Be prepared to explain and support your answer. (If you have trouble with questions 4 and 5, recheck the comments on page 47.)

## Coherence

Although the concept of coherence is abstract, a writer must understand and get the feel of it before he can be sure he is communicating. We have already discussed unity, the logical relationship between sentences that allows them to move in a single direction, and the oneness of tone that reenforces the oneness of subject. Unity's kinsman, coherence, differs from unity in that it is the mechanical connections that hold sentences or paragraphs together. When a writer uses certain writing techniques and devices to guide the reader smoothly from one thought to another, his sentences stick together; they cohere.

Coherence is not an inevitable result of unity; unity is a matter of *direction,* while coherence is a matter of *connection.* This connection is ordinarily supplied by the writer, either consciously or unconsciously, in writing that is already unified. Coherence is not a part of unity and, indeed, is not basically even a part of the thought of the paragraph or of the sentences being connected by a coherence device. Coherence is like a whole piece of chain with all the links interlocking. Interlock binds the whole together. Without it, there is no chain, only separate links. So it is with writing. The interlock in writing is the coherence devices that bind sentences and paragraphs into a whole.

Consider, for instance, these two sentences taken out of context:

**Mr. and Mrs. Vitek thought that under the circumstances there was only one course to take. The young man on my left saw several alternatives.**

These two sentences are on the same subject, but the second sentence appears at first glance to be on another subject because of the mention of an unnamed *young man.* The reader must pause to get his bearings when he reaches the second sentence because of this apparent change in subject. He is momentarily confused. Yet note that the addition of one word, *but,* before the first word in the second sentence avoids this confusion:

**Mr. and Mrs. Vitek thought that under the circumstances there was only one course to take. But the young man on my left saw several alternatives.**

Now, the reader can go easily from the first sentence to the second with no pause, with no confusion. The two sentences are drawn together by the one word *but.* The use of such a transition word is one method of achieving coherence. There are more.

### 1. Coherence through Consistent Point of View

Consider the following paragraph.

A year spent teaching in the "shacks" adjacent to the city schools provides a unique education to any teacher. The classroom temperature gets awfully cold sometimes. You cannot imagine how hard it is to teach when it is forty-six degrees inside the building. Field mice race over the student lockers just as the teacher begins an important assignment. As summer approaches with its rising temperatures and increased noise level, the teacher has decided that she would gladly trade her unique experience for anyone's traditional classroom. The water fountain is so far away that it occupies a good part of the class time for teacher and students to get a drink.

This paragraph is unified. In the first sentence, *unique education* is the pointer, and the remainder of the paragraph shows how the teacher gets this education from teaching in the shacks. But it is not coherent. The reader is not led smoothly from sentence to sentence. The reason is obvious; the writer has not maintained a consistent point of view. *Point of view* is the position from which the writer looks at his subject. In this paragraph, the writer has shifted his position from sentence to sentence, and the reader has difficulty following his shifts. You can see the shift by picking out the subject of each sentence after the topic sentence. The subject of the second sentence is *temperature*. The subject of the third sentence is *you*. The fourth uses *field mice;* the fifth, *teacher;* and the sixth, *water fountain*. Therein lies the trouble with coherence in the paragraph. Because the paragraph obviously concerns a teacher and her experiences, each sentence should be about the teacher. A simple revision of this paragraph, using *teacher* as the subject of each sentence, greatly improves coherence.

A year spent teaching in the "shacks" adjacent to the city schools provides a unique education to any teacher. *She* learns to adjust to a temperature of forty-six degrees inside her classroom, a condition that persists although all the radiators are working at full capacity. *She* learns to cope with the problem of field mice racing over the student lockers just as she begins an important assignment. As summer approaches with its rising temperatures and increased noise level, the *teacher* has decided she would gladly trade her unique experience for anyone's traditional classroom. *She* learns to control her thirst and teaches this lesson to her students, since the water fountain is so far away it is almost impossible to get a drink.

Now, the subject of all the sentences after the topic sentence is *teacher* (or its pronoun substitute, *she*), and as a result the point of view is consistent. Note that when you make the subject the same throughout, you make other improvements almost automatically, and the whole paragraph is better.

## 2. Coherence through Chronological Order of Sentences

*Chronological order* means simply the order in which events happen. This order is seen most often in narrative—writing that tells a story— and narrative is often a part of expository writing, particularly in illustrating a point. Narrative is not necessary, however, to the use of chronological order. For instance, a chronological order may be superimposed on the revised paragraph about the teacher, and the coherence of the paragraph becomes even stronger. Look at this revision.

A year spent teaching in the "shacks" adjacent to the city schools provides a unique education to any teacher. *In the fall,* the teacher learns to cope with the problem of field mice racing over the student lockers just as she begins an important assignment. *In the winter,* she learns to adjust to a temperature of forty-six degrees, a condition that persists inside the classroom although all the radiators are working at full capacity. *In the spring,* she learns self-control of thirst and teaches this lesson to her students, since a trip to the water fountain occupies a good part of the class time. *In summer,* with its rising temperatures and increased noise level, she has decided that she would gladly trade the unique setting for anyone's traditional classroom.

This version, as indicated by the italicized phrases, takes the teacher through the seasons in chronological order during the school year. Imposing the chronological order resulted in beneficial changes. Note here that there is not just one coherence device used in a paragraph but that methods are combined within any one paragraph.

## 3. Coherence through Repetition of Key Words

Read through the following paragraph and notice the words that are connected by lines.

This doctrine of the relativity of morals, though it has recently received an impetus from the studies of anthropologists, was thus really implicit in the whole scientific mentality. It is disastrous for morals because it destroys their entire traditional foundation. That is why philosophers who see the danger signal, from the time at least of Kant, have been trying to give to morals a new foundation, that is, a secular or nonreligious foundation. This attempt may very well be intellectually successful. Such a foundation, independent of the religious view of the world, might well be found. But the question is whether it can ever be a practical success, that is, whether apart from its logical validity and its influence with intellectuals, it can ever replace among the masses of men the lost religious foundation. On that question hangs perhaps the future of civilization.[2]

In this paragraph, the word *morals* appears in the first three sentences. *Foundation,* the key word repeated most often, appears five times. *Question* appears twice, and *trying* and *attempt* are synonymous enough to be repetitions. This repetition of key words would probably not be noticed on a first reading, if the words were not marked as they are here, and that is the way it should be. But this method of achieving coherence, when the paragraph is analyzed, appears to be the chief means of holding the paragraph together.

The author of the above paragraph is an experienced and successful writer; he uses this method of achieving coherence well. The beginning writer, however, must use caution to prevent the method itself from becoming obvious and obtrusive. In this example, a student has attempted to use repetition of key words to achieve coherence.

It is necessary for a student to receive a balanced education before he goes to college. This balanced education will help him decide what his goal is and how to achieve it. This balanced education will also help him if he fails in his endeavors by giving him the necessary background to start in another field of work. With this balanced education a student. . . .

In this example, the student has repeated *balanced education* four times in four sentences in an attempt at coherence. He has succeeded, however, only in annoying his reader by starting three of the four sentences with these same words. The student removed the annoying repetition and came up with this more successful version.

A student entering college needs a balanced high school education. It will help him decide what his goal in college is and how he will achieve that goal. It will enable him to choose from more than one college curriculum, if he finds his first choice unsatisfactory or if he fails in that field. With it a student. . . .

[2] W. T. Stace, "Man Against Darkness," *The Atlantic Monthly.* Copyright 1948 by *The Atlantic Monthly.* Reprinted by permission.

## 4. Coherence through Spatial Order of Sentences

In using a spatial order to achieve coherence, a writer explains or describes objects as they are arranged in space. To describe a room a writer might, from a position in the doorway to a room, begin describing the wall to his right, go to the wall opposite him, to the wall on his left, and from there to the center of the room. In this way, the writer imposes an order on his material that helps to give it coherence. Examine this paragraph.

The main characteristic of the little farm we had walked over was disorder. The winding, narrow road was bumpy and rough, and weeds grew rank and tall on each side of it. Near the barn stood a battered, unpainted tractor, plow, and rake. On the other side of the road, weeds sapping life-giving substances from the soil were also growing among the small, withered cotton plants. The house needed paint and repairs. The steps and porch were rickety, and several of their boards were broken. The fence around the pasture was badly in need of repairs. The broken window panes in the house had pieces of tin and boards over them. On one side of the road lay bundles of grain decaying from long exposure to wind, rain, and sunshine. The wire was broken in many places, and the wooden posts, rotten at the ground, were supported by the rusty wire. The yard was littered with rubbish—tin cans, broken bottles, and paper. The barn lacked paint; its roof sagged and some shingles needed to be replaced. In the pasture, diseased with weeds and underbrush, grazed thin, bony cattle, revealing their need for more and better food and shelter.

This paragraph has unity. The pointer in the topic sentence is *disorder.* All the details in the paragraph indicate the disorder on the little farm. But it lacks coherence because the description of the disorder is presented to the reader at random; the writer has not taken a position from which to describe the disorder. The result is that the paragraph itself is disordered, as an analysis of it will quickly disclose. The second sentence, following the topic sentence, tells of the road and the weeds on each side of it. The third sentence talks about the barn. The fourth goes back to the road again. The fifth jumps to the house, and the sixth, to the pasture. The seventh returns to the house, and the eighth the road. The ninth describes the fence around the pasture; the tenth, the yard around the house; the eleventh, the barn; and the twelfth the pasture and cattle. Now, if the writer rearranges the sentences so that they present the objects on the farm as he sees them from a position of walking up the farm road to the house, he will have a more coherent paragraph.

The main characteristic of the little farm we had walked over was disorder. The winding, narrow road was bumpy and rough, and weeds grew rank and tall on each side of it. On one side of the road lay bundles of grain decaying from long exposure to wind, rain, and sunshine. On the other side, among the small, withered cotton plants, weeds sapped the soil. The fence around the pasture was badly in need of repair. The wire was broken in many places, and the wooden posts, rotted at the ground, were supported by the rusty wire. In the pasture, diseased with weeds and underbrush, grazed thin, bony cattle, revealing their need for more and better food and shelter. Near the barn stood a battered, unpainted tractor, plow, and rake. The barn itself lacked paint; its roof sagged and some of the shingles needed to be replaced. The house, too, needed paint and repairs. The steps and porch were rickety, and several of their boards were broken. A screen hung on one hinge. The broken window panes were mended with tin and boards. The yard was littered with rubbish—tin cans, broken bottles, and paper.

The paragraph now has a logical spatial order; it takes the reader from the road to either side of the road, to the pasture, and to the barn and house.

### 5. *Coherence through Related Sentence Patterns*

Holding a paragraph together by repetition of sentence patterns within the paragraph is a relatively difficult means of achieving coherence because it requires more care in designing sentences, but it is an effective means. Look at this paragraph.

(1) To be genuinely civilized means to be able to walk straight and to live honorably without the props and crutches of one or another of the childish dreams which have so far supported men. (2) That such a life is likely to be ecstatically happy I will not claim. (3) But that it can be lived in quiet content, accepting resignedly what cannot be helped, not expecting the impossible, and thankful for small mercies, this I would maintain. (4) That it will be difficult for men in general to learn this lesson I do not deny. (5) But that it will be impossible I will not admit since so many have learned it already.[3]

Note that after the first sentence, the four remaining sentences are cast in the same form and are arranged in pairs, the second and third sen-

[3] Stace, "Man Against Darkness."

tence constituting one pair, and the fourth and fifth sentences another. Look at the second sentence in the paragraph. It starts with a dependent clause *That such a life is likely to be ecstatically happy* and then finishes with a short independent clause *I will not claim.* The third sentence starts with a *but,* which ties it to the second sentence, and continues with exactly the same structure as that of the second sentence: *That it can be lived in quiet content . . . this I would maintain.* The first pair of sentences, joined together with *but,* is complete. The fourth sentence starts out exactly as the others, *That it will be difficult for men in general to learn this lesson,* and finishes with the identical short independent structure as the others, *I do not deny.* The fifth sentence begins with a *but,* which ties it to the fourth. Then comes the same type of dependent clause that has started the last three sentences, *that it will be impossible* followed by the independent clause, *I will not admit.*

Such related sentence patterns are called *balance,* which can consist of *parallel structure, contrasting ideas* (antithesis), or both. Parallel structure is a matter of grammar and arrangement of words, so that successive words, phrases, clauses, or sentences form very nearly the same patterns; contrast results when ideas logically oppose one another. Here are some simple illustrations:

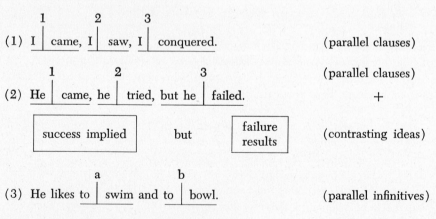

Balance is only one of many sentence patterns that can be used to add coherence. The author of the sample paragraph uses both types of balance to gain coherence, as illustrated in the following diagram.

**To be genuinely civilized means to be able to walk straight and to live honorably without the props and crutches of one or another of the childish dreams which have so far supported men.**

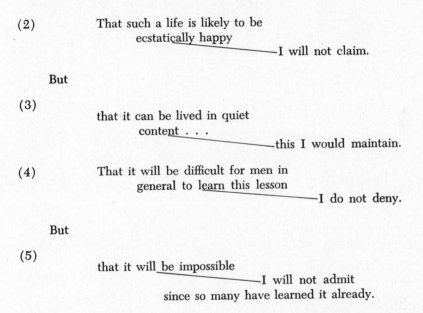

(2)       That such a life is likely to be
                ecstatically happy
                                    ——I will not claim.

        But

(3)
        that it can be lived in quiet
                content . . .
                            ——this I would maintain.

(4)       That it will be difficult for men in
                general to learn this lesson
                                    ——I do not deny.

        But

(5)
        that it will be impossible
                            ——I will not admit
                since so many have learned it already.

Both the four dependent clauses and the four independent clauses following them are examples of parallel structure. The *but* which begins the third and fifth sentences introduces contrasting ideas that force the reader to weigh them against the ideas of the preceding sentences. These balanced patterns force the ideas into a closer relationship; they give the paragraph coherence.

### 6. Coherence through Pronoun Reference

Look again at a paragraph quoted earlier, and another means of achieving coherence used in that paragraph becomes obvious.

This doctrine of the relativity of morals, though (it) has recently received an impetus from the studies of anthropologists, was thus really implicit in the whole scientific mentality. (It) is disastrous for morals because (it) destroys their entire traditional foundation. That is why philosophers who see the danger signals, from the time at least of Kant, have been trying to give to morals a new foundation, that is, a secular or nonreligious foundation. This attempt may very well be intellectually successful. Such a foundation, independent of the religious view of the world, might well be found. But the question is whether (it) can ever be a practical success, that is, whether apart from (its) logical validity and (its) influence with intellectuals, (it) can ever replace among the masses of men the lost religious foundation. On that question hangs perhaps the future of civilization.[4]

Note the number of times the pronoun *it* has been circled and tied to the antecedent noun. Any pronoun may be used for this purpose (*he, she, they, we, you,* or any other form). This method is a simple means of maintaining coherence, and it is closely allied to consistency in point of view and to repetition of key words.

## 7. *Coherence through Transition Words*

Probably the easiest, and most abused, method of pulling together the thought in a passage is through the use of transition words. Transition words or phrases bridge any gaps between sentences. They carry the reader from the thought of one sentence to that of another and indicate the relationship between the two sentences. An example of the way transition words work appeared earlier.

John and Mary Vitek thought that under the circumstances there was only one course to take. *But* the young man on my left saw several alternatives.

The word that bridges the two sentences is *but.* The reader immediately expects a *contrast* to the thought of the previous sentence, and he proceeds without pause to see what that contrast is. This word has made a transition between the two sentences and has shown their relationship—contrast.

The English language furnishes a sufficient supply of transition words to express any relationship between two sentences. The diagram below illustrates the uses of the transition words.

[4] Stace, "Man Against Darkness."

## ►—transition word►

| Thought of Sentence 1 | 1. To indicate a conclusion or result. | Thought of Sentence 2 |
| --- | --- | --- |
| | 2. To introduce an illustration. | |
| | 3. To add to a thought. | |
| | 4. To make a qualification or contrast. | |

*To Indicate a*
*Conclusion or*
*Result*

*Examples*

Therefore
As a result
Consequently
Accordingly
In other words
To sum up
Thus
Then
Hence

1. *Therefore,* his action can be justified by valid explanation.
2. *As a result,* hollow, vain aristocracies have been established on American campuses.
3. *Consequently,* the number of qualified voters remains small.

*To Introduce an*
*Illustration*

*Examples*

Thus
For example
For instance
To illustrate
Namely

1. *For example,* suppose I ask myself, "Will socialization ever come about?"
2. *For instance,* sophisticates can easily ridicule popular notions of government.
3. *Namely,* those who complain the loudest are often themselves the most guilty.

*To Add a Thought*

*Examples*

Second
In the second place
Next
Likewise
Moreover
Again
In addition
Finally
Similarly
Further

1. *Similarly,* the German university can profit by adopting the American practice of letting the student do most of the talking.
2. *Second,* human happiness feeds itself on a multitude of minor illusions.
3. Then *again* we work and strive because of the illusions connected with fame.
4. *Moreover,* the child assumes an attitude that he knows is false.

| *To Make a Qualification or Contrast* | *Examples* |
|---|---|
| On the other hand<br>Nevertheless<br>Still<br>On the contrary<br>By contrast<br>However<br>But<br>Or<br>Nor | 1. He was not, *however,* completely qualified for the task he had undertaken.<br>2. The Dobu, *by contrast,* are portrayed as virtually a society of paranoids.<br>3. *Nevertheless,* these theories do contain real insights into the nature of value judgments.<br>4. *On the contrary,* one should not blindly assume that our birthrate will continue to climb. |

The beginning writer will have to use some judgment to employ these transition words skillfully. Generally, he should keep two guidelines in mind.

1. *Use transition words sparingly.* The overuse of these words weakens writing style. Look at these sentences, for example:

James went to the resort planning to stay three weeks, *but* he became disgusted after the first day. *Consequently,* he packed and went home.

The weakness in this example is indicated by the string of three independent clauses joined together in thought by transition words. It is much better to delete at least one transition word and change one of the independent clauses to dependent.

James planned to stay three weeks at the resort, but after one day he became so disgusted that he packed and went home.

Here, the *consequently* has been dropped from the last sentence and the whole has been made into a dependent clause, *that he packed and went home.* This revision is an acceptable sentence; but why not add some meaningful details, and make a good sentence out of it:

Although James had planned a leisurely three weeks' stay at the resort, doing what he pleased when he pleased, he found himself caught up in so many planned activities—all arranged by a loud-mouthed, back-slapping "entertainment" leader—that he packed his bags and left in disgust after one day.

2. *Use transition words to indicate logical relationships.* Consider this example:

The College of Veterinary Medicine at Glory University is the only one in the state. *Therefore,* it is an excellent school.

In this example, the transition word *therefore* is not followed by a logical conclusion drawn from the evidence presented in the first sentence. Just because Glory University has the only College of Veterinary Medicine in the state, it does not necessarily follow that the college is excellent. This revision is much better:

Glory University's College of Veterinary Medicine, the only one in the state, is an excellent school.

Or consider this sentence:

Mary was healthy and robust, and she was born in Cincinnati in 1916.

The two parts of this sentence, *Mary was healthy and robust,* and *she was born in Cincinnati in 1916,* are not sufficiently related to be joined by a transition word. Apparently, the intent of this sentence is to comment on Mary's health for her age because her birth year is given. The place of her birth has nothing to do with any idea expressed in the sentence. The thought can be conveyed much better with a sentence such as this one:

At fifty-eight, Mary was healthy and robust.

Although the means of achieving coherence are considered separately in this chapter, it is not intended that only one of these means should be used in, say, one paragraph. The experienced writer may use several, even all, of them in any one paragraph to achieve the coherence he wants in his writing.

## EXERCISES

A. Examine this paragraph to see if its coherence can be improved.

1  One of the fastest-growing fields of study is wildlife ecology. The
2  growth is reflected in the increasing college enrollment in agriculture
3  and forestry. Student interest in conservation is the dominant force
4  behind the new popularity of these and such related fields as range
5  science, oceanography, and marine sciences. In the last decade col-
6  lege-bound students have become increasingly aware of the great need
7  for professionals trained in the management and conservation of natu-

8  ral resources. Reports from the Carnegie Commission on Higher Educa-
9  tion suggest that the job market for ecology-minded graduates will
10 continue to grow into the next decade.

## Analysis

1. Examine first the subjects of the sentences. The subject of the first sentence (line 1) is *one.* In the second it is *growth* (line 2), in the third it is *interest* (line 3), in the fourth, *students* (line 6), and in the fifth, *reports* (line 8). This examination shows that the student should maintain a more consistent point of view to give the paragraph coherence.

2. Examine the paragraph for evidence of other methods of maintaining coherence. There is some repetition of key words: *Growth* (line 2) and *grow* (line 10) echo *growing* (line 1), *fields* (line 4) repeats *fields* (line 1), *students* (line 6) repeats *student* (line 3), *conservation* appears in lines 3 and 7, *increasingly* (line 6) echoes *increasing* (line 2), and *ecology* appears in lines 1 and 9. Despite these echoes, the paragraph lacks coherence because the ideas have no clear *direction,* there are no transition words, there is no pronoun reference, and there are no related sentence patterns. Obviously, the coherence of this paragraph can be improved. Consider this revision.

1   The marked increase in the number of students enrolled in the field of
2   wildlife ecology has caused it to become one of the fastest-growing
3   professions. This increase also reflects the growing need for profes-
4   sionals trained in the management and conservation of natural re-
5   sources. Moreover, in the last decade college-bound students have
6   become increasingly aware of this need. Thus, the resulting student in-
7   terest in conservation has also become the dominant force behind the
8   new popularity of such related fields as range science, oceanography,
9   and marine sciences. Furthermore, reports from the Carnegie Com-
10  mission on Higher Education suggest that the job market for ecology-
11  minded professionals will continue to grow into the next decade.

Note the number of methods used to achieve coherence in this version. The most important change is in *direction:* There is a more logical movement from sentence to sentence, partly because the ideas have been rearranged and partly because sentence subjects are repeated. The subject of the first two sentences, for example, is *increase* (lines 1 and 3), while the subject of sentence four, *student interest* (line 6), echoes the subject of the third sentence, *college-bound students* (line 5). Moreover, the paragraph contains a number of transition words—*also* line 3), *moreover* (line 5), *thus* (line 6), *also* (line 7), and *furthermore* (line 9). Two modifiers (*this* in lines 3 and 6) and a pronoun reference (*it* in line 2) also add to the coherence. The paragraph repeats all the key words of the original version, but this time they appear in an order that improves the coherence. Note particularly the following sequence: *students* (line 1), *professions* (line 3), *professionals* (line 4), *students* line 5), *student interest* (line 6), and *professionals* (line 11). A similar repetition is seen in the use of *increase* and *growing*, and *ecology, need*, and *conservation*. Of 113 words in the paragraph, 30, or 26.5 percent, are key words repeated to maintain coherence. This is not an unusually high percentage. Explain why this version of the paragraph would (or would not) work as a developmental paragraph in a paper. How could you improve it?

B. In the following paragraphs, find the coherence devices and be able to point them out. Lines of the paragraphs are numbered for your convenience.

**1.**

1  I have given the impression that the Farm was remote, but this is not
2  strictly true. Not half a mile on each side of us was another farmhouse,
3  and clustering near the one to the east were three or four cottages.
4  We formed, therefore, a little community, remote as such; in Doomsday
5  Book, we had been described as a hamlet. The nearest village was two
6  or three miles away, but to the south, so that it did not count for much
7  until we began to go to school, which was not until toward the end
8  of the period of which I write. Northward our farm road ran through
9  two fields and then joined the highroad running east and west; but
10  eastward this road soon turned into a road running north and south,
11  down which we turned northward again, to the Church five miles away,
12  and to Kirby, our real metropolis, six miles away.[5]

**2.**

1  The farmhouse was a square stone box with a roof of vivid red tiles; its
2  front was to the south, and warm enough to shelter some apricot trees
3  against the wall. But there was no traffic that way: All our exits and en-
4  trances were made on the north side, through the kitchen, and I think
5  even our grandest visitors did not disdain that approach. Why should
6  they? On the left as they entered direct into the kitchen was an old ash
7  dresser; on the right a large open fireplace, with a great iron kettle
8  hanging from the reckan, and an oven to the near side of it. A long
9  deal table, glistening with a honey gold sheen from much scrubbing,

[5] From *The Innocent Eye* by Herbert Read. Copyright © 1947 by Herbert Read. Reprinted by permission of Harold Ober Associates, Incorporated.

10  filled the far side of the room; long benches ran down each side of it.
11  The floor was flagged with stone neatly outlined with a border of some
12  softer yellow stone, rubbed on after every washing. Sides of bacon and
13  plum dusky hams hung from the beams of the wooden ceiling.[6]

### 3.

1  By day it was the scene of intense bustle. The kitchenmaid was down
2  by five o'clock to light the fire; the laborers crept down in stockinged
3  feet and drew on their heavy boots; they lit candles in their horn
4  lanthorns and went out to the cattle. Breakfast was at seven, dinner at
5  twelve, tea at five. Each morning of the week had its appropriate ac-
6  tivity: Monday was washing day, Tuesday ironing, Wednesday and
7  Saturday baking, Thursday "turning out" upstairs and churning, Friday
8  "turning out" downstairs. Every day there was the milk to skim in the
9  dairy—the dairy was to the left of the kitchen and as big as any room
10  in the house.[7]

### 4.

1  At dinner, according to the time of the year, there would be from five
2  to seven farm laborers, the two servant girls, and the family, with
3  whom, for most of the time, there was a governess—a total of from ten
4  to fifteen mouths to feed every day. The bustle reached its height about
5  midday; the men would come in and sit on the dresser, swinging their
6  legs impatiently; when the food was served, they sprang to the benches
7  and ate in solid gusto, like animals. They disappeared as soon as the
8  pudding had been served, some to smoke a pipe in the saddle room,
9  others to do work which could not wait. Then all the clatter of washing
10  up rose and subsided. More peaceful occupations filled the afternoon.
11  The crickets began to sing in the hearth. The kettle boiled for tea. At
12  nightfall a candle was lit, the foreman or the shepherd sat smoking in
13  the armchair at the fireside end of the table. The latch clicked as the
14  others came in one by one and went early up to bed.[8]

### 5.

1  Many critics of our society have said that we lack standards. This
2  has been said so often by preachers and by the makers of com-
3  mencement addresses that we have almost stopped asking what, if
4  anything, it means to say that our society "lacks standards." But

[6] Read, *The Innocent Eye.*
[7] *Ibid.*
[8] *Ibid.*

5 that we do lack standards for welfare and standards for educa-
6 tion is obvious. Welfare turns into vulgar materialism because we
7 have no standard by which to measure it. Education fails because
8 it also refuses to face the responsibility of saying in what educa-
9 tion consists. Both tend to become merely what people seem to
10 want.[9]

### 6.

1 Duration is not the only political virtue, but it is a virtue. Constitutions,
2 by their name and function, can be deemed successes only if they last
3 long enough to give stability to the political life of the society they
4 are supposed to serve. The American Constitution passes that test. But
5 a constitution can survive in a form that makes it less and less adequate
6 for the needs of the society it purports to serve, and either that society
7 is cribbed, cabined and confined, held within an armor that forbids
8 adaptation or growth, or the constitution is disregarded and the true
9 political forces grow up beside it, paying only lip service to the antique
10 and obsolete forms, as Prussia grew up in the carapace of the constitu-
11 tion of the Holy Roman Empire of the German People. That has not
12 happened in the United States. The Constitution is still at the center
13 of American government and politics. It must be reckoned with every
14 day by the President, by the Congress, by the Courts, by labor, by
15 business. It has proved sufficiently adaptable to permit the expansion
16 of the thin line of newly emancipated colonies along the Atlantic sea-
17 board to the Pacific, the multiplication of the population fifty-fold, and
18 the extension of the armed power of the United States almost around
19 the globe. It has permitted the growth of these remote and, in 1789,
20 impoverished colonies to an economic power and a material wealth
21 unprecedented in human history. And it has done all this without distort-
22 ing its fundamental character or denying the political theories and
23 system of values on which it was based.[10]

### 7.

1 Studies serve for delight, for ornament, and for ability. Their chief use
2 for delight, is in privateness and retiring; for ornament, is in discourse;
3 and for ability, is in the judgment and disposition of business. For
4 expert men can execute, and perhaps judge of particulars, one by one;

[9] Joseph Wood Krutch, "Life, Liberty, and the Pursuit of Welfare," *Saturday Evening Post*, July 15, 1961. Copyright 1961 by The Curtis Publishing Company.
[10] From D. W. Brogan, *Politics in America*. Copyright 1954 by D. W. Brogan. Used by permission of Harper & Row, Publishers, and Hamish Hamilton Ltd.

5  but the general counsels, and the plots and marshalling of affairs, come
6  best from those that are learned. To spend too much time in studies is
7  sloth; to use them too much for ornament is affectation; to make judg-
8  ment wholly by their rules, is the humour of a scholar. They perfect
9  nature, and are perfected by experience: for natural abilities are like
10  natural plants, that need pruning by study; and studies themselves do
11  give forth directions too much at large, except they be bounded in
12  by experience. Crafty men contemn studies, simple men admire them,
13  and wise men use them; for they teach not their own use; but that is a
14  wisdom without them, and above them, won by observation. Read not
15  to contradict and confute; nor to believe and take for granted; not to
16  find talk and discourse; but to weigh and consider. Some books are to
17  be tasted, others to be swallowed, and some few to be chewed, and
18  digested; that is, some books are to be read only in parts; others to be
19  read, but not curiously; and some few to be read wholly, and with dil-
20  igence and attention. . . .[11]

[11] Francis Bacon, "Of Studies." Many editions.

# 4

# Writing Paragraphs

Discovery, organization, style. These are the three main subjects of this book. In the first chapter you learned about the organization of the whole five-hundred-word paper—its basic structure, its main parts, the relationship of the parts to the whole. In Chapter 2 you learned about discovering and limiting a broad subject, and about framing a thesis statement—you learned how to get started. The chapter you've just finished showed you how to give your paper unity and coherence. The next step is to learn how to write the paragraphs that make up the paper. You will be concerned mostly with two types of paragraph—introductory and developmental. For the first type, you will practice a simple, direct method to begin with; then you will be introduced to some other approaches. For the second, you will learn to develop paragraphs by use of *detail*, by use of *definition*, by use of *illustration* and *example*, by use of *comparison* and *contrast*, and by use of *reasons*.

## Introductory Paragraphs

Have you ever thought about how much information you've received by the time you've read through the first sentences of a writer's introductory pitch? Do you hear someone talking? Someone who seems aware of you as an audience? What is the writer's attitude toward his audience and his subject—bold or hesitant, quiet or loud, formal or informal, serious or playful, expository or argumentative? Do you get a sense of order and direction? How specifically does the writer state his subject? Although you will concentrate on only two major purposes of the introductory paragraph of the five-hundred-word paper, you should be aware of some of the other problems and possibilities.

A paper's opening paragraph is supposed to *introduce:* Quite independently of the paper's title, the introductory paragraph leads the reader into the subject and points him in a specific direction. Although both the leading and the pointing can be done in many ways, in all of the first papers you write, concentrate on two purposes: (1) Introduce the subject of the paper, and (2) in the last sentence of the paragraph specifically introduce the thesis statement to be supported in the developmental paragraphs that follow. The introductory paragraph need be only about fifty to seventy-five words, long enough to establish the subject of the paper. A paper longer than five hundred words might require a longer introduction reviewing the background of the subject to be discussed. In five-hundred-word papers, however, there is no space for lengthy exploration of the subject; state your subject as efficiently as possible. Then, you can use the allotted space to best advantage in developing and supporting your thesis.

An introductory paragraph starts with a broad, general statement introducing the subject of the paper, and then qualifies this subject statement by narrowing it to the specific thesis statement of the paper. This construction can best be seen in the following diagram.

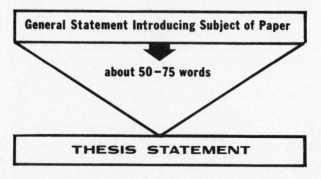

General Statement Introducing Subject of Paper

about 50–75 words

THESIS STATEMENT

Now, look at an example of a student's introductory paragraph that follows this pattern.

Women find various reasons for marrying: because it is convenient, or desirable, or highly acceptable to society, or sometimes even because it is necessary. But whatever her reasons, I contend that a woman should not marry a college student.

Note that this paragraph starts with a general statement about the reasons women marry and in thirty-nine words reduces this statement to a specific thesis statement to be established in the remainder of the paper. It wastes no time in getting to the main business of the paper, supporting the thesis statement in the developmental paragraphs.

Here is another example that does the same thing in seventy-eight words.

High school students, usually not avid readers of comic books, sometimes resort to substituting "classic" comic books for required reading. Basically honest, many of these students, under pressure of heavy assignments and extracurricular activities, think of the classic comic as merely a shortcut in completing an assignment. Although these students may be able to write a plot summary from their reading of the classic comic, they are cheating themselves when they take this easy way out.

Although that is the basic pattern you will follow at first, you will eventually want to try other kinds of introductory paragraphs and to practice ways of making your reader receptive to your ideas. For example, the first chapter tells you that the end-position for the thesis statement of the introductory paragraph is quite arbitrary. You could put it at the beginning of the paragraph or omit it entirely, letting the reader determine for himself the logical point supported by the evidence presented in the paper. The first chapter also tells you that the opening paragraph does more than merely introduce the subject in a thesis statement; it should establish tone and common ground with the reader, and it may provide a "blueprint" for the ideas to follow.

Here, then, is a more complete summary of the basic purposes of introductory paragraphs:

1. To introduce the subject (general statement)
2. To present a thesis statement with an argumentative bias (logical appeal)
3. To give a "blueprint" suggesting the order of ideas

4. To get the reader's interest (emotional appeal)
5. To get the reader to accept the writer and his views (ethical appeal) [1]

For the most part, you will concentrate on making your paragraph reflect the first two of these. The third reminds you that the order of the "because statements" in the thesis paragraph is usually the order they will follow in the developmental paragraphs. The result is a greater sense of direction for the reader. The last two purposes take care and practice, but they also give you a chance to be convincingly creative. First, a look at ethical appeal.

Your papers will be more successful if you always keep your audience in mind. Often, clear and well-supported logic is not enough to get the reader to say both "I understand" and "I agree." You can give your ideas an added push if you try to project a definite, positive image of yourself and your character. Here are a number of well-known ways to get your reader to accept and to believe you:

1. Use unemotional, calm, unprejudiced language.
2. Try to establish a common ground of understanding with your reader.
3. Praise your opposition (with restraint).
4. Give up part of your argument, admit that your position is weak (only in a minor way).
5. Tell the reader of your qualifications.

The words you use reveal your prejudices more than you think. Suppose, for example, you want to convince an audience of teenage readers that smoking marijuana is dangerous. Consider the effects of these two opening paragraphs.

**A.**

Young people are sadly mistaken if they think smoking marijuana is a fun-ride to freedom. A person is stupid to think that the only payment is the cost of the weed. Anyone who thinks at all knows that marijuana is dangerous

---

[1] Derived from the word *ethos*, the term *ethical appeal* is used to describe the appeal used in writing (and speech) that comes from the apparent, projected *character* of the person himself. To get his audience to trust him and to believe what he says, the writer (or speaker) tries to create in his work the *impression* that he is fair, or good, or intelligent, or sympathetic, or honest. The person may not actually possesss these qualities, but if his work *appears* to have them he could still convince his audience to accept him and believe what he says. Ethical appeal works best when the writer really possesses the qualities he tries to project in his work, when he really believes what he is saying.

because the stuff is illegal, it creates in the addicted user a sense of psychological dependence, and it turns users into bums who become dropouts from society.

Now compare Paragraph A with B:

**B.**

Smoking marijuana is not an easy way to freedom. The user always pays more than just the cost of the drug. Repeated use of marijuana is dangerous because it is illegal, it creates in the user a sense of psychological dependence, and it may turn users away from active participation in the community.

Paragraph B tries to tone down the prejudiced judgments of the first version by removing such negative words as *sadly mistaken, fun-ride, stupid, weed, thinks at all, stuff, addicted,* and *bums.* On the other hand, the first version might very well catch the favorable attention of a group of mothers who have seen their children arrested, dropped from school, and sent to jail. A calm tone is best if you want to appear *objective.*

Suppose Paragraph B started this way:

**C.**

I'm told it is fun to smoke marijuana, and I'm sure that is true. I'm told that legalizing the use of alcohol is not the cause of its abuse, that the same argument holds for marijuana, and I'm sure that is true. I'm told, also, that scientists have not proved that smoking marijuana harms the body, and I'm sure that, also, is true. But just because there is truth and sincerity in all these statements does not mean that smoking marijuana is not dangerous.

(Now, continue with Paragraph B.)

The writer of Paragraph C is trying to be personal, and he is trying to establish a common ground of understanding with his readers; he says he agrees with a number of arguments that oppose his view. By saying that these arguments are "true" and "sincere," he is praising the opposition and giving up part of his own argument (using marijuana is *dangerous*). Even with the toned-down language of Paragraph B following it, Paragraph C would probably not convince too many readers. Try to decide why.

The writer of these three paragraphs could add still one more ingredient to try to convince his readers that he and his views are acceptable. He could list his qualifications—personal experience, research, special skill. Try to add two sentences to the beginning of Paragraph C to make this final ethical appeal. Remember, however, that good writing demands *honesty* as well as supporting facts. If you assume that "anything goes" in order to convince your reader, you are likely to lose him when he spots insincerity because you overwork ethical appeal. Ethical appeal works best when the writer really possesses the qualities he tries to project in his work (intelligence, fairness, objectivity, for example), when he really believes what he is saying.

A final point: Introductory paragraphs should also try to get the reader's interest. Usually this means trying to get the reader involved psychologically or emotionally. If you compare the following opening paragraphs with the diagram for the introductory paragraph, you will discover changes in the pattern as well as other techniques of creating reader interest.

### D.

Strictness or permissiveness? This looms as a big question for many new parents. A great majority of them find the right answer in a little while. For a few parents it remains a worrisome question, no matter how much experience they've had.

I may as well let the cat out of the bag right away as far as my opinion goes and say that strictness or permissiveness is not the real issue. Good-hearted parents who aren't afraid to be firm when it is necessary can get good results with either moderate strictness or moderate permissiveness. On the other hand, a strictness that comes from harsh feelings or a permissiveness that is timid or vacillating can each lead to poor results. The real issue is what spirit the parent puts into managing the child and what attitude is engendered in the child as a result.[2]

Many writers use a provocative question to get started and to arouse the curiosity and interest of the reader. Here the author sets up a contrast to lead his reader into the work, withholding the thesis statement until the end of the second paragraph. But using a question or a series of questions to arouse interest and isolate a problem should be handled with restraint to keep the introduction from sounding insincere and overdone. Did you notice the series of questions used to introduce the "Introductory Paragraph" section at the beginning of this chapter?

If your subject is important and current, sometimes you can state it strongly in the first sentence of the introductory paragraph and get

---

[2] From "Strictness or Permissiveness?" from *Baby and Child Care* by Dr. Benjamin Spock. Copyright 1945, 1946, 1957 by Benjamin Spock, M.D. Reprinted by permission of Pocket Books/A Division of Simon & Schuster, Inc.

your reader involved immediately. Look at this opening to the first chapter of a highly successful book.

### E.

Time talks. It speaks more plainly than words. The message it conveys comes through loud and clear. Because it is manipulated less consciously, it is subject to less distortion than the spoken language. It can shout the truth where words lie.[3]

The author boldly asserts the thesis of his chapter in a two-word sentence stating that time is one of the silent languages. Perhaps a weakness in this beginning is that the reader gets well into the chapter before he understands the significance of the chapter title, "The Voices of Time."

There are, of course, many other ways of introducing the subject and pointing the way for the reader. You can begin by dividing the subject into its parts and then telling your reader which you will emphasize. You let the reader follow your thinking process: *Flight? Flight of birds, flight of planes, flight of animals, flight of men, flight from freedom, flight to avoid punishment, flight from responsibility.* Or you can present an explanation or justification of your paper, particularly if it is one based on personal observation. Some writers lead up to a thesis statement by beginning the introductory paragraph with a relevant quotation or incident, a striking illustration, or an anecdote. Others begin by stating a view which they will oppose, creating interest through contrast. Here are two final illustrations.

### F.

The philosopher Diogenes lived in a tub in the market place. He owned the clothes on his back and a wooden cup; one morning, when he saw a man drinking out of his hands, he threw away the cup. Alexander the Great came to Athens, and went down to the market place to see Diogenes; as he was about to leave he asked, "Is there anything I can do for you?" "Yes," said Diogenes, "you can get out of my light."

At different times, and in different places, this story has meant different things. . . .[4]

[3] Edward T. Hall, "The Voices of Time," from *The Silent Language.* Copyright 1959 by Edward T. Hall. Reprinted by permission of Doubleday & Company, Inc.

[4] From *A Sad Heart at the Supermarket* by Randall Jarrell. Copyright 1955 by Street & Smith Publications; copyright 1962 by Randall Jarrell. Reprinted with the permission of Atheneum Publishers.

**G.**

Childhood used to end with the discovery that there is no Santa Claus. Nowadays, it too often ends when the child gets his first adult, the way Hemingway got his first rhino, with the difference that the rhino was charging Hemingway, whereas the adult is usually running from the child. This has brought about a change in the folklore and mythology of the American home, and of the homes of other offspring-beleaguered countries. The dark at the top of the stairs once shrouded imaginary bears that lay in wait for tiny tots, but now parents, grandparents, and other grown relatives are afraid there may be a little darling lurking in the shadows, with blackjack, golf club, or .32-caliber automatic.

The worried psychologists, sociologists, anthropologists, and other ologists, who jump at the sound of every backfire or slammed door, have called our present jeopardy a "child-centered culture." Every seven seconds a baby is born in the United States, which means that we produce, every two hours, approximately five companies of infantry. I would say this amounts to a child-overwhelmed culture, but I am one of those who do not intend to surrender meekly and unconditionally. There must be a bright side to this menacing state of civilization, and if somebody will snap on his flashlight, we'll take a look around for it.[5]

Paragraph F uses an interesting anecdote to catch the reader. Illustration G gives the first two paragraphs of a serious article on children. Despite its serious subject, it is imaginative and humorous. It wins the reader over with its informal tone, teases him with a "fake" thesis statement at the end of the first paragraph, and then provides a genuine, contrasting thesis statement at the end of the second paragraph. The first *two* paragraphs provide the "introduction" to the article. The main aim of the first one is to create reader interest by overstatement and emotional appeal, with such statements as "gets his first adult," "running from the child," "offspring-beleaguered countries," "darling lurking," and "blackjack." The second paragraph uses less exaggeration and adds ethical appeal: The writer uses "I" and "we" to seem closer to the reader, adding that he will not "surrender meekly" and that "there must be a bright side" which *we* should look for (*together*, presumably).

Introductions that take more than one paragraph give the writer a chance to make both an emotional and an ethical appeal; they can be

[5] Copyright © 1960 by James Thurber. From "The Darlings at the Top of the Stairs," in *Lanterns and Lances*, published by Harper & Row, New York, and Hamish Hamilton, London. Originally published in *Queen*, England.

fun and they are always a challenge. However, a careless writer runs the risk of using appeals that fall flat: They can sound insincere and exaggerated rather than humorously honest, especially if the writer's main method of catching his reader is to entertain him. Before experimenting with emotional and ethical appeals, therefore, you should master the method of straightforward logical appeal (in *one* paragraph), as diagrammed at the beginning of this discussion. You must conceive and state your thesis clearly if your additional efforts are to succeed. Turn back to page 21 and check the student theme on "Law and Order" for emotional and ethical appeals. Do you think the appeals succeed? Or, you can study the examples of introductory paragraphs given on pages 157–61 in the section on tone; these also go beyond simple logical appeal.

### EXERCISES

A. By now you have probably written introductory paragraphs for several themes (see pages 23 or 39). Rewrite two of your introductory paragraphs, paying special attention to reader interest and reader acceptance, assuming that the reader is
   1. Your teacher
   2. Your best friend
B. Make a list of the kinds of changes you made in Exercise A, listing some examples (words, sentences, information, and so on). Be prepared to comment on the changes you needed to make most in order to alter the tone of your original paragraphs.

## Developmental Paragraphs

The developmental paragraphs are the meat of your paper because they present the evidence you have for your thesis statement. Again, a diagram explains the developmental paragraph. (See page 82.)

In this diagram, the space representing the first sentence in the paragraph is divided. The first part, labeled Transition, indicates that a word, phrase, clause, or sentence should ordinarily be used in this position to provide a connection between this paragraph and the preceding one. The second part is the topic sentence, which leads into the paragraph. For example, look at this opening sentence:

I am arguing, *then,* that there are *two readers distinguishable* in every literary experience. . . .

## THE DEVELOPMENTAL PARAGRAPH

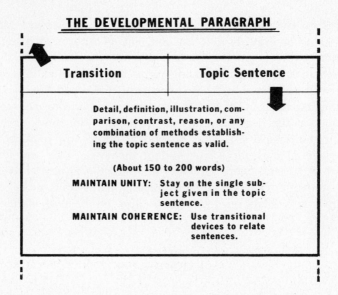

| Transition | Topic Sentence |
|---|---|

Detail, definition, illustration, comparison, contrast, reason, or any combination of methods establishing the topic sentence as valid.

**(About 150 to 200 words)**

**MAINTAIN UNITY:** Stay on the single subject given in the topic sentence.

**MAINTAIN COHERENCE:** Use transitional devices to relate sentences.

*Then* is a transition word that suggests a summing up and a continuation of the thought of the preceding paragraph. The *two readers* in the last part of the sentence are to be explained in the remainder of the paragraph.

I have given the impression that the Farm was remote, but *this is not strictly true.*

The first part of this beginning sentence points back to the preceding paragraph. The last part points forward to the remainder of the paragraph by announcing its topic.

Closely associated with *this distinction* between author and speaker, *there is another and less familiar distinction* to be made. . . .

*This distinction* in the first of the sentence is obviously the subject of the preceding paragraph. *Another and less familiar distinction* is the subject of this paragraph.

Although fraternity *expenses* are less hindrance to affluent members, the society *interferes* indiscriminately *with the studies* of its members. . . .

Here *expenses* refers to the subject of the preceding paragraph; *interferes with the studies* is the subject of the paragraph the sentence introduces.

These sentences all demonstrate transitional techniques necessary for the reader's easy progress from the main point of one paragraph to the main point of the next. Use these techniques to give your whole paper coherence and apply them within each developmental paragraph as well.

## Paragraph Development by Use of Detail

Have a look at two students' paragraphs and the discussion of them that follows. Here is the first one.

People who buy foreign economy cars are not getting what they think they are paying for. Foreign cars are not really any more economical to operate than are American cars. Those who talk about how good foreign cars are simply do not know what they are talking about. They should spend more time studying the durability record of American cars than just thinking about gas mileage. Many small foreign cars are worn out after 50,000 miles and have to be replaced. American cars will run much longer than this. So foreign cars are not good buys.

This paragraph was written by a student who had been assigned a paper to write in class at the beginning of the semester. After completing this paragraph and making several attempts to continue writing the paper, the student appealed to his instructor for help. What, he wanted to know, could he say next? The instructor explained that the broad ideas in the paragraph were undeveloped and that the student needed to use detail to support his ideas and to convince his reader. Consider, for instance, the general statement that foreign cars are not any more economical to operate than are American cars: What detailed facts could the student present to make this statement more than just an assertion? Without the facts, thousands of foreign car drivers may not agree with him.

Here is the second one.

The adoption of medicare can cause serious damage to our system of free enterprise and private medicine. It would ruin many medicinal-producing corporations and cause unemployment for thousands of workers. The control of medicine would pass from the doctors to the government. Our system of medicine has worked for over 180 years. Why destroy it now with medicare? Why take from the skilled hands of our doctors and give to untrained "butchers" of socialized medicine? This can not be allowed in the United States. Medicare must not be allowed to destroy our democratic system.

This student apparently feels quite strongly about his subject, so strongly, in fact, that he has let the discussion get out of hand. Personal belief in a subject is not enough to convince others. And no matter how the reader personally feels about medicare, he certainly must recognize this piece of writing as ranting and fanatic opinion unsupported by evidence. Logically, the paragraph is impossible. It equates free enterprise, private medicine, and democracy. These are not interdependent, as can be easily shown, and one does not necessarily collapse when one of the others does. How, for instance, can medicare ruin *medicinal-producing corporations* and cause unemployment? Why are the practitioners of socialized medicine called *butchers?* Are medicare and socialized medicine the same thing, as this paragraph asserts? How can medicare *destroy our democratic system?* How will it damage *free enterprise?* All these questions are unanswered, and we must conclude that this student needs to support his opinions with detail.

But he needs to learn more than this. He needs to learn to

**Use detailed FACTS:**
   **1. To support *ideas***
   **2. To support *judgments* or *opinions***

And he needs an understanding of the terms *fact, judgment, opinion,* and *inference.*

By definition, a *fact* is a verifiable statement, something everyone will agree to. For instance, the following sentences are all fact.

1. Yesterday there was a car wreck on Highway 6 about three miles south of the city limits. (This statement is easily verifiable by the police or the newspapers. Anyone will accept the validity of either source.)

2. The Weather Bureau reported that 3.00 inches of rain fell on the city yesterday. (Here the question of fact is not whether 3.00 inches of rain fell but whether the Weather Bureau reported it. Again, this fact is easily checked in the newspaper or at the Bureau.)

3. There are sidewalks on each side of the street. (Anyone who questions this statement can check it simply by looking at the street. Probably, no one would want to question it.)

4. In 1970, Texas had a population of 11,196,830. (Easily verified by the government census reports for 1970.)

5. John Jones told me that he saw a leopard change its spots. (Here again the question is not whether John Jones *saw* a leopard change its spots but whether he *told* me that he saw it. As long as John Jones will admit that he told it, the statement is verifiable. If he will not,

the question must be resolved by the reliability and reputation of the two people involved.)

An *opinion* is a conclusion or conviction formed about any matter. It is, of course, based on evidence, as all conclusions or convictions are, but the evidence can be logically sound or logically fallacious. An opinion is open to dispute and is not a soundly proved matter. It should be based on factual evidence, and a person expressing an opinion should be able to support it with fact and sound logic. Or he should have such a reputation for his experience with the subject and his knowledge of it that he is recognized as an authority. Without either fact or authority, an opinion holds little weight in any discussion.

Perhaps most often, human nature being what it is, opinions appear as judgments. A *judgment* is a statement indicating approval or disapproval of objects, happenings, persons, or ideas. Judgment, a form of opinion, is also based on some kind of evidence, but particular care must be taken in forming judgments and in expressing them. For instance, suppose your family bought a house from a real estate agent named John Jones and that before you made the down payment he promised to put a new roof on the house. When no workmen appeared to start work on the roof and you asked Jones when he was going to order the roof put on, he denied making any such promise. Your first reaction would probably be "John Jones is a crook," and you might make this statement to your friends. But wait. Even though Jones has wronged you, to call him a crook is to say that he has been a crook and always will be a crook in business dealings. On the basis of this one example only, such a judgment is hardly justified. About all you can say is that in this situation you think Jones dealt with you unethically. Or suppose you bought a Waumpum car two years ago and that you have now driven it for 75,000 miles with only a few minor repairs. You might well say, "The Waumpum is an excellent car." Yet the fact may be that yours is the only Waumpum to go over 50,000 miles without a major overhaul. Again, on the basis of experience with one car of one model, such a judgment is not justified. Judgments and opinions such as these should not appear in your papers unless they are firmly and soundly supported by factual evidence.

Imagine yourself in a situation such as this one: You observe a woman you have seen many times before, and you turn to your friend and say, "There goes that wealthy woman I see all over town." Your friend says, "Really? How do you know she is wealthy?" "Well," you reply, "she wears obviously expensive clothes, she drives a large, late model car, and she lives in a house that anyone would call a mansion." "That doesn't prove anything," says the friend. "She may just be deep in debt." Your friend would be right; you have not proved your point. But you did form an inference about the woman. An *inference* is a guess about the unknown based on the known. But an inference is not necessarily a valid conclusion, because there are usually other conclusions that you could just as logically derive from the evidence. For instance, suppose in the middle of a classroom lecture the student sitting next to you suddenly bangs his book closed, grimaces, rises, and stomps out of the room, slamming the door behind him. You might say to yourself, "Something the professor said made him angry." But again you might be wrong. The student may have had a sudden and uncontrollable stomach cramp from something he ate for lunch, and it became imperative for him to leave the room at once. There are other possible inferences to be drawn from the student's actions. Inferences cannot, therefore, be positively stated as if they were valid conclusions and absolute truth.

### EXERCISES

A. Identify the following statements as fact, opinion, judgment, or inference.
1. My history teacher has asked me a question in class every day for the past two weeks.
2. Don't take that history course—it's tough.
3. The referee penalized our team seventy-five yards in that game with Primitive University.
4. We lost that game to the referee.
5. We would have won that game with Primitive University if we had not been penalized so much.
6. That referee was no good.
7. Only twenty-five percent of that professor's students passed the last examination. It's time for an investigation of his teaching methods.
8. Termites have damaged the floor joists in that house.
9. I studied everything and went to class every time, but I still didn't pass because the teacher doesn't like me.
10. That's the worst teacher I ever had.

B. The first statement in this group is fact and the others are based on it. Identify them as judgment or inference.
1. There is a six-foot fence around their house.
2. They don't want people to visit them.
3. Their house looks like a prison.
4. They want privacy in their home.
5. There must be something wrong with those people.
6. Those people are crazy.
7. They must have something to hide.
8. I don't like that house with its high fence.

C. List the inferences that might be drawn from these sets of circumstances.
1. He was weaving as he walked along. He staggered several times. He suddenly sat down on the curb and held his head in his hands.
2. The man ran from the store in great haste. He jumped in his car and sped away. The store's owner ran out on the curb and shouted something after him.
3. After dinner she went straight to her room, took out paper and pen and spent four busy hours writing her English paper. She received a failing grade on it.
4. Everyone must be convinced by now that cigarette smoking does contribute to the high incidence of lung cancer. Yet the rate of cigarette consumption in the United States increases each year.
5. While the population of the United States has been increasing, church attendance has been decreasing.

D. Select from each of the lists you have written for Exercise C the inference you think is likely to be the most valid, and indicate your reasons for thinking so.

### Using Specific Details

Now that you have learned not to use opinion, judgment, or inference as fact, you can also learn to distinguish between the specific and the general in developing paragraphs by use of detail. You will want to learn to use the *specific* rather than the general in supporting ideas, opinions, or judgments.

The *general* includes all of a class, type, or group. For example *structure* is a general term, because there are several types of structures. The *specific*, on the other hand, refers to a *particular* in a class, type, or group. A building, a bridge, a television transmitting antenna, or a radar tower are each a particular of the general class, structure. Therefore, *building* is more specific than *structure*, because it is only one member of the whole class. In the same way, *box* is more specific than *container*, because a box is only one type of container. *Horse* is more specific than *vertebrate; boat*, more specific than *vehicle; meat*, more specific than *food;* and *furniture*, more specific than *household goods*.

But all these terms can be made yet more specific. *Building*, even though it is a type of structure, is still a general term that can be divided into types. A house, a service station, a garage, or a greenhouse can all be called buildings and are, therefore, more specific than *building*. Again, a filly is a type of horse, a wooden crate is a type of box, a chair is a type of furniture, beef is a type of meat, and a kayak is a type of boat. These terms can be made still more specific by reference to building material, color, location, shape, or size. For instance, *brick house* is more specific than *house*, and *red brick house* is still more specific. *The red brick house on Lincoln Street* will specify even further by pointing to a particular house.

Similarly, beef is a type of meat, steak is a type of beef, sirloin steak is a type of steak, and grilled sirloin steak is one type of sirloin steak. And the sirloin can be made more specific by describing its appearance: *grilled sirloin steak, charred on the outside, raw within.*

## EXERCISES

I. Select from the following groups the most specific in each group.

A. (1) dog (2) mammal (3) large bird dog (4) setter (5) canine

B. (1) a great boy (2) a witty and charming boy (3) a boy with a top-notch personality (4) a wonderful boy to know

C. (1) John and Mary served a large quantity of food. (2) Their table literally groaned with an abundance of viands. (3) They served a quantity of foods suitable for the Thanksgiving season and tempting to the most jaded palate. (4) In the center of their table was a large baked turkey surrounded by dishes of cranberry sauce, sweet potatoes, giblet gravy, rolls, and pumpkin pie. (5) Their cuisine was liberally illustrated by the delicious and nourishing products of culinary art distributed on the table in great number.

Answers: In *A*, *setter* is the most specific term, because it names the type of dog involved. In this group, *mammal* is the most general term, followed by *canine, dog,* and *large bird dog.* If you picked *witty and charming boy* in *B* as the most specific in this group, you were correct. In fact, of the choices here, this is the only one that gives any specific information about the boy. *C* is easy. Number 4 is the only one in this group that tells specifically what food was on the table.

II. Select the most specific from each of these groups.

A. (1) mosquito (2) blood-sucking insect (3) creature (4) invertebrate (5) insect with two wings

B. (1) man (2) person (3) individual (4) student (5) one

C. (1) a building with an established place in the history of one of our largest states (2) a historical shrine revered by Texans (3) an old stone mission where, in 1836, Santa Anna's 4,000 Mexican troops, after a thirteen-day siege, defeated and slaughtered Colonel Travis' Texas garrison of 180 men (4) a rambling structure, once a church, where Texas history was made (5) an old mission where the Mexican forces massacred the defending Texans

D. (1) He wore a battered brown derby, a new light-orange sport jacket, red slacks, frayed white spats, and black shoes. (2) He was extremely oddly dressed. (3) His hat and his spats were certainly from another era, but his coat and slacks were modern, although their colors were so loud they hurt the eyes of the onlooker. (4) No piece of his clothing matched any other piece. (5) He wore an old derby, a coat that clashed sharply with the color of his slacks, spats, and shoes.

E. (1) The book ends with a scene of mounting interest and excitement that leaves the reader sitting on the edge of his chair. (2) The ending of the book is simply magnificent in the gripping realism of its final scene. (3) At the end of the book, after Jack's followers, now complete savages, have set fire to the island and have hunted Ralph down to kill him, the reader understands with almost unbearable clarity the cruelty inherent in all mankind. (4) At the end of the book, after a series of highly interesting scenes, the reader is brought face to face with certain facts about modern life.

## Using Details in Paragraph Development

In diagram form, here is the paragraph developed through use of detail.

```
┌──────────────────────────────────────────┐
│   TOPIC SENTENCE  (Generalized)          │
├──────────────────────────────────────────┤
│                                          │
│        SPECIFIC FACTUAL DETAIL           │
│                                          │
│     (A series of related statements      │
│     giving particulars that support      │
│     the generalized topic sentence.)     │
│                                          │
└──────────────────────────────────────────┘
```

Here is an example of a paragraph developed through use of details taken from the work of a successful writer.

Freeman Halverson is tall, fast on his feet, and works hard. On his slender shoulders are laid many of the responsibilities of the little community. He is postmaster, storekeeper, driver of the school bus. He is chairman of the community study group, head of the newly organized conservation unit, president of the state alfalfa seed growers' association, editor of the Hub News. He is on the citizens' advisory board of the state agricultural college. He leads the Lonepine band. At times he trains the girls' chorus. And then toward the evening he plays the clarinet at home in the family ensemble.[6]

[6] From Baker Brownell, *The Human Community* (Harper & Row, 1950). Reprinted by permission of Harper & Row, Publishers, Inc.

This paragraph establishes the pointer in the topic sentence, *responsibilities*, by detailing the duties Freeman Halverson carries in the community. When the reader finishes the paragraph, he can only agree with the author that Halverson does, indeed, carry many of the responsibilities of the community.

Read this paragraph. You can recognize it as coming from the same work.

> Freeman Halverson is the downtown population of Lonepine, he and perhaps Ted Van der Ende, the cheesemaker. Freeman Halverson is postmaster and the owner and operator of the general store. His place is the rendezvous. *The post office is on one side of the room.* For a time the public library also was housed here. Below are freeze lockers. The butcher shop with its big refrigerator is at the back. In *this* building with its somewhat informal front porch may be bought a *wide variety of goods. Sales* are announced in the weekly *news sheet,* and the prices paid for local produce are revised to suit the season.[7]

You have already seen how effectively this author uses detail to support his ideas; therefore, you might be immediately suspicious of this paragraph, particularly if you examined the italicized parts. These parts indicate where detail might be used to good effect. The fact is that the author did not write this paragraph in quite this way. He supplied the needed details. Look at the way he actually wrote it. The details he used are italicized.

> Freeman Halverson is the downtown population of Lonepine, he and perhaps Ted Van der Ende, the cheesemaker. Freeman Halverson is postmaster and the owner and operator of the general store. His place is the rendezvous. The tiny post office, *not much larger than a telephone booth,* is on *the drygoods side* of the *big* room. For a time the public library also was housed here. Below are freeze lockers. The butcher shop with its big refrigerator is at the back. In this *rambling frame* building with its somewhat informal front porch may be bought a *modern cream separator* or a *pair of overalls, a pound of cheese or a tube of lipstick, a silken, western neckerchief, a saddle or a pound of old fashioned chocolate creams.* Brisk bargains are announced in the weekly *mimeographed* sheet of *news* and *market items,* and the prices paid for local *eggs* and *poultry, vegetables, seeds, potatoes,* and *fruit* are revised to suit the season.[8]

[7] Brownell, *The Human Community.*
[8] *Ibid.*

Now the paragraph is specific in its detail, and the reader has a much better idea of the effect the author intended to create.

Here are some students' paragraphs developed through the use of detail. Examine them carefully, for they will serve as models for your writing:

> The catcher is the "quarterback" of baseball. In effect, he runs the team. He is the only man who sees every player on the field and observes every move that takes place. He calls the pitches by giving signals to the pitcher. Sometimes he directs much of the defensive play by stationing the players in key spots and by directing the moves against the opposition. He is the one player on the team who can never for a moment relax, whether his team is in the field or at bat. He must know wind directions in every ball park, and he must study the opposing batteries, the mental condition of his own pitcher, and the spacing of his fielders. And he must watch runners on base, keeping track of the tactical situation and seeing that the rest of the team knows it also.

This paragraph uses the details of the catcher's job to establish the point that the catcher "runs" the baseball team. Enough detail is included to make the point of the topic sentence quite clear. Here is another example paragraph.

> We could not use the table he showed us. The wood was rough and saw-marked, and the finish was dull and spotty. The top was marked with several cigarette burns, although a label on the bottom promised that it was fire-proof. Stains and scuffs also marred the top. The construction was poor; the joints were ill-fitted, and one leg was held on by a wire. The metal cap on one of the legs, provided originally to protect the carpet, was missing, and the drawer, which had no handle, could not be opened more than three inches. Furthermore, the table was too long for practical use and too wide to be easily moved through the door.

In this paragraph, abundant detail is used to support the point of the topic sentence: The table was beyond use.

Here is a paragraph written by a student in business administration with previous business experience.

> Few people know the significant criteria that a financial manager must consider in devising a company's financial plan. He must keep abreast of the general level of business activity to determine the company's needs for assets and funds. To operate efficiently he must interpret and use money

and capital markets to the fullest extent. He must know the effects of tax rates and whether an increase or decrease in the tax rates will raise or lower the desirability of indebtedness. He must cope with seasonal and cyclical variations in business activity. To as great a degree as possible, he must know the nature and effects of competitors. He must use regulations and customs to the best practical extent. He must know the credit standing of his company and strive to keep it as high as possible.

The next paragraph was written by an expert bowler, a student who gave bowling lessons at the student union lanes.

Although the experts all claim that proper form is the most important aspect of good bowling, consistency is the real secret for a bowler. The bowler may push the ball away too fast, but if he does it the same way every time, his game will not suffer. He may backswing too high or too low, but if the ball reaches the identical spot in the backswing arc in each delivery, the high score compiled for each game will not reveal the weakness. He may take more or fewer steps than the recommended four, as long as he takes the same number in each approach. The bowler may even commit the unpardonable sin of releasing the ball while on the wrong foot, provided he can do it exactly the same way every time. In other words, the bowler can do everything "wrong" and still be an expert bowler, if he will do it "wrong" consistently.

This paragraph makes its point about consistency being the secret of good bowling by detailing the things a bowler may do wrong consistently but still bowl well.

This paragraph was written by a young high school teacher who had returned to college after teaching for a year on a temporary certificate.

Although many people think the work of a public school teacher is easy, the school teacher actually has the responsibility of many jobs. Before school opens in the fall, the teacher must attend meetings every day, sometimes for as long as a week, in preparation for the fall semester. During the semester, the teacher has official meetings, such as those for the faculty and the PTA, that he must attend. He is expected to sponsor clubs, coach athletics, and help promote such fund raising activities as carnivals. He has monitorial duties to perform when he is not in class. But, of course, his primary job is teaching. He must teach about five classes a day and sometimes conduct an additional study hall. In preparation for instructing his classes, the teacher spends about five to six hours a week preparing materials and reading to supplement textbooks. Still he must spend some of his "off" hours at school helping individual students having personal problems or difficulty learning the material. Furthermore, he must grade papers, evaluate the students' progress, make reports of various kinds, and even interview the parents of his students. But this is not all. To keep up with new teaching methods and programs the teacher himself must often go to school in the summer and attend conventions. And occasionally, he must take part in such community affairs as luncheons and civic organizations.

After reading this paragraph with its detailing of the teacher's duties, anyone must agree with the point stated in the topic sentence.

### Summary

1. Start a beginning paragraph with a general statement and narrow it to the thesis statement.

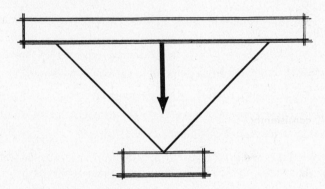

2. Learn to distinguish:

*Fact:* a statement that is verifiable.

*Inference:* a guess based on known fact.
   (May be valid but may not be)

*Opinion:* a conclusion, or conviction, established about a matter.
   (May be based on no fact)

*Judgment:* statement made of approval or disapproval.
   (May be based on no fact or insufficient fact)

3. In supporting inferences, opinions, or judgments (generalizations), use *specific facts.*

*General:* a broad term covering many particulars (the whole)

*Specific:* a narrow term specifying a particular (a small part of the whole).

*Thesis statements* and *topic sentences* are supported by related, factual, specific statements.

## EXERCISES

If you have trouble finding details for this assignment, you should check the "discovery exercise" on page 42 (Exercise D).

A. List the details that might be used to support five of the statements below.

1. The college student's life is full of (opportunity) (demands) (roles).

2. Dogs on the loose are a nuisance.

3. A young man can't get along without a car.

4. Car manufacturers are (are not) meeting human needs in automobile safety.

5. Television programs can be highly (instructive) (frustrating) (boring).

6. The dating game can be a (nuisance) (disaster) (threat) (joy).

7. Fixing a big breakfast is (fun) (messy) (challenging).

8. I didn't know where to start cleaning my room.

9. The clock I brought home from the discount house was incredible.

10. Horror movies create humor at the drive-in.

B. Rewrite these paragraphs and supply appropriate, specific detail at the italicized points. Freely add and change material that is here.

1. He stared at the carnival booth as if hypnotized. From it issued *highly amplified sounds* that almost overcame him with their intensity. Its *many* shelves were stacked with *a variety of flashy goods*. *Some men stood* at the booth's counter intently concentrating on looping hoops over a *stick some feet away*. *A few boys* chased each other through the *people* standing at the booth.

2. They entertained the *group of visitors* as best they could with such short notice. First, there was a *lunch outdoors*, followed by a long walk through *interesting gardens* of the city. After resting, the visitors were taken to *a local museum* where they were shown *relics of bygone days*, and in the evening they saw *a stage show of their choice*. At the end of the planned activities, the host took the entire group to his home, where they were joined by *friends of the hosts* for a *party to climax the delightful visit*.

3. *A manufacturing firm nearby* went all out to advertise their products and to establish goodwill in the community at the same time. They

ran a contest in the spring that offered a *costly grand prize* for the best slogan in praise of their products. In the winter, they offered an all-expense-paid trip *to the South* for the merchant who arranged the Ideal Display of the firm's products. For the consumer who could think up original ideas for putting the firm's merchandise to use, *there was a reward.* The community showed its appreciation *in many ways.*

4. The bride-to-be found it difficult to display all her lovely gifts in her parents' *small* home. Relatives from out of town had sent *lightweight but expensive knickknacks.* All these had arrived early and seemed to get choice spots in the living room. *Gifts of bedding and kitchenware* from nearby kinfolk covered the dining table and took all the space *on other furniture* in the dining room. Chums in her own age group had sent the bride more *"mod" gifts,* and these took over the TV room and what shelf space *there was in the house. Her gift from the groom's parents,* the one she treasured most highly of all, because of its resale value, the bride kept in her purse and brought it out for frequent praise from *interested parties.*

C. Using three of the lists you made in Exercise A write three paragraphs developed through the use of detail. If you have trouble getting started, check again the exercises beginning on page 41.

## Paragraph Development by Use of Definition

Before studying the means of using definition in paragraph development, read through this paragraph, a definition of *democracy,* written by the well-known historian Carl Becker. It will give you a good idea of what it means to use definition.

In this antithesis there are, however, certain implications, always tacitly understood, which give a more precise meaning to the term democracy. Peisistratus, for example, was supported by a majority of the people, but his government was never regarded as a democracy for all that. Caesar's power derived from a popular mandate, conveyed through established republican forms, but this did not make his government any less a dictatorship. Napoleon called his government a democratic empire, but no one, least of all Napoleon himself, doubted that he had destroyed the last vestiges of the democratic republic. Since the Greeks first used the term, the essential test of democratic government has always been this: the source of political authority must be and remain in the people and not in the ruler. A democratic government has always meant one in which the citizens, or a sufficient number of them to represent more or less effectively the common will, freely act from time to time, and according to established forms, to appoint or recall the magistrates and to enact or revoke the laws by which the community is governed. This I take to be the meaning which history has impressed upon the term democracy as a form of government.[9]

This paragraph starts with a conventional topic sentence using *implications* as the pointer to give the paragraph unity. It explores these implications chronologically by use of examples starting with the Greeks (Peisistratus) and ending with France's Napoleonic Empire. When the paragraph comes to a statement of the principal implication, which is Becker's one-sentence definition of democracy, it maintains coherence by reference to the Greeks, mentioned early in the paragraph. After the one-sentence definition, . . . *the source of political authority must be and remain in the people and not in the ruler,* the paragraph explains in more detail what this definition means. In the final sentence, the paragraph declares that this is the meaning of democracy that Mr. Becker is to use throughout his book, and the reader need have no misunderstanding of what he means when he uses the word.

As Becker has done in his paragraph, you must also define the terms you use in writing, if there is any chance that your reader may use a different meaning from the one you intend. Many a verbal argument has ended with some such statement as "It has become obvious that we are not defining our terms in the same way, and I won't accept your definitions." This usually ends the argument, because without acceptable definitions there is no real communication. One group talks about one thing and the other group is arguing another, although they seem to be talking about the same subject. Throughout one presidential campaign, for instance, there was a running argument over whether the United States is a republic or a democracy, but nowhere in the campaign were these two terms satisfactorily defined, nor was the distinction between the two made clear. Consequently, the argument carried little weight with the voting public. So make the meaning of the terms you use in writing clear to the reader. Defining terms will not necessarily make the reader agree with you, but without adequate definitions, he cannot tell what you are saying.

When you decide a term needs defining, you will not want to copy verbatim the dictionary definition and use it in your paper with some phrase as "Webster defines socialism as. . . ." Such a practice defeats your purpose, which is to make clear the exact meaning *you* are attaching to a word. You can devise your own definitions. There are five methods of doing so.

[9] Carl Becker, *Modern Democracy.* Copyright 1954 by Yale University Press. Used by permission.

1. Classification
2. Synonym
3. Example or Illustration
4. Enumeration
5. Function

Consider these methods one at a time.

### Definition by Classification

This is also called the Aristotelian method, and it is the one most often found in dictionaries. Its use is quite simple and involves only two steps:

1. Place the word to be defined in its family (genus).
2. Differentiate the word from all others in its family.

For instance, if you wanted to define the relatively simple word *bridge* (to indicate that you do not mean the card game or a part of the nose or of a pair of spectacles or an arch to raise the strings of a musical instrument or a raised platform on a ship or a transition in music), you would first place the word in its family:

**A bridge is a structure.**

You have already seen that *structure* is a general term including many particulars, a bridge being one of them. The second step, then, is to differentiate *bridge* from all other structures—buildings, houses, towers, and so forth. This can be done by naming its function:

**A bridge is a structure *carrying a roadway over a depression or obstacle.***

Examine these definitions by classification:

| Word | Family | Differentiation |
|------|--------|-----------------|
| Bird | vertebrate | covered with feathers and having wings. |
| Insect | invertebrate | having head, thorax, and abdomen, three pairs of legs, and one or two pair of wings. |
| Chair | seat | having four legs and a back, for one person. |
| House | building | serving as living quarters for one or more families. |

In defining by classification, there are three missteps to guard against.

1. Look at this definition of *net* from Samuel Johnson's dictionary:

A net is any reticulated fabric, decussated at regular intervals, with interstices at the intersections.

Since you know what a net is, you can probably make out what this definition says. But suppose you do not know what a net is. Could you possibly make sense from this definition without looking up several words in the dictionary? Probably not. So when you see the necessity of defining a word, follow this rule:

Do not use words that might not be clear to the reader (that is, obscure, ambiguous, or figurative).

Suppose you read this definition: *A democracy is a government in which the citizens are sovereign.* This is a perfectly good definition as long as you know what the word *sovereign* means. The writer could have avoided the use of this word by spelling out its meaning. For instance, he might have written this clearer definition: *A democracy is a government is which the citizens hold supreme power by periodically electing, either directly or indirectly, their representation in the government.*

2. Consider this definition: *A democracy has a democratic form of government.* Here no defining has taken place, because the definition offered leaves the reader at the same place he started. The writer has used a form of the defined word in the definition itself. This definition has the same trouble: *A good man is one who performs good deeds.* The word that is being defined here is *good,* but this word has also been used in the definition of it, so nothing has been clearly defined. Stick to this rule, also:

Do not use any form of the defined word in the definition of the word.

3. Look at this definition: *Democracy is when the citizens are sovereign.* You have probably been told throughout your scholastic career that you cannot define by saying that something "is when. . . ." Logically, you cannot make the adverbial construction (showing condition), *when the citizens are sovereign,* equal to the noun, *democracy;* but the use of the verb *is* says that they are. In defining, then, you must also remember this rule:

The word defined must always be equal to the definition.

That is, wherever the defined word is used, you should be able to substitute your definition in its place. You can say, for instance, *The government of the United States is a democracy*, but when you try to substitute for the word the definition of democracy just considered, complete nonsense results: *The government of the United States is when the citizens are sovereign*. So a good definition of democracy is needed, one that can be substituted wherever the word itself is used. Here is a definition that will work: *Democracy is a form of government in which the citizens are sovereign*. Now we can substitute this definition for the word *democracy* in the sentence, *The government of the United States is a democracy: The government of the United States is a form of government in which the citizens are sovereign*. Note that placing the word in its family and then applying differentiation corrects this misstep.

### Definition by Synonym

Using other words that mean the same thing as the defined word but that are likely to be more easily understood is one of the easiest ways to define. For instance, if you are not certain your reader will know what *prevaricating* means, you can define it by saying that it means *lying* or *fibbing*. Or you can say that to *limit* is to *restrict* or to *define*. Or you might define *bad* as meaning *bath* in German, but as meaning *evil, wicked,* or *naughty* in English. In using synonyms to define, you must understand two points.

1. Synonyms are useful in definition only when they are closer to the reader's experience than is the word defined.
2. Usually synonyms are not definitions but only approximations. They may best be used to clarify other kinds of definitions.

### Definition by Example or Illustration

Sometimes it is possible to make a word unknown clear to the reader by pointing out an example of something that is known and that is the same thing. For instance, you can define the color green by pointing to a plot of live grass and saying, "Green is the color of that grass." Or if you happen to have anything at hand of the color you want to define, you can simply hold it out and say, "Magenta is this color." Or if you do not have any of the color at hand you can say, "Magenta is red with some blue in it—a purplish red." To define by illustration you can give a brief narrative (a story) that explains what is being defined. Here is an example of how you might define *spoiled child*.

When Roger is asked to do something he doesn't want to do, he sticks out his tongue or simply turns away with no response at all. He demands what he wants and gets it, or else he lies on the floor and screams until it is forthcoming.

### Definition by Enumeration

In defining words that are the names of general classes of objects, you can sometimes define the word by simply listing the members of the class represented by that word. For example, you can define *decathlon* by listing the athletic events included.

The decathlon is an athletic event in which each contestant competes in the 100-meter, 400-meter, and 1500-meter runs, the 110-meter high hurdles, the javelin and discus throws, shot put, pole vault, high jump, and broad jump.

Or you can define the Pentateuch by listing the books of the Bible that compose it.

The Pentateuch is Genesis, Exodus, Leviticus, Numbers, and Deuteronomy.

Some classes are too large to enumerate, but most frequently you can list enough of the members of the class so that the definition is made understandable. For instance, to list all the seasonings would take up more space than the definition is worth and would make tedious reading. But some of the seasonings can be listed and the effect is the same as if they were all listed.

Salt, pepper, thyme, oregano, marjoram, are common seasonings.
Fruits such as lemons, oranges and grapefruit are citrus fruits.

Note that the definition admits the listing is not complete. And, again, you must be sure that the reader will be more familiar with the members of the class than with the name of the class itself.

### Definition by Function (Operational Definition)

Frequently you can define by describing how an object functions or operates. Definition by function is particularly useful in defining the name of a machine or mechanism, because showing what a machine does will usually be sufficient. The functional definition is not limited to defining the names of objects, however. For instance, you might define *prejudice* by using the functional method. A dictionary definition of prejudice might appear in some such form as this: *A preconceived, especially unfavorable, judgment or opinion.* A functional definition would show how prejudice operates.

A prejudice is a judgment or opinion about a person, race, religion, nation, or any particular group or object without careful consideration of facts. To feel antagonism at first meeting toward a student from a rival college without actually knowing the student is to be prejudiced toward him.

Or, *claustrophobia* might be defined in a dictionary as *morbid fear of enclosed or confined places.* A definition by function, which might be added to this definition by way of further explanation, would come out in this way:

Persons who, when confined in a small, enclosed space such as an elevator, experience a rapid quickening of heart beat, acute agitation, and a desperate desire to leave the enclosed space are suffering from a mental disturbance known as claustrophobia.

### EXERCISES

A. If any of these statements is not acceptable as a definition, indicate specifically what is wrong with it. If any is acceptable, mark it *C.*

 1. Lapidation is when you hurl stones at someone.
 C 2. A lanyard is a rope used in firing certain types of cannon.
 3. A proletarian is a member of the proletariat.
 4. Syneresis is closely associated with dieresis and synizesis because all of them concern the coalescence of two vowels or syllables. *UNKNOWN WORDS*
 5. English is where expository writing is learned.
 6. Gamosepalous is the same as synsepalous. *NOT DEFINED*
 C 7. Tabasco is the trade name of a sauce made from red pepper.
 8. Tetrameter is a line of verse consisting of four metrical feet.
 9. Second childhood means senility or dotage.
 10. Debate is an element basic to any democracy. *NOT EXPLAINED*

B. Write your own definitions of the following words, using two methods of defining for each. Do not consult your dictionary.
 1. Magazine
 2. House
 3. Free speech

4. Enemy
5. Chair
6. Money
7. Laws
8. Vehicle

### The Extended Definition

Now that you have learned the methods of defining, you are ready to write an extended definition. An extended definition is ordinarily a paragraph, but it can be much longer, using a combination of definition methods to explain the defined word explicitly, and starting with a definition by classification. A diagram of the paragraph developed by an extended definition will help clarify.

---

**DEFINITION BY CLASSIFICATION**

**Clarification (usually of differentia) by any pertinent means: illustration, examples, contrast, comparison, detail, synonyms, enumeration, function.**

---

To further clarify, here are some students' extended definitions.

Jargon is a special vocabulary understandable only to the users. In Elmstown, one has only to pay a visit to Joe's Wagon Diner, at Tenth and Canal, to hear examples of its use. Table orders are taken by the waiters and given to the kitchen in such a manner that one hears expressions like, "One-eyed jacks up, no hog," meaning an order of two eggs fried on one side and no bacon; or "One brown with dogs, add straight," meaning an order of hash brown potatoes with sausage, and coffee without cream or sugar; or "Cream it with hens," meaning creamed eggs on toast; or "Dunk one all the way," meaning doughnut and coffee with cream and sugar.

This paragraph starts with a definition by classification and then extends the definition by adding a series of short examples to explain what jargon is. Here are three more example paragraphs of extended definitions.

A "turista" is any human being who finds himself in strange surroundings that he is not able to appreciate. The word is usually employed to describe middle-aged persons who have just started traveling. It is a fit description for a woman who upon arriving at the Grand Canyon rushes to the gift shop to buy postcards before she has had a look at the sight she has traveled to see. The word, although it has a feminine ending, is applied to the male traveler who goes to the Louvre and stares at female forms in the flesh and not at the Venus de Milo. The "turista" is constantly comparing his present surroundings with the heaven-on-earth where he lives, making all listeners wonder why he had not remained in that choice place. He is a steak-and-potato man and is constantly griping about the food. He refuses to eat reindeer meat in Norway, but longs for it as he is eating lasagna in Italy, proving to the uninterested listeners that he has been to Norway. The word is never applied to anyone except Americans, meaning anyone from the United States, and is used by persons in foreign countries to show their dislike for individuals who spend their money ostentatiously while traveling.

Elephant jokes, popular some time ago, are humorous devices consisting of two lines—a question and an answer—in which an elephant is pointlessly involved. An example of this joke would be, "What was the elephant doing on the expressway?" and the answer, "About three miles an hour." Or, with a side flavor, "What do you call the black stuff between an elephant's toes?" Answer, "Slow natives." Or, with a risqué twist, "How do you make an elephant fly?" Anwer, "First, you get an eight-foot zipper." Often these jokes are presented in a series, each joke related to the last. A short example would be, "How do you tell an elephant from a bluebird?" Answer, "Elephants live in trees." Question, "How did the elephant get flat feet?" Answer, "From jumping out of trees." Question, "Why do elephants jump out of trees?" Answer, "How else could they get down?"

A thunderstorm is a weather disturbance having lightning and, consequently, thunder within it. There need not be rain falling, but without lightning it is merely a rain shower and not a thunderstorm. Thundershowers come in three types—air mass thunderstorms, frontal thunderstorms, and thunderstorms caused by unstable air over mountains. Air mass thunderstorms are common along the Gulf Coast in the afternoon during the summer. Frontal thunderstorms occur in the fall, winter, and spring along and ahead of cold fronts. Since there are no mountains in this area, the third type of thunderstorm never occurs here. Sometimes towering to heights of 50,000 or 60,000 feet, thunderstorms can be quite severe, bringing rain and hail and sometimes spawning tornadoes.

**EXERCISES**

Select three of these topics and write a paragraph of extended definition for each.

| | |
|---|---|
| Rock music | Trial marriage |
| Beauty of soul | Adequate diet |
| Courtesy in everyday affairs | Vivacity of youth |
| "Decency" at the beach | The home remedy |
| Unethical behavior | Jokes |
| Worthwhile fishing trips | Slang |
| Any new slang word | Free enterprise |
| Well-dressed man | Political liberals |
| Good teacher | Classical music |
| Soul brother | Promiscuity |
| Obscene picture | Happiness |
| Integrity | Dirty politics |
| Sportsmanship | Practical jokes |
| The joys of Christmas | Excellent teachers |
| | Social fraternities |

## Paragraph Development by Use of Illustration

Illustration, as used to support a topic sentence in the developmental paragraph, is narrative, that is, it tells a story. It usually gives a chronological account of what happened in a certain situation that would give validity to the topic sentence. Illustrations can be either real or hypothetical. You can use an account of some event you actually know about, or you can, in effect, "make up" one, provided the reader understands that the illustration is hypothetical. Usually the hypothetical illustration starts with something like "Suppose such-and-such a thing happened. What would be the result?" Then the writer goes on to supply a narrative of what would happen in the hypothetical situation.

Paragraphs may be developed by two kinds of illustrations—short and extended. A collection of short illustrations, all supporting the topic sentence, may be used as a paragraph. Usually, the narrative in a short illustration is quite brief. Or an extended illustration, a single, relatively long narrative, may constitute the paragraph. Of course, any combination of extended and short illustrations may be used to support the topic sentence.

The paragraph developed by the use of illustration appears as in this diagram.

```
┌─────────────────────────────────────┐
│                                     │
│     TOPIC  SENTENCE                 │
│   ═══════════════════════════════   │
│                                     │
│   A narrative or a number of nar-   │
│   ratives, in any combination, that │
│   specifically illustrate  the va-  │
│   lidity of the topic sentence.     │
│                                     │
│                                     │
└─────────────────────────────────────┘
```

Now, look at some examples of students' paragraphs using illustration. The first paragraph uses a series of short illustrations in support of the topic sentence.

American history is a record of courage. During the Revolution, Paul Revere, a Boston silversmith, rode his horse through the night to warn the Massachusetts colonists that the British were coming. Daniel Boone, Kentucky trailblazer and Indian fighter; Davy Crockett, hero of the Battle of the Alamo; and Lewis and Clark, leaders of the trail expedition to Oregon, all did their share in shaping the growth of a young country struggling against unknown obstacles. In more recent times, Charles Lindbergh, who by making the first nonstop flight from New York to Paris established the importance of air power to our country; General Douglas MacArthur, victorious against the Japanese after early defeat; and John F. Kennedy, who nearly lost his life as a PT boat commander in World War II but lived to become president of the United States, all displayed the personal bravery so apparent in American history.

That paragraph used seven short illustrations, arranged chronologically in American history, to support its topic sentence. The next paragraph is an example of the extended illustration.

Poor communication between the administration and staff results in misunderstandings among the employees of the Chemist's Laboratory. Recently, for instance, the department head told a graduate student employee, a good worker who had been carefully trained by another administrator in the same department, to go home and change out of Bermuda shorts or to consider himself fired. The incident, which occurred while several women employees were present, embarrassed the student so deeply that he determined not to work for such a man. The student resigned, and the department lost a well-trained and efficient worker because neither administrator had taken the responsibility of telling the employee what dress was acceptable for work.

Here is another example of the use of a series of short illustrations.

Many people in show business have become famous because of a "gimmick." In the thirties, for example, such entertainers as Helen Kane with her "boo-boop-a-doop," and Joe Penner with "Wanna buy a duck?" rose to national prominence. In the fifties, Elvis Presley achieved adulation and stardom as a rock-and-roll singer by wiggling his hips and charming the teenage world by his wild gyrations. Frank Fontaine became popular because of a humorously stupid laugh. And more recently, the Beatles, an English singing group, were an immediate sensation, not so much for their singing as primarily for their clothes and long hair.

Here is another use of extended illustration, a hypothetical one.

Despite the general opinion that it is recreation, an all-night fishing excursion is more work than pleasure. Suppose, for example, a typical fisherman decides to fish in his favorite lake, an afternoon's drive from his home. Since he plans to spend the night, he will spend all morning packing his gear—boat, fish lines, bait, food, cooking utensils, tent, bedding, and clothing. Then, after driving all afternoon to reach the lake, he will begin the tiring job of establishing camp. This task completed, he must back his boat trailer to the edge of the lake and laboriously ease his boat into the water. He then must find what he considers the perfect spot for setting out and baiting his lines. On his return to camp, he will perspire over an open fire while preparing his supper. After supper and again at two o'clock in the morning, he must run his lines, rebaiting where necessary. If he is lucky, he may net a fish or two before returning to camp for a few minutes of rest. As the sun appears on the horizon, he will cook and eat breakfast and begin to repack his gear for the long journey home. Four hours later, after an exhausting drive, he will walk into the house and collapse on the bed for a well-earned rest.

You will note that this paragraph does not contain an actual illustration, that is, the experience recounted in the paragraph did not happen to a specific person, necessarily, but it simply indicates what would likely happen to anyone on an overnight fishing trip.

The next sample is similar to the preceding one in that it involves a hypothetical individual and situation. But this example was written by a respected, published writer.

The tribes we have described have all of them their nonparticipating "abnormal" individuals. The individual in Dobu who was thoroughly disoriented was the man who was naturally friendly and found activity an end in itself. He was a pleasant fellow who did not seek to overthrow his fellows or to punish them. He worked for anyone who asked him, and he was not filled by a terror of the dark like his fellows, and he did not, as they did, utterly inhibit simple public responses of friendliness toward women closely related, like a wife or sister. He often patted them playfully in public. In any other Dobuan this was scandalous behavior, but in him it was regarded as merely silly. The village treated him in a kindly enough fashion, not taking advantage of him or making a sport of ridiculing him, but he was definitely regarded as one who was outside the game.[10]

The next two paragraphs from the same book indicate how the author uses an extended illustration about a real individual as he has been observed in the Zuñi society. Note that the illustration extends over two paragraphs but that each paragraph makes its own point with its own topic sentence.

The dilemma of such an individual is often most successfully solved by doing violence to his strongest natural impulses and accepting the role the culture honors. In case he is a person to whom social recognition is necessary, it is ordinarily his only possible course. One of the most striking individuals in Zuñi had accepted this necessity. In a society that thoroughly distrusts authority of any sort, he had a native personal magnetism that singled him out in any group. In a society that exalts moderation and the easiest way, he was turbulent and could act violently upon occasion. In a society that praises a pliant personality that "talks lots"—that is, that chatters in a friendly fashion—he was scornful and aloof. Zuñi's only reaction to such personalities is to brand them as witches. He was said to have been seen peering through a window from outside, and this is a sure mark of a witch. At any rate, he got drunk one day and boasted that they could not kill him. He was taken before the war priest who hung him by his thumbs from the rafters till he should confess to his witchcraft. This is the usual procedure in a charge of witchcraft. However, he dispatched a messenger to the government troops. When they came, his shoulders were already crippled for life, and the officer of the law was left with no recourse but to imprison the war priests who had been responsible for the enormity. One of these war priests was probably the most respected and important person in recent Zuñi history, and when he returned after imprisonment in the state penitentiary he never resumed his priestly offices. He regarded his power as broken. It was a revenge that is probably unique

10 From Ruth Benedict, *Patterns of Culture.* Copyright 1934 by Ruth Benedict. Reprinted by permission of Houghton Mifflin Company.

in Zuñi history. It involved, of course, a challenge to the priesthoods, against whom the witch by his act openly aligned himself.

The course of his life in the forty years that followed this defiance was not, however, what we might easily predict. A witch is not barred from his membership in cult groups because he has been condemned, and the way to recognition lay through such activity. He possessed a remarkable verbal memory and a sweet singing voice. He learned unbelievable stories of mythology, of esoteric ritual, of cult songs. Many hundreds of pages of stories and ritual poetry were taken down from his dictation before he died, and he regarded his songs as much more extensive. He became indispensable in ceremonial life and before he died was the governor of Zuñi. The congenial bent of his personality threw him into irreconcilable conflict with his society, and he solved his dilemma by turning an incidental talent to account. As we might well expect, he was not a happy man. As governor of Zuñi, and high in his cult groups, a marked man in his community, he was obsessed by death. He was a cheated man in the midst of a mildly happy populace.[11]

## EXERCISES

A. Select two of these topic sentences and write two separate paragraphs. In one, use a series of short illustrations to support the topic sentence. In the other, use an extended illustration.

1. College (high school) freshmen have a rough time.
2. The principal did not always act so wisely.
3. The clean-up drive produced noteworthy results.
4. Students are uncomfortable in the new high school.
5. Cheating is (is not) widespread in .............. High School.
6. Today's hair styles are ridiculous.
7. Seventeen is a frustrating age.
8. Country music has distinctive qualities.

B. This exercise reviews some of the material already covered.

1. Look again at the paragraph about American history on page 105, and answer the following questions.
   a. What is the pointer in the topic sentence?
   b. Are there any sentences that do not help to establish this pointer as valid?
   c. What is the purpose of the phrases *During the Revolution* and *In more recent times?*
   d. What is there in the last sentence that ties it to the first sentence?

[11] *Ibid.*

e. Would you say, then, that this paragraph is coherent? Why or why not?

2. Answer these questions on the paragraph about fishing on page 106.
   a. What is the pointer in the topic sentence?
   b. Examine the subjects of the sentences. Is a consistent point of view maintained?
   c. In what other ways is coherence achieved?
   d. About two-thirds of the way through the paragraph the word *perspire* is used. Would you prefer another word here? Why or why not?

3. These questions concern the two paragraphs about the Zuñi society on pages 107–8.
   a. What is the pointer in the topic sentence of the first paragraph? Of the second paragraph?
   b. In the first paragraph, what coherence device is employed in the sentence that starts *In a society that thoroughly distrusts. . . .* and in the next few sentences?
   c. What is the purpose of the phrase *At any rate* about half-way through the first paragraph? Has the principle of unity been violated just before the use of this phrase?
   d. Look at this sentence a little more than halfway through the first paragraph: *This is the usual procedure in a charge of witchcraft.* As you read through the paragraph (try it aloud), this sentence seems to be out of the tone of the rest of the paragraph. What makes it seem so? Try to rewrite it to make it fit in better. You might try including it in the preceding sentence.
   e. What is the purpose of *however* in the first sentence of the second paragraph?
   f. What purpose is served by *As we might well expect* in the third sentence from the end of the second paragraph?
   g. Is the second paragraph coherent? What means of achieving coherence are used?

# Paragraph Development by Comparison or Contrast

Comparison and contrast, as developmental methods, are so much alike that they can be considered together. First, the two terms must be defined.

**Comparison:** indicates similarities between two objects, people, places, or ideas for the purpose of clarifying or explaining one or the other.

**Contrast:** indicates differences between two objects, people, places, or ideas for the purpose of clarifying or explaining one or the other.

Comparison shows similarities, and contrast shows difference. Developing a paragraph by comparison or by contrast is not difficult, but it is better to compare or contrast point-by-point than to take the whole of the first object of comparison and then the whole of the other object. For instance, if you were comparing two cars it would be better to compare, say, the performance of one to the performance of the other, next their economy, and finally their appearance, than to describe these three points for one car and then describe them for the other.

Here is a diagram of the paragraph developed by comparison or contrast.

---

**Topic Sentence**

---

**A point-by-point comparison
or a point-by-point contrast that illustrates
the soundness of the topic sentence.**

---

Note how the following student paragraph makes this point-by-point comparison between a school and a game of basketball.

School is like a game of basketball. In both, the time is short, and the student uses all his resources in the class as the player does in the game. The student has a background of knowledge that enables him to meet the challenges in class; the player relies on ability he has acquired previously. The student begins on registration day a period in which he matches wits with his opponent, the professor. The first whistle of the basketball game starts the player matching his wits with the opposing team. The student relaxes over the weekends, taking this time to catch his breath; time out in the basketball game allows the player to catch his breath. The student can slow down the class, if he is tired, by turning it into a bull session. The basketball player can also slow the game. Each is aware that he runs the risk of being punished, as the professor can give a pop quiz, or the referee can call a foul. Each participant is striving for a measure of his ability, a grade for the student and a score for the player. At the end of the term, the student looks anxiously at the bulletin board just outside the classroom for the final verdict. The player's eyes scan the scoreboard for the outcome of his efforts. The result is the same. If the student makes a good grade or the player has the high score, both are pleased with their efforts. If either loses—but that is too horrible to think about.

And here is a paragraph written by a student who was very fond of her new foreign car. She planned her paragraph around the same point-by-point comparison.

The proud owners of big American automobiles look with scorn at my little foreign car and with contempt call it a beetle. Well, I suppose it is almost a beetle. Nature carefully designed oval-shaped, low bodies for beetles to decrease air resistance, and my tiny horseless carriage is as smooth, oval, and low as any real beetle. Most beetles are actually poor flyers and indeed, some like my car, never fly. A true member of the beetle family is powerful but slow; my small auto cannot go over sixty miles per hour, but it can climb steep curving roads well in spite of ice, rain, or standing water. Bugs take in energy-giving food anteriorly, and my bug-car has its gasoline tank near its nose also. Real beetles have posterior air intake tubes just like my little foreign car, although the real beetles have more of them. Normally I dislike bugs, but I am so fond of my beetle-like Volkswagen that I may grow to like all beetles.

This paragraph compares first the appearance of the two objects, next the performance of the two, and finally the position of fuel and air intake openings.

This next paragraph is developed by use of contrast. Note that again the point-by-point plan is used, but here in contrasting rather than in comparing.

The modern kitchen is different from the old-style type. It even looks different. The charm of the old kitchen lay in its design, from the wallpaper to the curtains to the tablecloth; but the modern kitchen has no designs, only shiny chrome and brilliant color. There's a different atmosphere, too. Grandma's kitchen was a place to talk things over, to have a hot drink and relax while savoring the odor of bread baking in the oven, to leisurely plan and put loving thought into every meal prepared there. But the modern kitchen is constructed for speed, for the fastest and easiest way to get the food on the table and the dishes washed so that the cook can go on to other activities. The modern kitchen seems to have a different role to play in our lives. Instead of being a center of family life, it has become a laundry, dining room, and office for the increasingly complicated job of the home-maker.

This paragraph compares the old and the new kitchen on three points: their appearance, their atmosphere, and their roles in family life.

The next paragraph, a comparison, was written by a disgruntled married student.

Special words have been used to sympathize with the "golfer's widow," but no terms directly apply to the amateur mechanic's wife, who is no better off. Both are often left stranded for hours with no cars while the laundry waits to be washed and the pantry to be filled. The golfer cannot stand the thought of his friends putting on the green without him, and the auto maniac insists on being present after each exciting mechanical failure. Either situation may leave the wife floundering in a welter of broken social engagements. Although it is worse in some ways to break appointments for lack of transportation or an escort, the mechanic's wife and the golfer's wife are placed at further social disadvantage by knowing that, come spring, when afternoon picnics and cook-outs are enticing, they dare not plan them. After a winter of being cooped up in the house, the amateur mechanic wants to polish his car as well as those of his buddies, and the golfer wants to join his cronies on the golf course. Both leave their wives to wonder how the myth of "family companionship" persists.

## EXERCISE

Select two of these topic sentences. Write one paragraph using comparison as a means of development and another paragraph using contrast.

1. The P.E. teacher insisted that the class would benefit far more if they chose swimming rather than fencing (archery, golf, badminton, field hockey, handball) for the second semester's work.
2. Death is like sleep.
3. The prospective buyer has little choice among today's cars.
4. I didn't know whether to ask the tall blonde or the little, dark-eyed brunette.
5. Mrs. Smith said that one conversation piece in the living room was enough.
6. Fear is like fire (ice).
7. Youth has "rebelled" before.
8. Men and women are similar (opposites).
9. I have not found college so different from high school (or the opposite).
10. The feud between the Suffles and their neighbors included even the landscaping of their lawns.

## Paragraph Development by Reasons

The use of reasons in paragraph development has already been discussed in the section about maintaining unity in the paragraph. Recall that example paragraphs in the section gave two or more reasons for the validity of the topic sentence and then supported those reasons. Also recall that this pattern of development is the one suggested in the first chapter for the whole paper, except that in the paper the reasons (topic sentences) support the thesis statement of the paper. Therefore, because a paragraph is like a small paper, the same method of development can be used within the paragraph.

In one of the exercises of an earlier chapter, you were asked to analyze a paragraph by E. B. White. This paragraph was developed by using reasons. Have another look at it.

It is a miracle that New York works at all. *The whole thing is implausible.* Every time the residents brush their teeth, millions of gallons of water must be drawn from the Catskills and the hills of Westchester. When a young man in Manhattan writes a letter to his girl in Brooklyn, the love message gets blown to her through a pneumatic tube—*pfft*—just like that. The subterranean system of telephone cables, power lines, steam pipes, gas mains and sewer pipes is reason enough to abandon the island to the gods and the weevils. Every time an incision is made in the pavement, the noisy surgeons expose ganglia that are tangled beyond belief. By rights *New York should have destroyed itself long ago,* from panic or fire or rioting or failure of some vital supply line in its circulatory system or from some deep labyrinthine short circuit. Long ago the city should have experienced an insoluble traffic snarl at some impossible bottleneck. It should have perished of hunger when food lines failed for a few days. It should have been wiped out by a plague starting in its slums or carried in by ships' rats. It should have been overwhelmed by the sea that licks at it on every side. The workers in its myriad cells should have succumbed to nerves, from the fearful pall of smoke-fog that drifts over every few days from Jersey, blotting out all light at noon, and leaving the high offices suspended, men groping and depressed, and the sense of world's end. It should have been touched in the head by the August heat and gone off its rocker.[12]

12 From pp. 24–25 in *Here Is New York* by E. B. White. Copyright 1949 by E. B. White. Used by permission of Harper & Row, Publishers, and Hamish Hamilton, London.

The topic sentence of this paragraph is the first sentence. Its pointer is *miracle*. The two reasons that support this topic sentence are italicized in the paragraph. In its simplest outline form, the paragraph appears like this:

*Topic Sentence:* It is a miracle that New York works at all.
*Main Reason 1:* The whole thing is implausible.
*Main Reason 2:* New York should have destroyed itself long ago.

This outline as it stands could be assembled into a paragraph.

It is a miracle that New York works at all. The whole thing is implausible for a number of reasons. There is so much congestion that New York should have destroyed itself long ago.

But you have learned that this is not a good paragraph because it does not supply details as supporting reasons. White did it like this:

*Topic Sentence:* It is a miracle that New York works at all.
   *Main Reason 1:* The whole thing is implausible.
      *Supporting Reason 1:* Water must come from a distance.
      *Supporting Reason 2:* Mail is carried through tubes.
      *Supporting Reason 3:* Subterranean lines, cables, and pipes are hopelessly tangled.
   *Main Reason 2:* New York should have destroyed itself,
      *Supporting Reason 1:* From insoluble traffic snarls.
      *Supporting Reason 2:* From hunger through failure of food lines.
      *Supporting Reason 3:* From plague through slums or rats.
      *Supporting Reason 4:* From the sea.
      *Supporting Reason 5:* From workers' nerves.
      *Supporting Reason 6:* From insanity.

A paragraph from the section on comparison and contrast may also be used to illustrate paragraph development through reasons. Look at it again.

The modern kitchen is different from the old-style type. *It even looks different.* The charm of the old kitchen lay in its design, from the wallpaper to the curtains to the tablecloth; but the modern kitchen has no designs, only shiny chrome and brilliant color. *There's a different atmosphere,* too. Grandma's kitchen was a place to talk things over, to have a hot drink and relax while savoring the odor of bread baking in the oven, to leisurely plan and put loving thought into every meal prepared there. But the modern kitchen is constructed for speed, for the fastest and easiest way to get the food on the table and the dishes washed so that the cook can go on to other activities. *The modern kitchen seems to have a different role to play in our lives.* Instead of being a center of family life, it has become a laundry, dining room, and office for the increasingly complicated job of the home-maker.

The topic sentence is the first sentence in the paragraph. The pointer is *different*. The paragraph lists three reasons for the difference. In diagram form, the paragraph looks like this:

*Topic Sentence:* The modern kitchen is different from the old-style type.
  *Reason 1:* It has a different appearance.
  *Reason 2:* It has a different atmosphere.
  *Reason 3:* It plays a different role in family life.

The development of each of the three reasons is accomplished by the use of contrast, that is, contrasting the old kitchen to the new on each of these three points. The paragraph, then, is developed by two methods —reasons and contrast.

### EXERCISES

A. Using two of these topic sentences, write two outlines for paragraphs to be developed by reasons. You may take the opposite point of view of any of these topic sentences.

  1. We lost the game because of our star player's mistakes.

  2. Dormitory life teaches the freshman self-reliance (caution) (tolerance).

  3. Sally did not want to have a date with him.

  4. Dress helps to make the man.

  5. Her teaching methods were directed toward making the student think.

  6. Downtown business centers in cities are certain to decrease in importance.

  7. A universal metric system would allow freer world trade.

  8. (Your school) was the proper choice for me.

  9. Charlie decided not to attend the play.

  10. Bicycles are dangerous.

Follow this outline form:

*Topic Sentence:*
> *Main Reason 1:*
>> *Supporting Reason 1:*
>> *Supporting Reason 2:*
>
> *Main Reason 2:*
>> *Supporting Reason 1:*
>> *Supporting Reason 2:*
>
> *Main Reason 3:*
>> *Supporting Reason 1:*
>> *Supporting Reason 2:*

Your outlines must have at least two main reasons plus as many as you may need to develop the paragraph adequately. Each main reason must also have at least two supporting reasons.

B. Write paragraphs from the two outlines composed for Exercise A.

## Methods of Development in Combination

Ordinarily, paragraphs are not developed solely by one of the methods you have just studied but by any combination of them. The methods selected are those that seem to the writer the most suitable to explain and establish the topic sentence. And, ordinarily, the experienced writer does not deliberately determine to develop a paragraph by any specific method. He unconsciously selects methods as he writes; nevertheless, he does use methods. For example, here are some paragraphs written by experienced writers. Note how they combine methods in a single paragraph.

1  Lasers—there are several varieties—are rather surprisingly simple
2  devices which generate highly disciplined and coherent light rays. To
3  appreciate their impact one must first realize that until a few years
4  ago an important dividing line cut across the electromagnetic fre-
5  quency spectrum just above the upper limits of the microwave region.
6  Below this divide there were transistors and electron tubes which could
7  generate the coherent signals necessary for communications or com-
8  puters or any of the other tasks of modern electronics. Above it, in the
9  infrared and optical regions, there were only incoherent thermal sources
10  —the sun, light bulbs, arc lamps, flames. The electromagnetic radiation
11  from these sources is highly undisciplined, containing waves traveling in
12  all possible directions and made up of a scrambled mixture of all pos-
13  sible frequencies.

14    The development of the laser as a coherent light source means that
15    this division is now gone. Note that most lasers emit considerably less
16    total power than, say, a hundred-watt bulb. But the light bulb, which
17    is incoherent, emits its energy into so many frequencies and directions
18    that the amount emitted into any single specific frequency and direction
19    is minute. By contrast, the laser, which is coherent, emits all of its
20    energy at a single frequency and in a single direction and in some
21    cases does so in a single brief but extremely intense burst. Within its
22    single frequency and direction, therefore, the laser is incomparably
23    brighter than, say, the sun or any other thermal light source.[13]

These two paragraphs are definition paragraphs. They attempt to define lasers in nonscientific terms so that an ordinary reader can understand. Several methods of development are used in the definition. Note that the first sentence is a simple definition by classification. From lines 2 through 8, the author uses explanation of background reinforced by reason. In line 10, he defines *incoherent thermal sources* by enumeration. The last part of line 11 starts a definition by classification of the word *un-disciplined* as applied to electromagnetic radiation. Lines 15 through 23 offer contrast as a method of development. Note that *incoherent* and *coherent light sources* are defined in this contrast. The last sentence is a conclusion, as shown by the transition word *therefore*.

Here is another paragraph by an experienced writer.

(1) An Indian coffeehouse, like an Indian bazaar, has its own peculiar atmosphere. (2) It is a cheerful, unpretentious place in which to dawdle, encounter friends, talk, discuss, gossip. (3) Students make fiery speeches to each other; women meet for a break in the morning's shopping; idlers stop by for a rest, to watch the world go by, to pick up a chance colleague. (4) The actual drinking of coffee is the least important part of the whole affair. (5) Looking around at the tables, I couldn't help thinking that this particular sort of place doesn't exist in Moscow. (6) There, one can find restaurants (mostly rather expensive by any standard), or "Parks of Culture and Rest," or hotel dining rooms, and several varieties of bar ranging from the *pivnaya*, where as a rule you can't even sit down, where women are seldom seen, and where the customers walk to the bar, order a drink, down it and leave, all within the space of five minutes, to the *stolovoye*, which is considered more refined, more suitable for women, and where ordinary vodka is not served, though wines and brandy are brought to your table.

13 Anthony E. Siegman, "The Laser: Astounding Beam of Light," *Stanford Today*, Autumn, 1964. Reprinted by permission of *Stanford Today*, Leland Stanford Junior University, Stanford, California.

(7) But India is not a drinking country—even in the states where there is no prohibition. (8) The sight of drunks being thrown out of restaurants with the offhand ruthlessness that Russians employ for such occasions is extremely rare in India.[14]

In this paragraph, sentences 2, 3, and 4 use detail to explain the atmosphere of the Indian coffeehouse. Sentences 5, 6, 7, and 8 are concerned with a contrast between the drinking habits of Indians and of Russians. Note that sentence 6 is filled with detail to describe the Russian bars.

## EXERCISES

A. Throughout this chapter you have written many paragraphs. Choose any three and rewrite them to change the tone to fit any of the following (use a different one for each paragraph): *formal, informal, personal, impersonal, critical, emotional, more argumentative, humorous, absurd.* You may want to discuss these tags before you begin this exercise.

B. Choose one of the six paragraphs involved in Exercise A and rewrite it to improve reader interest and reader acceptance (assume you are writing to a close personal friend). (If you have trouble with this assignment, reread pages 76, 77, 80, 81.)

C. 1. Think about each word in the following list and decide whether your feeling about the word is "favorable" or "unfavorable." Place a plus (+) beside those you respond favorably to, and a minus (−) beside those you respond unfavorably to. Those that don't fit either class or fit *both* label "neutral" (0).

| | | | |
|---|---|---|---|
| crash | shout | eye | scold |
| rush | sit | fire | listen |
| cool | honest | foolish | cheer |
| talk | fair | hand | brag |
| walk | crush | careful | agree |
| quiet | say | clash | define |
| slap | frigid | stoop | jeer |
| wise | warm | silly | assure |
| run | stand | trip | beg |

2. a. Be prepared to discuss your classification.
   b. What can you conclude about words and a person's feelings?
   c. Compare your list with others in the class. Why are there differences?

[14] Santha Rama Rau, "Return to India," *The Reporter,* June, 1960. Published by The Reporter Magazine Company. Copyright 1960 by *The Reporter.* Reprinted by permission of William Morris Agency, Inc.

d. Try to spot the "feeling" words in the paragraphs you wrote for A and B, above.

D. Now that you have worked Exercise C, turn back to page 10 to the theme, "Dogs on the Loose." Make a list of all words that imply a "judgment" to you (for example, *restrain, fear, nuisance, damage, scare, affectionately*). After you have completed this list of "tone" words (you should be able to find several dozen), classify the words in the same way you did in Exercise C, above, but use only two classes, "favorable" (+) and "unfavorable" (−).

1. Which "tone" words appear more frequently, (+) or (−)?

2. Compare your list with others in the class. Why are there differences?

3. On the basis of your classification, what do you think the person "speaking" in the theme feels about dogs? Do you think the *writer* of the theme and this "speaker" are in agreement? Explain.

4. Your instructor may ask you to repeat this exercise using the theme on "Law and Order" (page 21).

# 5

# Putting the Parts
# Together:
# The Whole Paper

Now that you have studied the parts of the five-hundred-word paper, it is time to put them all together. First, as a reminder, look again at the five-hundred-word paper in a diagram, presented this time in a slightly different version because of your knowledge of it. (See the diagram on page 121, facing.)

This is the pattern you will use in writing your papers. But you are better prepared now than you were when you wrote the five-hundred-word paper at the end of Chapter 1. Your writing should reflect what you have learned in the meantime. Also, you should have a better idea of what your instructor looks for when he reads your papers. But before you write any new themes review the basic things he will be checking. The grade he assigns will be a composite evaluation of how well you do on three or four main points:

A. *Content*—Your instructor will decide whether you have a meaningful, limited subject and whether your development of it has been full and logical.

B. *Organization*—He will determine whether you have an acceptable thesis statement supported by topic sentences that are in turn supported by evidence in the developmental paragraphs.

C. *Tone*—He may also bring to your attention problems concerning reader interest and reader acceptance, the way in which the writer's "voice" is coming across. Remember that the kind of "voice" the reader hears as he goes through your paper will influence his judgment of it.

D. *Mechanics*—And finally, your instructor will mark unacceptable spelling and punctuation, poor sentence structure (for instance, incomplete sentences that don't work), disunity and lack of coherence, and poor diction (that is, word choice, including listless verbs and overuse of adverbs).

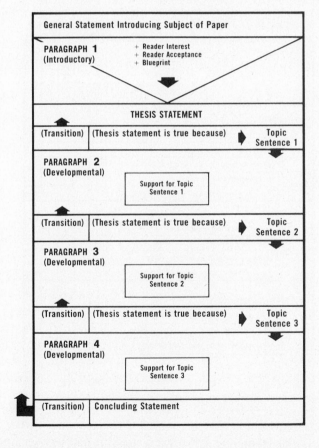

Keep in mind that a real weakness in any *one* of these major basic areas will influence your grader. You can, for example, show good content and organization, but if the mechanics of your paper are poor, your grade could be disappointing. Similarly, your mechanics can be perfect and your organization good, but if your paper lacks ideas of consequence or is dull, the result may be the same. A word about dullness.

Usually the dull paper that is good in all other respects has a problem in *tone;* that is, it may have no reader interest, or it may lack ethical appeal (getting the reader to accept the writer and his views). Or it may have an informal tone where a more formal one is demanded by the subject; or it may sound insincere because the words are far too fancy for the subject. You will learn more about tone in the next chapter (see page 155). Meanwhile, if tone becomes a problem, study pages 76–81 on introductory paragraphs.

Here is a check sheet that summarizes the four basic areas your instructor will evaluate; note that it also lists some of the details within each of the four areas to help you revise your own work.

### SIMPLIFIED CHECK SHEET FOR THE WHOLE PAPER

|  | Excellent | Good | Acceptable | Weak | Poor |
|---|---|---|---|---|---|
| **A. THOUGHT** | | | | | |
| 1. Does the paper have a meaningful subject? | | | | | |
| 2. Is the subject limited and pointed? | | | | | |
| 3. Do developmental paragraphs give factual support? | | | | | |
| 4. Is the support adequate and detailed? | | | | | |
| 5. Does the whole paper have unity of thought? | | | | | |
| **B. ORGANIZATION** | | | | | |
| 6. Is the thesis statement adequate? | | | | | |
| 7. Do all topic sentences support the thesis? | | | | | |
| 8. Is there a "blueprint" to order the ideas? | | | | | |
| 9. Does the whole paper have coherence? | | | | | |
| **C. TONE (The Writer's "Voice")** | | | | | |
| 10. Does the paper create reader interest? | | | | | |
| 11. Does the paper try to get reader acceptance? | | | | | |
| 12. Does the tone fit the subject and the reader? | | | | | |
| **D. MECHANICS** | | | | | |
| 13. Good word choice: strong verbs, care with adverbs? | | | | | |
| 14. Spelling, punctuation, grammar? | | | | | |
| 15. Sentence structure? | | | | | |

Use this check sheet before you turn in your papers to note those elements which need revision. Of course, if you don't reread your papers before turning them in, you won't be able to evaluate their success. The check sheet has several other uses: You can exchange papers with a classmate to spot each other's strengths and weaknesses; your instructor may want to use the check sheet for similar purposes, having the entire class evaluate its own papers; or he may use it to point out your problems quickly (especially if he doesn't have time to comment at length).

To further understand what your instructor will be looking for, consider the next three students' papers, which are analyzed as an instructor might do it. Examine them one paragraph at a time.

### The Student and Classic Comics

High school students, usually not avid readers of comic books, often resort to substituting classic comics for required reading books. Basically honest, many of these students, under pressure of heavy assignments and extra-curricular activities, think of the classic comic merely as a short cut to an assignment. Although students may be able to write a plot summary, they are cheating themselves when they take the easy way out.

This paragraph fulfills the requirements for a short introductory paragraph. It starts with a general statement and ends with a specific thesis statement: Students cheat themselves when they take the easy way out (by substituting classic comics for required reading). The remainder of the paper must show why students cheat themselves through this procedure. Look at the first developmental paragraph.

The student who depends on the comic book version of the world's great literature often deprives himself of an accurate presentation of the original story. For example, if he reads the comic version of Twain's *A Connecticut Yankee*, which eliminates any attempt at satire, he receives the impression that Twain was making an early effort at some type of science fiction. A student who relies on the comic classic of *Huckleberry Finn* misses many of Huck's adventures, such as the Grangerford episode, and finds the story ending in a manner that would startle the author. The unfortunate student who makes his book report from the comic classic *The House of Seven Gables* will overemphasize the Pyncheon ancestors and the family curse, saying little about Hepzibah, Clifford, and the other characters because mysterious deaths and family curses create better mystery stories than the effect of these circumstances on characters.

This developmental paragraph has a proper topic sentence, as the first sentence in the paragraph, indicating one reason that the thesis statement is valid: The student does not get an accurate presentation of the original story. To give support for this topic sentence, three short illustrations are used from three famous works of fiction to show how each story is twisted in its comic book version. Because the pointer in the topic sentence is *deprived* and each illustration indicates how this deprivation comes about, the paragraph has unity. Each of the sentences in the paragraph uses *student,* or its substitute *he,* as the subject; therefore the paragraph maintains coherence through a consistent point of view. There are no mechanical errors.

Now, look at the second developmental paragraph.

(1) In addition to being deprived of accurate presentations of literature, each time the student resorts to the comic classic version of a novel he misses practice in critical reading and evaluation of literature. (2) The student has no concept of the underlying theme of a particular story or of persistent themes that recur in one author's works. (3) Since the comic classics present only what the characters say, the reader has no way of interpreting the author's purpose for writing a story. (4) Further, since symbolism and point of view cannot be adapted to comic book presentation, the reader misses these artistic devices. (5) Finally, the student fails to see the structure of the novel because the emphasis is always on plot and action. (6) Regardless of the importance of setting or characters in the original version, the student will see plot as the dominant factor.

Again, in this paragraph, the first sentence is the topic sentence. The pointer is *misses practice;* the remainder must show why this practice is missed. The paragraph is developed through reason, and three reasons are given to indicate the validity of the topic sentence. The first is in the second sentence—the student misses the underlying theme or themes that recur in one author's work. The second reason is in the fourth sentence—the student misses symbolism and point of view. The third reason is in the fifth sentence—the student misses the structure of the novel because emphasis in classic comics is on plot and action only.

The paragraph maintains unity. The three reasons given directly support the topic sentence. The other sentences also contribute to the unity of the paragraph. The third sentence, for instance, explains the first reason given in the second sentence, and the sixth sentence explains the third reason given in the fifth sentence. The paragraph holds together well. The subject of each sentence is *student* or a pronoun or noun standing for student. To increase coherence, transition words are used twice. *Further,* in the fourth sentence, introduces the second reason, and *finally,* in the fifth sentence, introduces the third reason. Note further that the first part of the first sentence is used as transition to link this paragraph with the preceding one to improve the coherence of the whole paper.

Now consider the final paragraph.

(1) Of equal importance to the student who substitutes the comic classic version for the original novel, he does not enjoy the power and majesty of the English language as it has been used by our greatest authors. (2) He finds no new and interesting words to challenge him. (3) Because these books are intended primarily for a young, nonliterary audience, he encounters only simple, everyday words that he already knows. (4) Comparing the comic version with the author's, he finds the vocabulary confined to words with little, if any, connotative meaning. (5) The student will also find that most descriptive passages have been eliminated or reworded. (6) The author has described the actions and scenes in vivid, carefully chosen words, but the comic book reader sees only the crude and oversimplified drawings. (7) He discovers that he need not use his imagination to create a character because he has access to the stereotyped picture drawn by the comic strip artist. (8) Thus, he does not need the figurative language that enriches and encourages imagination. (9) Not only does the student miss the artistry of word choice and description, he cannot see the different combinations of words in sentences and sentences in paragraphs used by authors to create distinctive styles. (10) Since he is reading a condensed and altered version of the novel, he is not aware of the vividness of an author's use of dialect or his ability to make the most ordinary things seems out of the ordinary. (11) He misses the artistry of an author like Poe who chose words for sounds and then placed these words in sentences, almost rhythmic and poetic. (12) By reading this inaccurate presentation of the world's great literature, the student denies himself the opportunity of reading the literature of the past, the value of developing a critical attitude toward literature, and the pleasure of enjoying the power and beauty of his own language.

This paragraph, like the other developmental paragraphs, starts with the topic sentence. The point it develops is that the student who reads comic classics as substitutes for the real thing misses the full effect of the artistry as used by our geratest authors. The developmental method is the use of detail—the piling up of reasons for what the student misses. The last sentence is the concluding statement. It contains the three reasons for the validity of the thesis statement that make up the topic sentences of the paragraphs.

Again, this paragraph is coherent and unified. All the sentences directly support the topic sentence. All the sentences use *student,* or the pronoun *he,* as subject. Notice, too, the use of the transition words *also,* in the fifth sentence, and *thus,* in the eighth sentence. Further, the beginning of the ninth sentence, *Not only does the student miss the artistry of word choice and description,* provides transition to the next group of ideas. The first part of the topic sentence, *Of equal importance. . . ,* connects this paragraph with the preceding one.

An outline will demonstrate the overall organization of the whole paper.

| | |
|---|---|
| *Thesis statement:* | Student cheat themselves when they choose the "easy way" of reading classic comics instead of required books. |
| *Reason 1:* (Topic Sentence) | They deny themselves an accurate presentation of the original story. |
| *Reason 2:* (Topic Sentence) | They miss the opportunity to practice critical reading and evaluation of literature. |
| *Reason 3:* (Topic Sentence) | They lose enjoyment of the power and majesty of the English language. |

This paper could be marked *good* on organization, *good* on content, and *good* on mechanics, and it should earn a *good* grade.

When you write a five-hundred-word paper, it will need a title; so far, nothing has been said about titles. These eight guidelines will serve you well:

1. Use no more than five words, usually.
2. Use no final mark of punctuation.
3. Make no reference to your title in the first lines of your paper.
4. Capitalize the first and last words of your title. Do not capitalize articles (a, an, the), conjunctions (and, but, or, and so forth), or prepositions.
5. Make your title honest. (Don't try to be "cute.")
6. Summarize your paper in the title.
7. Do not make your title a sentence.
8. Never put quotation marks around your own title.

Take, for example, the title of the paper just analyzed. "The Student and Classic Comics." It requires only five words, has no final mark of punctuation, and has all words capitalized except the conjunction *and*. It is an honest title; it summarizes the paper; and it is not a sentence. It fulfills the requirements for a good title.

Now look at another paper.

### The Library, the Teacher, and the Student

Students in the high school I attended have certainly lost the inquiring mind, if they ever had it, and they no longer even want to think for themselves. It seems, in fact, that our whole society has lost the zest for inquiry because of the loss of ideals and qualities. I cannot account for society's loss, but among students in my school I can see at least two reasons: inadequate libraries and prejudiced teachers.

This introductory paragraph is not bad. All the parts are there, but they are not organized. The first sentence is apparently the thesis statement. But this sentence is composed of two independent clauses: *Students in the high school I attended have certainly lost the inquiring mind* and *they no longer even want to think for themselves.* You have learned that this construction is not acceptable for a thesis statement because the clauses carry equal weight and there is no way for the reader to determine which is the subject of the paper. If you look at this sentence closely, however, you will realize that its author is saying the same thing in both parts. What he intends to be his thesis statement is that students no longer want to think for themselves. This idea should be given the important position in the sentence; it should be placed at the end of the first paragraph with the two reasons given in the third sentence, because they are apparently going to be used as topic sentences in the paper. The second sentence in the introductory paragraph is a general statement about all people, not just students, and it needs to be recast and used as the first sentence of the paragraph. But take care in recasting to avoid such general words as *ideals* and *qualities,* because as they are used in the second sentence, they are not specific enough to be meaningful. Even so, this paragraph holds together. Note that *lost* in the first sentence is repeated in the second and that it appears as *loss* in the third. All three sentences are tied together by repetition of a key word. The whole paragraph, however, could use some reorganization.

The first developmental paragraph discusses the first reason students do not want to think for themselves.

In my high school, the library was pathetically inadequate. If we wanted to know about the latest scientific developments, we had no reference books to examine except a fifteen-year-old encyclopedia more suitable for the primary grades than for the high school. We could read no recent scientific magazines, because there were none, not even any fifteen years old. The most weighty current magazine in the library was *The Reader's Digest,* hardly the one in which to research a topic in, say, biology. If we were interested in literature, about the best we could do for modern fiction was *Seventeen* by Booth Tarkington or perhaps *The Virginian.* No teacher of any subject ever assigned us library work or outside reading. On the few occasions one of us did venture into the library on his own initiative, old Miss Spence, who had been librarian for twenty years, made it clear that she could not care less. If we came into the library, it only meant trouble for her. Under these conditions it is not surprising that the students did little inquiry into important human problems. They did not even know what these problems were; they had no way of knowing.

This paragraph appears to be a good one. It starts with a topic sentence that has a pointer, *pathetically inadequate*. Basically, it gives three reasons in support of the validity of this topic sentence: (1) resources for scientific research were nonexistent; (2) literary research, particularly modern, was equally difficult; and (3) the teachers and the librarian were uninterested in encouraging library work. Each reason is supported by illustration, and the paragraph ends with a summary sentence. The paragraph reads well as a unit. Note, for instance, the repetition of *fifteen* in the first part of the paragraph and of *library* and *librarian* in the last part to help in achieving coherence. Unity is maintained because all the evidence offered supports the topic sentence.

Here is the last paragraph.

(1) We have modified our society a great deal in the past few decades. (2) With the new advances in knowledge and in working and living conditions, we have come to expect more from other people than from ourselves. (3) Students revel in the new prosperity, buying things, having fun, and joining clubs. (4) The sole aim of their lives has become to have pleasure, so much so that they simply do not have time for school or studies or satisfying their natural curiosity. (5) In fact, they do not even notice these things, because they do not contribute to what they consider their pleasure. (6) Teachers foster this pursuit of pleasure in their students by trying to make their students all conform to what they think students ought to be and to think. (7) Students are expected to parrot on quizzes the ideas the teacher has given out in class. (8) They do not want us to think for ourselves but to go to established authorities for even simple ideas and explanations. (9) These teachers, and other forces in society, who rebel against nonconformity (something may or may not be right, but they won't try to find out if it is or not) make certain that a teacher with other ideas is not allowed to exist in their little world. (10) This is well illustrated by the case of Mrs. Jane Doe, a former teacher of mine. (11) In her English classes, she discussed everything, always taking the view opposite that of the majority of her students. (12) She would rant in class in her attacks on the established order of society or politics or tradition, and actually spoke in favor of Communism just to get her students to argue with her. (13) Her attacks forced her students to think to support their views. (14) Forcing her students to think was the best thing she did for her students. (15) But Mrs. Doe was accused of being a Communist and fired because the other teachers, the school administrators, and the community did not appreciate her value. (16) With the lack of research facilities in the school library and with this sort of narrow-mindedness from our teachers, students at the high school I attended cannot think for themselves.

This paragraph is a jumble of ideas without unity, and what seemed to be a promising paper falls to pieces. The introductory paragraph announces that the paper will develop two reasons for the validity of the thesis statement: Students do not want to think for themselves because (1) the library is inadequate and (2) the teachers are prejudiced. This paragraph should be the one that develops the pointer *prejudiced,* but the word does not even appear in the paragraph.

What has happened to this student? He may have started writing the paper without thinking it through. Then when he reached this last paragraph, he was not sure what he would use to support his idea about the teachers being prejudiced. Rather than going back and reorganizing—not much change needed—he plunged ahead and ruined his paper. Or, he may have failed to see that his last paragraph discusses two subjects, not one. He changes direction in the middle of the paragraph. Through the fourth sentence, the paragraph has to do with the hectic life students lead and how it stops them from thinking. The remainder of the paragraph, however, is concerned with teachers' narrowminded conformity and the way it restricts student thinking. Each of the two main ideas should have been developed in a separate paragraph. This paragraph is a good example of the use of hazy, undefined terms *(advances in knowledge and in working and living conditions, forces in society)* that allow the writer to wander off in all directions with no particular point being supported.

The third paragraph might be questioned at several points. The trouble is largely a matter of diction—the use of hazy, general words instead of specific ones that convey exact meaning. For instance, look at the beginning of the second sentence: *With the new advances in knowledge and in working and living conditions. . . .* What precisely does the general term *advances* mean to the writer? How does he intend for the reader to know what he means? We can guess at the meaning, but we cannot be certain. In addition, how have these *advances* led us *to expect more from other people than from ourselves?* Because the writer does not answer this question and he does not define *advances,* the sentence seems meaningless. The instructor might mark this sentence simply with a question mark in the margin. If you should see this mark on your paper, it indicates that the reader cannot determine what you mean and that you need to clarify.

The seventh sentence will also have to be questioned. It begins *These teachers, and other forces in society, who rebel against nonconformity (something may or may not be right, but they won't try to find out if it is or not). . . . ,* and stops the reader cold. He cannot possibly continue into the sentence after this point without rereading this beginning carefully to determine precisely what is being said. The parenthetical material is confusing; something is being defined, but what? Further, the sentence introduces a new subject, *other forces in society*, that appears irrelevant to the discussion. The dependent clause following this phrase, *who rebel against nonconformity*, is twisted in such a way that the reader must stop to figure it out. Ordinarily, we speak of rebelling against conformity rather than against nonconformity. We rebel against what is established. Nonconformity could hardly be said to be the established way of life in our society. So the reader is confused by this clause. *Who support conformity* is a much better way of saying it here.

The illustration of the teacher who refused to conform is not a satisfactory one. It makes the reader wonder whether the school board was not perhaps justified in firing the teacher. She was apparently hired to teach English, but the illustration suggests that she taught everything but English. If she *ranted* in her classroom, it would make the school board's case more secure. But maybe this is another instance of the writer's difficulty in choosing precise words.

Read the next paper all the way through before any comment.

### Exercise in Our Daily Lives

Exercise should play a very large role in daily life. Everyone, no matter what age, needs exercise every day. However, with modern life being what it is, few older people get the daily exercise they need. Probably television as well as other modern inventions plays a part in producing the physically unfit American.

There are many kinds of exercise that will help people keep physically fit, if they are done every day. First, there are setting-up exercises that anyone can perform for a few minutes every day. If more people would do setting-up exercises on a regular schedule, fewer people in America would be sick. Younger people need to play games to keep themselves physically fit. Football is one of the best games a young person can play for this purpose. But any game that requires running and bending and stretching will do the same thing. Of course, young people should take advantage of the athletic programs in their school and of the school gymnasium on every occasion. Body-building centers are springing up all over the United States. In these centers, anyone from the youngest person to the oldest can set up an exercise program under the supervision of an expert in body building. Or, of course, a family can always buy exercise equipment such as stationary bicycles, barbells, and slant boards on which to exercise daily. If more people would exercise daily, they would find that they feel better all the time.

Television and other modern inventions could possibly be a factor that produces the physically unfit American. Television can be very educational. There are many educational programs for adults as well as for the young generation. "Face the Nation," for example, and news programs such as "Sixty Minutes" can help the people of the United States learn more about the advancing world. But mostly, television is just a waste of time, being concerned altogether with entertainment programs. Another modern invention that contributes to the physically unfit American is the automobile. People no longer walk any place. If they have to go only two blocks to the grocery store, they get in the car and ride there instead of walking. Even the young people don't walk, but expect their parents to give them a car at an early age. If people are going to sit for hours in front of their television sets and ride in their cars everywhere, they need to get exercise by doing setting-up exercises or working out on gym equipment.

In our progressing world, everyone seems to be looking for more and more entertainment and for easier ways of doing things. It is easier for a mother to have her children watch entertainment programs on television while she does her work around the house than it is to put her housework off while she takes her children outside for some healthy exercise or outdoor play. By doing this is the mother making things easier for herself or is she thinking about her children's welfare? A good mother will let her children play outdoors while she does her housework. Under the same conditions, adults will watch television rather than exercise as they should.

You recognize at once that the paper is poor, and you are able to point out its chief weaknesses. If an instructor attempts to mark everything unacceptable in this paper, the margins will not accommodate his marks and comments. Perhaps personal conferences with the instructor will guide this student writer.

One of the chief weaknesses of this paper is its content. The very title, "Exercise in Our Daily Lives," suggests emptiness and dullness. When the reader sees the thesis statement, *Exercise should play a very large role in daily life,* the first sentence, he knows the paper will not be vital. First, *very large* is not precise. How much exactly is a *very large role?* Second, who wants to read about so commonplace a subject, one that everyone knows about already?

Despite the confusion apparent in the introductory paragraph, the reader may discern three points the paper uses to support the thesis: (1) Everyone needs exercise every day; (2) few older people get the daily exercise they need; and (3) television and other modern inventions produce the unfit American. None of these supports the thesis statement as given. We need go no further into the paper than the brief introductory paragraph to predict the results—an unacceptable paper. The rest of the paper bears out such a prediction. The paragraphs are not unified. Each of them jumps from subject to subject, changing direction every sentence or so. Some second-paragraph material is discussed in the third, and some in the third is discussed again in the fourth. Therefore, the paragraphs cannot be coherent; no use of coherence devices will help these paragraphs, unless they are first rewritten for unity. Diction and sentence structure will have to be revised. Some sentences, possibly the result of too little thought or too hasty revision, come out unintentionally humorous. Look, for instance, at the last sentence. The writer has just explained that many mothers allow their children to waste time watching television because it speeds up housework. The last sentence says: *Under the same conditions, many adults will watch television in their spare time rather than exercise as they should.* The reader is tempted to counter, "Under what conditions? While their mother is taking care of them?"

## WRITING ASSIGNMENTS

A. 1. Select one of the following general topics (your instructor may add to this list).

| | |
|---|---|
| Advertising | Movies |
| College | Parents |
| Commercials | Planes |
| Dating | Politics |
| Education | Sports |
| Flight | Television |

If your instructor is going to ask you to do Writing Assignment B or C, you may want to read them before choosing your subject for paper A.

2. Restrict your selected general topic by dividing it into its parts and by choosing one of these restricted parts as suitable for development in a five-hundred-word paper.

3. Write a good thesis statement.

4. Decide on at least three reasons for the validity of the thesis statement. (Your instructor may want to check what you have done before you go on.)

5. In one paragraph, use reasons as the basic method of development; in another, use either comparison or contrast; and in another, use illustration, either a series of short illustrations or one extended illustration. (Your instructor may substitute other methods for these.)

6. Underline your thesis statement and all topic sentences.

7. Write in the margin, beside each developmental paragraph, the principal method of development used in that paragraph.

8. Before you turn in your paper, use the check sheet given on page 122 to evaluate what you have written.

B. After you get back the paper for A, read it again and then try to answer the following questions:

1. Does the paper still sound convincing?

2. Does it seem to have a definite reader in mind?

3. Does it try to create interest? How?

4. Check the exercises on page 118; then try to list the "feeling" words in your paper.

Now rewrite Paper A, or its first two paragraphs only, trying to improve reader interest and reader acceptance, but this time assume that you are writing to one of the following:

a. Your best friend (same sex)

b. A group of traditional old men

c. Junior high school students

d. Your mayor or congressman

Keep your ideas, thesis, organization, and illustrations basically the same as they were in Paper A. Concentrate on changing the interest and tone to fit the readers. In parentheses immediately below your title, give your reader, like this: (Reader: My best friend, Agnes).

C. Here's another way to learn about creating a specific tone in a paper. First read these three student paragraphs (all by one student) and try to determine what three "voices" are used.

1. I took the ball on the handoff from the quarterback. I hid the ball behind my outside thigh as one does on a bootleg. The ball was hidden so well it fooled the end and the linebacker. Then I simply outran the rest of the clods to the goal.

2. Charlie's fake on that play was great—he was the fullback who took the first fake and dived into the line. The end and linebacker tackled him, thinking he had the ball. This enabled Fred to turn the end and cut up the field for the score.

3. The Slip Yeomen slid by the Elm Lions by a score of 7–0. The only score came late in the last half, when the right halfback took the ball from the quarterback and cut up field for 70 yards. But the play was a team effort: all the blocks and fakes were perfectly executed because the team had worked the play for the past two weeks.

What other things have changed in these paragraphs with the change in "voice"? (Consider such things as choice of words, pronouns, and general "feeling.")

Now try to do something similar with the first two paragraphs of Paper A or B. This time, assume a *role;* pretend you are someone other than yourself with characteristics you know well. Again, keep your ideas, thesis, organization, and illustrations basically the same as they were in Paper A (or B); make changes to fit the new "voice" you have assumed in the paper. Here are some role suggestions (you may use others):

a. Your father (or mother)

b. An excited young girl (or boy)

c. Your grandmother (or some other relative)

d. A housewife with no high school education

e. A salesman who never stops selling

f. A person much younger than you

In parentheses immediately below your title, identify the "voice" you are trying to project, like this: (Writer: Agnes, age 12).

D. If you study the techniques you used in B and C, you should be able to write a theme on one of the following:

1. Changing Tone in a Paper

2. Creating Reader Interest in a Paper

3. Some Effects of "I" and "He" in a Paper

You should discuss this paper in class before trying to write it; your instructor may want to give you some additional suggestions.

# REVISION
# AND
# STYLE

# two

# 6

# Revising Your Paper–
# Diction

The preface tells you that your writing will take on strength and life if you practice the two skills emphasized in this book—clearly explaining a main point with supporting evidence, and projecting a convincing attitude with self-confidence. "But why," you may be asking, "aren't my papers more convincing? Why can't I sit down and *just write?*" You *can* make your papers more convincing, but no one can sit down and "just write"—freely, easily, seemingly without thought and preparation and without rewriting. Good writing demands patience and discipline; even established writers find writing hard work and know the value of revision. Thinking, organizing, explaining, supporting, illustrating—all the skills emphasized in the first five chapters cannot, by themselves, result in a truly finished work. And although Part One stresses focus and organization, it also introduces some of the problems you must solve to make your writing convincing and interesting. Part Two, Revision and Style, looks more closely at these and related problems.

## Aids to Strength, Clarity, Directness

### The Importance of Revision

Serious revision is vital to all successful writing. All professional writers revise because revision makes a writer's work stand out: It carries his mark, not accidentally, but because a work *is* the writer and because he consciously revised it to make it do exactly what he wanted it to. These last two chapters ask you to revise *seriously* to achieve the two broad purposes you are striving for:

1. Strength, clarity, and directness of *thought*—getting the reader to say "I understand."
2. A *tone* of self-confidence and conviction—getting the reader to say "I agree."

You will first study diction (word choice), then sentences, and finally, you will begin to think about your own "style."

The first complete copy of your five-hundred-word paper is the rough draft. Though that is the copy some students turn in, it is only the first stage of the actual writing process described in the first five chapters. At this point you will have managed merely to get organized ideas and evidence down on paper. Now you'll need some systematic revision, perhaps using the check sheet given on page 122. Go over your paper slowly and thoroughly, checking unity, coherence, and convincing support of thesis statement and topic sentences. It is at this point, too, that you will look for reader interest and reader acceptance. Mark out and change words and lines liberally as you see the need. Supply transitions where you've neglected them and change any words that don't seem to fit the tone you are trying to create. Then make a copy of the paper as revised. Give this second copy the same close scrutiny you gave the first, making additional changes where you think they are needed. You may need to make still another copy before you are satisfied that you have written a paper as exact in idea and as polished in expression as you can make it. Never turn in a paper that has not gone through this revision process.

When you are satisfied that the revision is as good as you can make it, recopy it as neatly as possible. Although manuscript neatness is not a virtue in itself, you shouldn't make it difficult to read; there is

no need to prejudice your reader (in this case your instructor) against your ideas with a messy-looking paper. Similarly, don't try to hide emptiness of thought by following precisely and neatly a specified form; the emptiness will show through. And if your reader is an employer, he will not be likely to tolerate messy work. Whether you write or type, get into the habit of making the final copy a finished product you can be proud of.

After you have had some experience, you should become so conscious of the elements that go into the making of a good paper that you'll be able to avoid some of the effort of revision by using greater care in the rough draft. It is this kind of added care that will greatly improve your performance in a short, fifty-minute class period. Keep the following suggestions in mind when writing the rough draft and when revising it.

### Change the Passive Voice to Active Voice

English verbs have two voices—active and passive. For example, consider these sentences:

Andy | hit the ball.

The ball | was hit by Andy.

The first sentence is in the active voice. The subject, *Andy,* is doing the action expressed in the sentence. The second is in the passive voice. The subject of this sentence, *ball,* is receiving the action. Or, to put it another way, the first sentence (active) follows the normal word order for English sentences—subject, verb, complement (or actor, action, receiver of action). The second sentence (passive) turns this normal word order around. What was the complement of the first sentence becomes the subject in the second sentence. Its order is receiver of action, action, actor.

Look at this example.

(1) To call a telephone on your own party line proceed as follows: Lift the receiver and wait for dial tone. (2) The regular seven-digit number of the desired station is dialed, the busy signal will be heard, and the calling party then places the receiver on the hook. (3) The desired station is then signaled. (4) After a reasonable time, remove receiver and start talking.

The writer of these directions has shifted from active to passive and back to active in four brief sentences. The resulting jumble is enough to cause any telephone subscriber to hesitate calling a neighbor on his own party line. The first sentence is in the active voice. The subject *you*, the actor, is understood. *You* are to lift the receiver and *you* are to wait for the dial tone. The second sentence, however, shifts to the passive. There is no one dialing, and no one is hearing the busy signal. The last part of the second sentence shifts again to active voice. The calling party acts. Again, in the third sentence, no one is signaling the desired station, and the sentence is passive. The final sentence returns to the active voice with an understood *you* as the actor. These directions do not communicate clearly to the reader; they confuse him. If the understood *you* had acted throughout (that is, if the author had remained in the active voice), there would be no confusion about following the directions.

The passive voice is not always inappropriate, of course, or there would be no need to have it in the language. But you must be careful to use it where it is appropriate and unobtrusive. If, for instance, you do not know who performs the action, or if the actor is too unimportant to the thought of the sentence to be worth mentioning, it is often appropriate to use the passive verb. If you write, "Highway 6 was completed last May," no one is going to insist that you change this passive construction into an active one by naming the engineering firm that built the road. But you probably do not need to leave this sentence in the passive voice. You can easily make it a phrase and put it into a longer, active sentence, for example: "Highway 6, completed last May, has increased trade in Boonville by fifty percent," or "Completion of Highway 6 last May boosted trade in Boonville."

This example has acceptable use of the passive voice:

**After the operation, Ernest was moved to his room and was given a sedative by the nurse who was to watch over him during his long convalescence.**

In this sentence, we can take it for granted that a doctor performed the operation and that an orderly moved Ernest to his room. There is no point in mentioning them, for they are unimportant in this context. Notice that the remainder of the sentence continues in the passive, *was given by the nurse*, instead of *the nurse gave*. This use of passive is appropriate because to change it to active would change the point of view in mid-sentence. To make it active, this part of the sentence would have to become an independent clause preceded by a comma: . . . room, *and the nurse who was to watch over him during his long convalescence gave him a sedative*. A second objection to this active form of the verb is the distance between the subject of the clause, *nurse*, and its verb, *gave*. Ordinarily, they should be as close together as possible. Here they are too far separated.

The passive, then, can be used with care when the actor is unknown or unimportant or when the active voice would interfere with style or cause a clumsy construction. Usually you should change any passive sentences to active ones. Sometimes students use passive constructions to avoid using the first person *I.* For example, sentences such as this one appear frequently: *C. Goehring's* Life in the Jungle *was selected for a book report because of the interest of its subject matter to this reader.* Note that no one has selected a book in this sentence. *This reader* may have, but who is he? Better by far to say in a forthright manner: *I selected C. Goehring's* Life in the Jungle *for a book report because its subject matter interested me.* Furthermore, do not refer to yourself in writing as "the author" or "this writer." Attempting to avoid the first person almost always leads to a poor use of the passive or to clumsy circumlocutions.

Here are more examples of poor use of the passive taken from student papers.

Coffee had to be drunk and cookies eaten before games were played. (No one in this sentence is doing anything. Change to something like: The visitors had coffee and cookies before playing checkers and monopoly.)

Games to be played were checkers and monopoly. (Again, no one is playing the games. Make it active this way: They will play checkers and monopoly.)

8:15 was shown by the clock on the wall. (Very simple to change. The clock should be doing the action expressed here, so make it the subject of the sentence: The clock on the wall showed 8:15.)

### EXERCISE

Change any passive construction to active in these sentences.

1. Her skirts were always too short, Jane's parents insisted, and when she got a veto on her white leather suit, tears were shed, enough to fill Thompson's creek.
2. When the fourth child came, all plans to move to Bardtown in the spring were given up by the Guy family.
3. More than ten pounds of fish and sixteen sacks of ten-cent peanuts were consumed by the two dieters per week on their carbohydrate diet.
4. In 1910, his case was called incurable by every doctor in the north woods of Maine.
5. "All that I hope to be, I owe to my beloved oilwell," was the twist Miss Susie gave the Lincoln quote.

6. The centerpiece was arranged by the office secretary, while doughnuts and coffee were set out on card tables in the foyer by the clerk-typist.

7. Plans to attend the first session of summer school were made by the Douglass girls.

8. The hay was thrown over the fence by Farmer Swenson, whose cows were then called by their owner to "Come and get it!"

9. J. R.'s closet held more than fifty sports shirts, but every time, he chose the blue-gray plaid.

10. The house on Suffolk Street was pink and brown with a most vulgar green on the roof, and the color combination was loudly bemoaned by the neighborhood, as it was by the new owner.

11. Facts could not be ascertained, and so no decision was reached by the Committee to Remove Uncooperative Members from the club rolls.

12. Lee pranced home to stun his father with the news that he would be blasted off to California for the summer with the guys.

13. Complaints were heard by the young man when he announced to his parents that he had just quit his new job.

14. The mystery of the missing hymnals was finally solved by the rector at the Saturday meeting of the acolytes.

15. Because of the development of seven new cavities, the afternoon was unpleasantly spent in the dentist's office.

16. Excellent recommendations were given on the application sent by the artist from Arkansas.

17. The practice was continued until the target was hit by every marksman.

18. On November 15, agreement was reached among the Brechner Boulevard neighbors over rights to the water tank.

19. Amazing progress has been made by the Bell County Chamber of Commerce.

20. All the potato salad, as well as the Greek olives and the pickles, was eaten before mid-afternoon.

### Avoid Listless Verbs

They deaden your writing. As you revise, change as many of these as possible to lively verbs.

| | |
|---|---|
| ARE | GO |
| IS | SAY |
| IT IS | SEE |
| HAD | THERE ARE |
| HAS | THERE IS |
| HAVE | |

Look at the italicized verbs in this paragraph:

The Volkswagen *is* unexcelled for dependability. It *is* well-behaved under driving conditions in which other cars *are* kept off the road. Unlike conventional cars with their engine over the front wheels, the VW engine *is* in the back, which gives superior traction to the rear wheels. As a result, the VW can *climb* steep, slippery hills with ease or it can *go* with sureness through ice, snow, mud, and sand. Furthermore, other cars *are* easily outperformed by the VW even under the most extreme temperature conditions because *there are* no radiator problems in the VW. The VW engine *is* air-cooled; thus *there are* no leaks, rust, or antifreeze problems peculiar to conventional cars. Any time, summer or winter, day or night, the VW *is* ready to go anywhere.

Every verb in this paragraph, with the exception of *climb*, is on the list. Further, a poor use of the passive appears in mid-paragraph. Can you spot it? It marks a change in point of view.

This paragraph as it stands is not the worst one ever written, but making it better is simple. Just change the verbs (automatically taking care of the passive construction).

Unexcelled for dependability, the Volkswagen *behaves* well under driving conditions that *frighten* other cars off the road. Unlike conventional cars with their engines over the front wheels, the VW, with its engine's weight in the back of the car, *allows* the rear wheels superior traction. As a result, the VW *climbs* steep, slippery hills with ease or *cruises* securely through ice, snow, mud, and sand. Further, the VW outperforms other cars even under the most extreme temperature conditions, because it *needs* no radiator. The air-cooled engine thus *develops* no leaks, rust, or antifreeze problems peculiar to conventional cars. Any time, summer or winter, the VW *stands* ready for anything.

In this revision, none of the listless verbs appear. No change in point of view mars the paragraph's coherence. No weak use of the passive confuses the reader.

Occasionally, you will find it necessary to use some of the listless verbs. Fine! As long as you do not overuse them to the point that your writing becomes boring. A good rule to follow is: *Change any verb that does not draw a picture.*

### EXERCISE

Change all colorless verbs in these sentences to stronger, active ones.

1. The tour conductor said that we could not lean over the wooden railing.

2. There is a fat little green pig with roses on his back placed on the dresser.
3. The painter came down the shaky ladder and put his pan and brush down on the floor in disgust.
4. The driver drove his truck down the road, passing cars on the icy road very carelessly.
5. The girl was crying when she said that the police were after her.
6. The governess could see the dusting powder all over the floor, and some of it was on the bedspread and some on the study table.
7. Sylvia gave a loud cry when she realized that the telephone call was long distance from her sister Laura in Philadelphia.
8. Every time one of the carbonated drinks was opened, out came a gush of purple pop with a hissing noise, and I had to put it down and run to keep from getting wet from the spray.
9. Jackson had a stomach-ache, so he said, and he told us that there were six other leading athletes who had stomach-aches, too.
10. We went first to Los Angeles and then went on to Kansas City, not getting to the convention until Thursday afternoon.

### Examine All Uses of "Who" and "Which"

The overuse of *who* and *which* weighs writing down with deadwood (that is, unnecessary words). These words introduce dependent adjective clauses. Reducing the clauses to phrases almost always results in economy in wording and an increase in interest. Here is an example.

Terry's *Guide to Mexico,* which was first written over fifty years ago, has gone through nine revisions, of which the latest was in 1965.

If you drop the first *which* and the first *was,* along with the *of which* and the same listless *was,* you will have a stronger and more economically worded sentence.

Terry's *Guide to Mexico,* first written over fifty years ago, has gone through nine revisions, the latest in 1965.

In the next two sentences, the *who* and *which* are unnecessary.

Jack Jones is a man who calls every trick. (Let us assume from his name that Jack Jones is a man. Then strike *is a man who,* and you have cleared away four words of deadwood. Yet the meaning is intact.)

Jack Jones calls every trick.

Peterson's poem, "The Way to Heaven," is a poem which needs no explanation. (As in the previous sentence delete *is a poem which* and you have eliminated a weak *is* and an unnecessary *which*.)

Peterson's poem, "The Way to Heaven," needs no explanation.

Note the number of who's, which's, listless verbs, and other deadwood in this paragraph.

1    The university catalog *can be used* to good advantage by the fresh-
2    man *who is* bewildered by university life. *It is* revised every year *in order*
3    *that* it *will be* up-to-date. *First, of all, there is* in this catalog a list of all
4    the courses *which are* offered by the university. These courses *are* ar-
5    ranged alphabetically by department *in order that* the student may
6    choose *which* courses he wants to take. *It is also* from this list of courses
7    *of* each department that a degree plan for the student *can be* devised,
8    *which will be* within the limits of the regulations of the university.

Line 1: Listless verb, *can be used.*

Line 2: A *who* followed by the listless verb *is*. Write it *the freshman be-wildered by university life* and avoid both. *It is* at the beginning of the next sentence needs revision. Why not leave this whole sentence out and substitute the one word *current* before *university* in the first line?

Line 3: Listless verb *will be*. Problem avoided if you delete this whole sentence as suggested. *First of all.* Do not use this expression. If you must use a *first*, be certain you also use a *second*. In any case, delete *of all.* Do not use *firstly* or *secondly* at any time.

Line 4: *Which* followed by listless verb *are* needs examination. Listless verb *are* needs revision.

Line 5: *In order that.* Do not use this phrase; . . . *to allow the student choice of courses* is better here.

Line 6: *Which* avoided by the revision suggested for line 5. *It is,* at the beginning of the next sentence, needs to be removed by revision. *Of courses of each department* has too many *of's.* Remove one *of* by writing *of departments' courses.*

Line 7: Listless verb *can be* needs changing.

Line 8: *Which* followed by listless verb *will be* also needs revising. *Of the regulations of the University.* Delete one *of* by writing *of university regulations.*

All lines: The passive construction in every sentence underlies most of the problems in the paragraph. The active voice will eliminate *which*, *who*, and listless verbs.

Here is a revision of the paragraph. Notice the difference in length when the deadwood is deleted.

The current university catalog offers help for bewildered freshmen. It lists all university courses alphabetically by department, allowing the student, if he follows university regulations, to choose his own courses and devise his own degree plan.

Look now at a paragraph by Robert Louis Stevenson. Here no *which* or *who* clutters the thought. No overuse of listless verbs deadens it. Some passive constructions appear. Can you spot them? Verbs are italicized.

These long beaches *are* enticing to the idle man. It *would be* hard to find a walk more solitary and at the same time more exciting to the mind. Crowds of ducks and sea gulls *hover* over the sea. Sandpipers *trot* in and out by troops after the retiring waves, *trilling* together in a chorus of infinitesimal song. Strange seatangles, new to the European eye, the bones of whales, or sometimes a whole whale's carcase, white with carrion gulls and poisoning the wind, *lie* scattered here and there along the sands. The waves *come* in closely, vast and green, *curve* their translucent necks, and *burst* with a surprising uproar that *runs* waxing and waning, up and down the long keyboard of the beach. The foam of these great ruins *mounts* in an instant to the ridge of the sand glacis, swiftly *fleets* back again, and *is* met and buried by the next breaker.[1]

Three listless verbs appear in this paragraph—*are* in the first sentence, *be* in the second sentence, and *is* in the last sentence, and these are all passive. But these are the only listless verbs and the only passive constructions in the paragraph. Notice the preponderance of strong, active verbs—*hover, trot, lie, curve, burst, runs, mounts, fleets.* Note also the absence of *which* and *who.*

### EXERCISE

Revise the following sentences to eliminate *who, which,* listless verbs, and other deadwood.

1. Bill decided to take the road to the east, which would get him to Troy fifteen minutes sooner.
2. Grace sold the book which had been given to her last Christmas in order to buy a ticket to Calico Rock.
3. Geoffrey Chaslin, who played the lead in *A Man for All Seasons,* which

[1] Robert Louis Stevenson, in "The Old Pacific Capital," first published in *Frazier's Magazine,* November, 1880.

is a play about Sir Thomas More, visited London last year in order to become better equipped to play the role.

4. His grandfather, who is also his godfather, gave him an air rifle, which his parents stole and hid, he said.

5. The tall elm tree, which had replaced the scrubby oak, lost all its leaves and turned sick, which worried Frances, who had done all she could to keep the homestead pretty.

6. She decided to wear the black and white piqué, which her mother made and which was far prettier than any of the others wore, which included Sharon, whose dad is Dean of Everything on campus.

7. He went through all of the cancelled checks of the Bank of Commerce in order to try to find the one which he had sent to the mortgage company to make his house payment for the month of January.

8. Joe McCown is the man who contributed all his ranch income to the orphan whom the police found in the house which was deserted. (Note: If you have to use them, how do you decide between *who* or *whom?* It is simple. *Who* and *whom* will be found only in dependent clauses. Remove the clause from the sentence and substitute *he* or *him* in place of the *who* or *whom*. If *he* fits, then *who* is proper; if *him* fits, choose *whom*. For example, in this sentence *who* is found in the clause *who contributed his ranch income*. If you try both *he* and *him* in place of the *who*, you will find that the only *he* will fit properly: *He contributed his ranch income*. So *who* is correct here. *Whom* is found in the clause *whom the police found*. You will find that only *him* can be substituted for *whom: The police found him*. So *whom* is proper in this clause. If it is plural, substitute *they* for *who* or *them* for *whom*.)

9. The choice which was made was between Bill and him, neither of whom had any experience in typing, which was required of the person who was to be employed. (Is this *whom* proper?)

10. There is no reason for the chairman, who is Vanessa Jones, to take offense at the motion, which is aimed at electing a vice-chairman who is to help her with her duties.

### Avoid Anything Trite

Some words and phrases are used so much that they become worn out. Yesterday's slang, for instance, is trite today. Not many of you would want to "cut a rug" or to "put a bee" in someone's "bonnet," nor would many now use a phrase like "crazy, mixed-up kid." These are out of date. The same happens to certain combinations of ordinary words, as in these sentences.

**He not only started sweeping like mad, but also gave me a list of items**

to buy for the party, such as the following: party hats, confetti, horns, and so forth. These things proved to be so much fun that we had a ball.

The trite words and expressions are listed below.

| | |
|---|---|
| not only . . . but | and so forth |
| like mad | proved to be |
| such as | we had a ball |
| the following | items |

### Or Any Exhausted Phrase

Each of these sentences contains at least one exhausted phrase, a phrase that is used over and over. They are *italicized*. Avoid them and others like them.

*Due to the fact that* I had gained too much weight in the past month, I *turned down* his invitation to dinner. (Always substitute *because* for *due to the fact that*. It works every time.)

This apathy has spread over the *entire world.* (Why not just *world?*)

Our *ever-growing population* will be a problem in *just a few short years.*

*To this rule I was no exception.*

We crossed the street *in order to* avoid meeting him. (We crossed the street to avoid meeting him. Always delete *in order.)*

*In this fast moving world,* the scientist must *keep abreast of* technological advances.

*In this land of ours today,* no one can really be a *rugged individualist.*

*So for many years to come* we will feel the effect of Sputnik.

*Yes, truly it can be said that* young pople today are rebellious.

Ours is becoming a *push-button society.*

Texas Avenue will soon reach the limit of its capacity, *as far as* traffic *is concerned.* (A particularly poor one.)

These expressions only fill space. They add nothing to the thought of the sentence. Avoid them *like the plague* (another one!).

### EXERCISES

A. Pick out all trite and exhausted words and phrases in this paragraph.

Yes, truly the American way is the one which is best suited to serve the needs and desires of the people of this far-flung world of ours today. Even if one of the various and sundry philosophies which oppose our way of life were to win out and conquer our country as well as all others, there are various means through which we could make a comeback. We could pull the rug out from under our enemies by stirring up a hornet's nest of far-flung, ever-increasing destruction of enemy materiel, that is, as far as their supply lines are concerned—trains, airplanes, and so forth—so that they would not have a leg to stand on, as far as fighting us is concerned. It would, therefore, prove to be the case that in order to keep us under their thumb, our enemies would have discovered that they have bitten off more than they can chew and would be facing an impossible task.

B. Rewrite these sentences with a fresh approach so that exhausted words and phrases are removed.

1. She had clearly suffered the ravages of time.
2. We sat under the sheltering arms of the gnarled old oak.
3. Would you believe half a million trading stamps?
4. He is twenty-three and not getting any younger.
5. Heaven only knows and time will tell which way the cookie crumbles.
6. She is the motherly type and talks to me like a Dutch uncle.
7. She left no stone unturned to find happiness at any price.
8. He felt a fierce loyalty for his native Arkansas.
9. The little children played at games and such until dinner.
10. Restitution will be made by June 20.
11. When we asked him about the missing cookies he looked as guilty as the cat that ate the canary.
12. When the going got rough, Becky decided to turn the job over to Susan.
13. He soon discovered that a rolling stone gathers no moss and settled down to a steady job.
14. In my opinion, I think he was just whistling in the dark all the time he was smiling like a Cheshire cat.
15. On the other side of the ledger is the fact that he was driving like a bat when the accident occurred.

### Avoid Forcing Your Reader to Love It

If you grow too enthusiastic about your subject, you may stretch your reader's credibility by making statements intended to convince him of the worth of your subject. You are, in effect, attempting to force him to fall in on your side. These sentences do just that:

Horseshoes is a delightful game that can always be enjoyed by everyone, young and old. (Maybe horseshoes is delightful, but there is *no* game that *everyone* will *always* enjoy).

There's nothing as exciting as a good football game. (To some people there may be activities that are considerably more exciting—reading a book, for instance.)

*Irma's Last Love* is the most fascinating book ever written. (To the writer, but perhaps not to the reader.)

No one will regret making this trip into the depths of Devil's Canyon. (Not even someone who slips and breaks a leg on the descent?)

The point: Do not tell your reader how wonderful something is; make him feel it through the quality of your writing. Then you will not need to tell him.

### Do Not Preach

"Preaching" usually takes the form of moralizing in writing. Rarely does a reader want a lecture on what his moral positions should be or on what he should believe. If you present convincing evidence, you will not have to draw the moral conclusions so odious to the reader. Look at these examples of student moralizing.

Young people should try to understand their parents.

If we all love our country, no foreign ideology can ever take us over!

Everyone should strive to live a more moral life.

Students, awaken! We must not let our sacred traditions be taken away from us.

Examination of these "preachy" sentences discloses the use of certain words that make the sentences preachy. These words divide naturally into two classifications.

1. *False words.*

| | |
|---|---|
| always | everything |
| ever | never |
| every | nobody |
| everybody | no one |

When you use these words without qualification you say something about everyone or everything in a class. Almost no conclusion about everyone or everything can be valid. You can write that everyone must die some day or that everyone has been born; but otherwise, someone, somewhere, proves the exception to most statements about all people. (Note that in this last sentence we carefully avoided writing that someone proves the exception to *all* statements about all people.) The ridiculousness of using these words becomes apparent when you see a sentence such as this one:

Everybody always likes everything about every film that Hitchcock makes, and no one ever criticizes his techniques.

2. *Commanding words.* Such words as *must, ought to, should,* and *had better* demand obedience to the writer. Such admonishment is more likely to make the reader resentful of your ideas than receptive to them.

### Avoid Stilted Wording

When a writer attempts to impress his reader by using big words and flowery phrases inappropriately, he is stilted in his writing. He goes out of his way to make a simple statement complicated by using longer words and more words than the thought warrants. The result is lack of communication because ideas are obscured rather than clarified by the clutter of words. Look at these examples and their simplifications:

The consumption of alcoholic beverages among the younger generation is escalating. (Young people are drinking more.)

Felicitations on the auspicious occasion of your natal day. (Happy birthday.)

I desire to pen my memoirs. (I want to write an autobiography.)

He matriculated with the earnest desire to graduate in three years, but due to certain problems that presented themselves, he was forced to accept a grade of failing in two courses of study and finally found it necessary to withdraw from two others, which left as a remainder only one course, on which his instructor awarded him a grade of C—. (Although he wanted to graduate in three years, he failed six hours, dropped three, and barely salvaged three in his first semester.)

### EXERCISE

Revise all moralizing and stilted wording in these sentences.

1. The surgeon hesitated, his features drawn and sorrowful, as he ap-

proached to verify our deep and foreboding premonition that the immediate ancestor of our parent was expected to expire before the sun rose to shine upon the world again.

2. Everyone should consume some of the leafy green products of the garden every day because of their nutritional value.

3. The happy cries of the darling children reached the ears of their delighted parents.

4. Despite warnings of friends and family, of the government, and even of the tobacco manufacturers themselves, Hubert continued to partake of tremendous amounts of nicotine.

5. His employment was terminated due to the fact that his employer felt that an excessive number of hours per day were being spent in other than gainful pursuits.

6. She has the ability to discuss at length any topic of conversation that is introduced, despite the fact that she sometimes is less than expert in the field under discussion.

7. And so in conclusion, let me say that we should all strive in unison to extirpate from our society the evils of gambling.

8. The babe still lay quietly, lost in slumberland, as the wee hours of the morning ticked on and sounds of dawn reached the ears of the drowsy parents.

### Avoid "Fine Writing"

Some beginning writers believe that a fancy and elaborate style is elegant. Be warned that it is not. For instance, a freshman English student had difficulty understanding why her instructor marked her down when she wrote the following:

> Lush, well-maintained grounds combine with the harmonic grace of the buildings to give a deep majestic glow to the grounds. Flying everywhere, beautiful birds lend their melodious tones, while squirrels flit from tree to tree, chattering ecstatically.

In trying to be artistic, the student said nothing. English instructors usually call this "fine writing," and they are not giving it a compliment. A good rule to follow is this: Write briefly, plainly, and sensibly. Do not put on airs or use flowery words. Say what you mean.

### Avoid "ly" Words

Most "ly" words are adverbs and modify verbs or adjectives. When used to modify a verb, the "ly" word allows the author to deaden his writing by selecting a listless verb instead of searching for the strong active verb to make his writing more lively. For instance, you could write "He ate voraciously," but "He gobbled his food" draws a better picture. Sometimes the "ly" words are unnecessary, as they are in these sentences:

I have completely exhausted my supply. (Delete *completely.* If you have exhausted it, it is exhausted. There is nothing more to say.)

There was really no reason for his success. (Delete *really.* It is a filler word, as are most of the "ly" adverbs.)

His remarks were truly nonsense. (Delete *truly.* If they were nonsense, that is all there is to it. Another word used as a filler.)

There are some "ly" words you might want to avoid. Check your papers to be certain that you do not overuse these words.

| | | |
|---|---|---|
| absolutely | positively | truly |
| completely | purely | undoubtedly |
| extremely | really | unfortunately |
| fortunately | surely | unquestionably |

### Avoid Vague Words

Vague words are those the writer can use from habit or without thought, as substitutes for specific words that convey exact meaning. Vague words convey little meaning because they are general. For instance, this sentence says nothing: "The many different factors involved created various problems for many people." Nothing specific can be communicated to the reader through this sentence, and there is no point in writing it.

Here is a list of vague words to avoid. When you are tempted to use one of them, mark it out and select a more specific term.

| | | | |
|---|---|---|---|
| a lot | factor | many | pretty |
| aspect | field (of) | much | provide |
| characteristic | innumerable | nice | several |
| consideration | interesting | people | thing(s) |
| contains | item | pertains | variety |
| deal | large | phase | various |
| different | lots of | | very |

It takes special effort for most beginning writers to avoid the words on this list, but the successful are rewarded. Remove these words from your vocabulary. Otherwise, you may end up saying nothing, as did the students who wrote these sentences:

There are lots of ways to consider making a living.

There are many and various sweaters to be made in all sizes and colors.

The many different aspects of socialized medicine are interesting.

## Intention and Audience—Tone

As the heading to this section suggests, tone has to do with a writer's intention as found in his finished work and as perceived by the reader (audience). Another way of looking at tone is to think of it as the writer's "voice"; in your papers it is your "voice" as your readers hear it, and it may not be the "voice" you intended at all. Once you freeze a word on paper, it loses much of the added power it would normally have if you spoke it. For example, try to *hear* how each of the following would *sound* if spoken according to the instructions given:

1. Good bye. (firmly, straightforwardly)
2. Good bye. (softly, almost with fear)
3. Good bye. (whispered, with love)
4. Good bye! (loudly, meaning "get lost")
5. Good bye. (loudly, to people at distance)

Not everyone would say these in exactly the same way. Still, it is obvi-

Used by permission of John Hart and Field Enterprises, Inc.

ous that a writer loses some "voice power" when he puts his words down on paper. An added problem, too, is that a reader may not hear what a writer intends; we read into things, we hear what we want to hear. Inexperienced writers often try to supply this missing intention by using adverbs excessively (as you learned earlier in this chapter).

You can see, then, that tone involves the three-part relationship represented in this diagram:

## INTENTION AND AUDIENCE—TONE

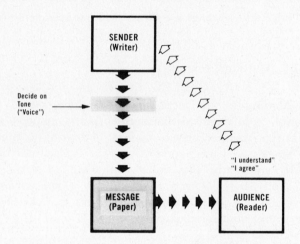

The diagram suggests that you, as the writer (sender), need to decide on the tone or "voice" you will try to project in your paper (message); then you must make sure that it is this tone that accompanies your message to the reader (audience). In the classroom, the reader (usually your instructor) will let the writer know that he "understands" and "agrees"; or he may disagree with you, and ask you to add more factual support. With published papers the information returning to the writer (through sales, criticisms, personal comment, perhaps) is less certain.

Tone is related to changes in the sound of the voice in speech, where it is usually easy to spot a tone that is approving (or disapproving), serious (or humorous), personal (or impersonal), direct (or sarcastic), formal (or informal), calm (or excited), and so on. It is this tone in a work that helps determine a writer's control of the reader's attitude toward the ideas presented. If you recheck the section on introductory paragraphs, you'll find that you already know a lot about tone—how to get the reader's interest, how to get him to accept you and your ideas (see pages 76 to 81). Study and use this definition of tone:

*Tone consists of those qualities in a work through which a writer hopes to get a specific response in his reader.*

"Qualities" implies logical thought as well as the psychological appeals used to create reader interest and to get reader acceptance. And since the "qualities" in question must be conveyed by words, they must be your starting point in controlling and projecting the tone you want your reader to hear.

This chapter has already shown you many ways inexperienced writers unknowingly create an undesirable tone by using passive voice, listless verbs, too many adverbs, trite expressions, "fine writing," and *who* or *which* constructions that lead to "deadwood." The following illustrations have been chosen for study because in each the writer has tried to create a specific tone. Also, all are introductory paragraphs, chosen because a writer must establish tone and interest at once if he is to keep his reader moving into the work. The first is by a student; all the others are by professional writers.

**A.**

Of all the *enemies* of mankind that have ever existed upon the face of the earth, there are some that simply *do not deserve* to be here. Ranked third in the all-time top ten *worst enemies*, just behind the *devil* himself and the *notorious snake*, is the cockroach. This *disgusting* little insect far exceeds his nearest competitor, the mosquito (who, for the sake of *those who may be curious*, could manage only an eighth-place finish behind such *powerful contenders* as *rats, buzzards*, lions, and piranha) because of his superior size and strength, and his *too-horrible-for-words* appearance. The cockroach should be *wiped out* at Glory U. because he is an eye *sore*, he *interferes* with one's learning, and he is a *hazard* to one's health.

Even a quick check of the italicized words in this paragraph reveals a negative tone: *enemies, worst, notorious, disgusting, horrible, eye sore.* This student clearly dislikes cockroaches; his thesis is that this insect "should be wiped out," and his paper develops the reasons pointed to in the rest of the thesis statement. But there is more to the success of this paragraph than a clear statement of disapproval. How, for example, has the student prevented the passage from becoming too serious? Do you think this passage would be as effective if both the subject and the tone were serious? He maintains the tone of playful seriousness through-out the paper with such comments as: "one of the little monstrosities galloping across the room," "he may be seen a few feet away just sitting and staring," "squatting in the corner surveying the situation," and "con-verge upon him armed with sticks, shoes, books, chairs." Professional humorists are well aware that exaggerating little things usually creates humor; do you think this student has carried exaggeration too far?

**B.**

I am a gun nut, I suppose. My father made me a gun nut. He taught me how to shoot, and ever since what I would really rather be doing than anything else is shooting at small, innocent birds.[2]

You could never tell from introductory Paragraph B that Stewart Alsop is seriously attacking computerized bureaucracy. There is no thesis statement at the beginning, only a calculated tone of sarcastic playfulness created at once by the first sentence. The first sentence of the second paragraph echoes this tone: "To the non-gun nut, this may seem as mysterious as the nuttiness of the young does to the middle-aged." Maintaining his tone, he leads the reader surely toward the thesis (about half-way through) with the following statement: "What, indeed, you gonna do? So I took off most of an afternoon to be fingerprinted for J. Edgar Hoover's files, a messy and demeaning business." Only in the next-to-last paragraph does he give his reader a thesis:

But surely there is a better way. Surely it is better to go to the root of the evil. Invention should have halted with the flush of the toilet a century ago— what sensible man has a good word to say for the ballistic missile or the bomb, or even for the automobile, and the airplane? But the worst invention of the lot was the computer.[3]

But the tone of sarcastic playfulness persists, partly because of exaggeration and partly because no reader can be expected to remain wholly serious as he reads about the "flush of the toilet." Notice, too, that the first-person "I," used throughout, disappears in this paragraph. Why has the writer left it out?

**C.**

When I hear about some *flagrant violation of human rights* in a far-flung place on the globe I react violently as any free, red-blooded American does. I get filled with righteous indignation. I get stirred. I get—*I get nervous is what I get.*[4]

---

[2] "A Call to Revolt" by Stewart Alsop, from *Newsweek*, December 22, 1969. Copyright Newsweek, Inc., 1969. Reprinted by permission.

[3] *Ibid.*

[4] From "Peace Is Hell," by Goodman Ace. Copyright 1967 by Saturday Review Co. First appeared in *Saturday Review*, August 5, 1967. Used with permission.

Example C is the introductory paragraph to a short political article on the tense peace in the Middle East. Again the author chooses to with-hold his thesis and concentrate on getting the reader interested and sympathetic. Aside from the personal "I," how does Goodman Ace keep you smiling as he heads toward a rather serious comment on peace? What is the effect of the contrast between the two comments in italics?

A main function of the "I" in Paragraphs B and C is to create a personal tone that can readily be turned into playfulness. Properly used, the "I" usually adds a feeling of first-hand observation; but it can be used to gain interest for very serious observations without the sugar-coating of humor seen in these first paragraphs. Here are some examples.

**D.**

*A few mornings ago* I rescued a bat from a swimming pool. The man who owned the pool—*but did not own the bat*—asked me why. That question *I do not expect ever to be able to answer,* but it involves *a good deal.* If even *I* myself could understand it, *I* would know what it is that seems to distinguish *man* from the rest of *nature,* and why, despite all she has to *teach* him, there is also something he would like to *teach* her *if he could.*[5]

Paragraph D begins a fairly long paper on nature, the individual, and the species. The author concludes that nature has a "passion for mere numbers," disregarding individuals, and that some men have also become too "careful of the type" and too "careless of the single life." Only when the reader reaches the last two paragraphs of the paper does he fully see the author's main point. In what ways does the author try to keep the paper from becoming too formal? What might you conclude about this writer's intention and tone from the italicized words? How does he create reader interest? How does the writer get you to think of him as serious, thoughtful, and questioning?

**E.**

*A couple of years ago* I became involved on a panel for the Western Psychological Association which was about *something called* "The Psyche of a Scientist." It turned into *a kind of* psychodrama because *here were* all these psychologists, sociologists, and anthropologists, but I was the only *real live* scientist. The *tribe I* belong to is called biochemistry, which is sort of a subgroup in the *pecking* order of science somewhere below physical chem-

[5] From *The Desert Year* by Joseph Wood Krutch. Copyright 1952 by Joseph Wood Krutch. Reprinted by permission of William Morrow & Company, Inc.

istry and above geology. And what *I* was listening to was a fantasy, or, *you might say,* the results of a *con job* by the *natives* on some *poor hapless explorers* who did not understand the *terrain* at all.[6]

The author of Paragraph E is beginning an outspoken attack on certain practices in the "science jungle," concluding (several pages later), "Until we become aware of these evils of big science we cannot hope to eradicate them." Judging from the words in italics, what would you conclude about the tone of this introductory paragraph? Which of the following descriptive terms would you use to describe the tone: *impersonal, objective, personal, formal, informal, casual, serious, direct, indirect, sarcastic.*

**F.**

*I feel* that this award was not made to me *as a man,* but to *my work*—a *life's work* in the *agony* and *sweat* of the *human spirit,* not for glory and least of all for profit, but to create out of the materials of *the human spirit* something which did not exist before. *So this award is only mine in trust.* It will not be difficult to find a dedication for the money part of it *commensurate* with the purpose and significance of its origin. *But I would like* to do the same with the acclaim too, by using this moment as a pinnacle from which *I might* be listened to by the young men and women already dedicated to *the same anguish* and *travail,* among whom is already that one who will some day stand here where *I am standing.*[7]

In this famous address William Faulkner concludes that "man will prevail." He has chosen a moment of triumph to call for action. The tone he projects might be called "urgent"—a bid for attention in a time of need. How many personal "tags" can you discover in this paragraph? What is the effect of words like *travail, commensurate, anguish, human spirit?* Comment on the nature of the "ethical appeal" here. (See pages 76 and 78 for additional information.)

**G.**

The School System has much to say these days of the virtue of reading widely, and not enough about the virtues of reading less but in depth. There are any number of reading lists for poetry, but there is not enough talk

---

[6] From "The Science Jungle" by Paul Saltman in *Harper's Magazine,* February 1967. Copyright © 1967 by Harper's Magazine.

[7] William Faulkner, "Nobel Prize Acceptance Speech." Reprinted from *The Faulkner Reader.* Copyright 1954 by William Faulkner (Random House, Inc.).

about individual poems. Poetry, finally, is one poem at a time. To read any one poem carefully is the ideal preparation for reading another. Only a poem can illustrate how poetry works.[8]

The thesis statement at the end of introductory Paragraph G asserts firmly what this poet-critic will be discussing. Although the "voice" you hear is authoritative, it doesn't have quite the sense of personal argument that most of the previous paragraphs have. Of all the paragraphs, it is probably the most clearly *expository,* setting up a thesis and then supporting it in a fairly long paper. The writer decides to use the personal "I" very sparingly (there are only two or three, and they appear later in the discussion). Does he write in a way to create interest? What is the effect of the *parallelism* and *antithesis* in the first two sentences? (See page 62 for some hints.) Although there is no "I" in the paragraph, could you call it "impersonal"? Why not? (See page 34 for some comments about challenge and strength in thesis statements.)

To summarize. The questions you must ask yourself when thinking about tone in a work include at least the following:

1. What is the specific response the writer is seeking from his reader? "I understand"? "I agree"? "I sympathize"?
2. How does the writer create interest?
3. What kind of person does the writer sound like? An authority? Objective commentator? Involved participant? A lively human being?
4. Are the words strong and expressive or weak and colorless? Is their effect "negative" or "positive"? Personal or impersonal?
5. Are the sentence patterns simple or complex? What effect do they have on the tone?
6. How serious is the thought presented? Is there any attempt to tone down the seriousness with humor or sarcasm?

If you look back at the diagram on page 156, you should see immediately how these questions apply to your writing and to the decisions you make before you begin writing. The diagram shows that you, as writer, decide on the "voice" or tone *before* you begin to write the paper. If you are clear on "who you are," how serious, how informal, how personal, how assertive, you should be able to carry this attitude into the paper itself, giving it the unity of tone a good paper must have (see the two shaded areas in the diagram).

8 "Robert Frost: The Way to the Poem" by John Ciardi from *Saturday Review,* April 12, 1958. Copyright 1958 by Saturday Review Inc. Reprinted by permission of the author and publishers.

## EXERCISES ON TONE

1. Here is a simple exercise that will make you aware of some of the limitations most of us have when we grab words from our vocabularies in a hurry.

   The list below consists of words you probably learned before you went to school. Look at them quickly and decide their meanings.

   | | | |
   |------|--------|-------|
   | arm | knife | dish |
   | eye | nose | cup |
   | worm | chair | can |
   | elbow | finger | egg |
   | spoon | hand | table |

   You probably thought of them as nouns (names of things), just as you first learned them. But these "baby" words can become strong *tone verbs* if you think about them. For example: *Arm* yourself with strong verbs; don't *finger* your hair that way; she *wormed* her way into my affections; *spoon* out the chemicals carefully; can you take it as well as *dish* it out?

   List another ten words that you consider preschool words (hint: think of pets, body parts, furniture, food, things around any home, including kitchen, dining room, and bathroom).

   Now write ten short sentences which turn these common words into strong tone-creating words you can use.

2. Come to class prepared to discuss *denotation* and *connotation*. Why are these two words important clues' to tone? (Recheck Exercise C on page 118.)

3. Recheck Exercises C and D, pages 133 and 134. Using Exercise C as your model, write three different paragraphs on one of the subjects listed for you in Exercise A, page 94. Your instructor may want you to repeat the assignment with other topics in the list to practice creating tone.

## REVIEW EXERCISES

On the basis of the material in this chapter, revise these sentences in any way necessary.

1. World War II was over, and he was coming in on a wing and a prayer.

2. Marjorie Ann is gorgeous, but to hear her tell it, she is plain, unless she is too modest, as not many of her age group are.

3. He was on Cloud 9 when he inherited enough money to live in the manner to which he had become accustomed.

4. They knew, moreover, that the malady was to be a lingering one and that insidiously it would increase in seriousness until the dear one's life itself would be snuffed out, as a candle is suddenly relieved of its light-giving pleasure when its usefulness is ended.

5. They were too tired to move, but they walked home, slowly as though they resented every step of it, but they did not have bus fare, and they did not know what else to do but to walk.

6. His own father, who was to Paul a financial wizard, and whom Paul hoped to imitate, knew now that the cards were down and that it would be tough sledding and uphill all the way from now on along the road to Wall Street.

7. To whom should she appeal for funds for the Scouting outing, she asked herself. Who cares enough to give, and from whom can I seek aid?

8. They hurried to church fast, because they knew that the choir director would not be happy if they came into rehearsal late again, and they did not like to walk the full length of the building up to the choir loft while she looked at them with anger in her eyes.

9. At least we can say with certainty that nobody can deny Charles the praise he deserves for making the organization run more smoothly than Tommy was able to, or Buster, either.

10. You haven't lived until you've sat at the lake's edge while the sun goes down, with a hired hand to mix up the refreshments and swat away the mosquitoes.

11. Freddie refused the invitation due to the fact that his aunt was expected, whom he had not seen since her third marriage, which was three years ago.

12. Nothing is more charming than Delilah with an armful of tulips and a smile on her face.

13. The doorbell had been loudly rung, and it was too late for anything but hope.

14. The figs preserved by Mrs. Wenglar, the ceramics painted and baked by Mrs. Hill, the doillies embroidered by Mrs. Pearl—all were truly lovely and all well deserved the blue ribbon.

15. The large family, including innumerable in-laws, showed interesting characteristics and aspects in lots of ways, especially as pertained to the various occupations and different hobbies they were involved in.

# 7

# Revising Your Paper–
# Sentences

More than any other animal, human beings seem to need to communicate with each other. They build complex communities that demand a subtle mixture of freedom and control. They invent machines, buildings, and ideas in response to their environment. They develop elaborate social systems and governments and territories that play on the harmonious interaction of natural hostilities. Cities, skyscrapers, computers, planes, love, democracy, country, war—without an efficient, effective communication system, these products of man's labor wouldn't be possible. If you think about it, you'll see that there are three basic ways people communicate:

1. Through physical touch—a handshake, a pat on the back, a kick in the shins

2. Through body movement in space—pointing a finger, smiling, winking, nodding the head
3. Through visible and audible symbols—words and sentences, written and spoken

The subject of this book has been *written* communication—a complete paper, paragraphs, words, sentences.

But you have already seen from the discussion of tone in the previous chapter that one of the major problems in writing is to make the written message represent the "voice" you have in mind and—equally important—to make sure that the reader of your message receives what you want him to in thought and tone. The tone of voice, the wave of the hand, the pat on the back are absent in the sentences you write. One aim of your sentence revision should be to compensate for the loss of these in written communication; another is to be certain that you choose sentence patterns that give the most important ideas the strongest position.

## Sentences in General

Good sentences are not born automatically. Not for anyone. They are created, with patience and skill, out of the accumulated knowledge of many years, out of the thoughts, feelings, words, and word-patterns *you have available to you*. But unless you—and, in fact, anyone who wants to improve his writing skill—consciously study how to improve, you may find that what is "available to you" are the simple sentence patterns of your childhood. This chapter should help you recognize those basic patterns, improve them, and encourage you to experiment with them to gain new strength and emphasis.

There are many things you know about sentences already. *Length*, for example. Short sentences move fast. Long ones, on the other hand, tend to move somewhat more slowly toward their final destination. You need them both in your writing, and you need to know when to use them. You also know that there are many *kinds* of sentences, depending on how you classify them:

1. Grammatically—simple, compound, complex, compound-complex
2. Rhetorically—loose, periodic, balanced, antithetical
3. Functionally—question, command, statement, exclamation

Why so many "kinds"? Each performs a specific job in communication. Because of their structures, some keep the reader involved by withholding the full meaning until the end of the sentence (as this one has done). Others make their point at once. Still others balance part against part, meaning against meaning. The five sentences immediately preceding this one, for example, illustrate five kinds. Which are they? Using different kinds of sentences gives your writing *variety* and prevents monotony. You can gain variety in sentence patterns in four basic ways: *balance* (which you learned about in the chapter on coherence, page 62); *inversion* or unusual word order, a pattern different from the one a reader might expect; *repetition* of phrases or clauses for effect, for emphasis; and *omission* of certain words supplied by the sense of preceding passages. (Meaningful sentence fragments are an example: "How do you feel?" *Sick.*) Most of the material on revision in this chapter can be studied under the three broad headings just discussed: *length, kind,* and *variety.*

## The Simple Sentence

A sentence isn't necessarily *a group of words containing a subject and a verb and expressing a complete thought.* Modern grammarians are cautious in defining a sentence, for the pat, conventional definition doesn't always fit. Perhaps it is best to think of a sentence as just a complete thought. Thus, single words like *help* and *incredible* can be sentences, when properly capitalized and punctuated, without our having to be concerned about what is understood; they are both units of expression.

Sentences come in all *lengths:* minute, medium, and mammoth. Some of the most effective in English are quite brief. For instance, the famous, shortest verse in the Bible, *Jesus wept,* expresses in its context more feeling and emotion than a longer sentence might. Similarly, at the end of *Hamlet,* Shakespeare uses four words, *The rest is silence.* On the other hand, sentences can be quite long. But extremely long sentences are used infrequently and only for a special effect that might not easily be conveyed by a series of shorter sentences. For instance, Ernest Hemingway tried to give the feeling of a bullfight in 151 words.

Cagancho is a gypsy, subject to fits of cowardice, altogether without integrity, who violates all the rules, written and unwritten, for the conduct of a matador but who, when he receives a bull that he has confidence in, and he has confidence in thém very rarely, can do things which all bullfighters do in a way they have never been done before and sometimes standing absolutely straight with his feet still, planted as though he were a tree, with the arrogance and grace that gypsies have and of which all other arrogance and grace seems an imitation, moves the cape spread full as the pulling jib of a yacht before the bull's muzzle so slowly that the art of bullfighting, which is only kept from being one of the major arts because it is impermanent, in the arrogant slowness of his veronicas becomes, for the seeming minutes that they endure, permanent.[1]

Ordinary sentences are much shorter than this one, for the reader has trouble following long involvements. Shorter units of thought, cast for the most part in normal, expected English word order, are more desirable; the reader can recognize such sentences almost automatically. Lewis Carroll, the author of *Alice in Wonderland,* recognized this fact long ago when he wrote the nonsense poem "Jabberwocky":

> 'Twas brillig and the slithy toves
> Did gyre and gimble in the wabe;
> All mimsy were the borogoves,
> And the mome raths outgrabe.

Even though you don't know what *toves* or *borogoves* look like, or what *brillig* and *slithy* mean, you can still easily recognize that this verse is made up of English sentences. You can spot these unknowns as parts of speech: *brillig, slithy,* and *mome* are obviously adjectives; *toves, wabe, borogoves,* and *raths* are nouns; *gyre, gimble,* and *outgrabe* are verbs.

Any group of nonsense words arranged in the patterns of English sentences can be recognized as sentences, as long as articles and prepositions are real. Look at these different sentence patterns using nonsense nouns, verbs, and verbals:

> The junbig cranned a biglou.
> A biglou was cranned by a junbig.
> Cranned by a junbig was a biglou.
> After cranning a biglou, the junbig
> zlon up the donnen.

Each of these represents a recognizable English sentence pattern. The first uses normal word order for English sentences.

### Normal English Word Order

| Subject | ....... | Verb | ....... | Object |
|---|---|---|---|---|
| | | or | | |
| Actor | ........ | Action | ........ | Goal |
| (The boy | ....... | hit | ....... | the ball.) |

---

[1] Reprinted with the permission of Charles Scribner's Sons from *Death in the Afternoon* by Ernest Hemingway. Copyright 1932 Charles Scribner's Sons; renewal copyright © 1960 Ernest Hemingway. Used also by permission of the executors of the Ernest Hemingway Estate, and the publishers in the British Commonwealth, Jonathan Cape, Ltd.

It is "normal" and "expected" because the *subject-verb-object* pattern is by far the most common and because it is probably the one we all learn first. When you study style at the end of this chapter, you will see that special sentence effects are possible *because* we are so accustomed to expect the "normal" one.

Most English sentences are written in this "normal" order with these parts, though there are often modifiers (words, phrases, or clauses) of any one or all the parts. For emphasis and sentence *variety,* the normal word order can be varied: *Up the stairs ran the girl* reverses normal word order. The subject comes in last position. Such a sentence used rarely is acceptable, but overused, it draws attention to itself, as most unusual word order does.

To be called complete, in the conventional sense, a sentence must have at least two of the parts indicated above—a subject and a verb. The subject may be understood (*you*); the verb may not. A complete sentence expresses ONE complete thought. If it has more than one, it is not unified, that is, it does not move in one direction but in as many directions as there are topics in the sentence. Look at this sentence:

My car broke down twice on the way to the campus, and I spent all day Monday at registration.

Here there are two complete thoughts in two independent clauses. One complete thought has no necessary relationship to the other. In effect, they move in different directions. This sentence, then, has MORE THAN ONE complete thought; consequently, it is not a good sentence. For the same reason, neither is this sentence a good one:

Iris Stone was a healthy girl who was born and bred in Tampa.

Here the dependent clause, *who was born and bred in Tampa,* has no necessary connection with Iris Stone's being a healthy girl. There are two topics here also, and each should probably be put in a sentence of its own.

On the other hand, a group of words without a complete thought is a sentence fragment. Look at these groups:

We arrived at 8:00 o'clock. Before the game started.

The first of these is one complete thought. The second is not. The presence of *before* turns this group of words into a dependent clause and demands the addition of an independent, complete unit. We can add this dependent element to the end of the other group of words by replacing the period with a comma. Then the dependent clause (with its incomplete thought) is attached to a complete thought:

**We arrived at 8:00 o'clock, before the game started.**

Look at these two groups:

**He preached against three sins. Cards, whisky, and tobacco.**

The second group is made up of three nouns and one conjunction, but it is missing a verb to express action. It has LESS THAN ONE complete thought. Because the first group of words is a complete sentence, the second group can be attached to it, as it obviously should be:

**He preached against three sins: cards, whisky, and tobacco.**

Some "sentence fragments," however, do communicate complete thoughts because the context supplies the missing meaning. Here are some examples:

**No one can write well without practice. *No one.***
***Now for the second point.***
**What did he do? *Nothing, as usual.***
***And the result? Chaos.***

### EXERCISE

Try your hand at spotting which of the nonsense word groups are complete sentences. Write *F* for fragments, *C* for complete sentences.

1. The junbig cranned a biglou.
2. The junbig cranning a biglou.
3. After the junbig had cranned a biglou.
4. There is the biglou the junbig cranned.
5. Since cranning a biglou, which was done by the junbig.
6. A biglou was cranned by the junbig.
7. The biglou being cranned by the junbig.
8. The biglou cranning junbig.

### *Emphasizing Words and Ideas in a Sentence*

Ideas and words gain emphasis if they are placed in strong positions within the sentence. In normal word order of English sentences, the opening and the closing positions are most emphatic. For instance, look again at this simple sentence:

| Actor | Action | Goal |
|-------|--------|------|
| The boy | hit | the ball. |

The most important words in this sentence are in the most important postions. Boy (the actor) and the ball (the goal) are the important key words. In this normal English sentence, *boy* opens the sentence, and *ball* closes it. The key words are then in the emphatic positions—the beginning and the end. The end position is stronger, however, because words and ideas in that position are the last ones the reader sees.

This diagram will illustrate the importance of sentence positions.

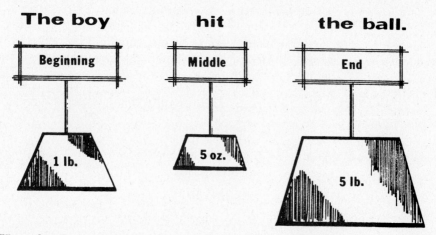

Here the three sentence positions are assigned weights to indicate their relative importance. The beginning position has been given a weight value of one pound; the middle position, five ounces; and the strong end position, five pounds. Now, by applying these weight values to the key words in a sentence, we can assign a weight to the whole sentence to indicate the strength of its emphasis. Look at this group of sentences.

1. However, *she* was an excellent *cook*.    5 lbs., 5 oz.
2. *She* was an excellent *cook*, however.    1 lb., 5 oz.
3. An excellent *cook she* was, however,    1 lb., 5 oz.
4. *She* was, however, an excellent *cook*.    6 lbs.
5. An excellent *cook*, however, was *she*.    6 lbs.

These weights are assigned by taking the key words (*she* and *cook*) and giving them the value of the position in which they appear in the sentence. Thus, in the first sentence, *she* is in the middle position and gets a weight of only five ounces. *Cook,* in the end position, gets a weight of five pounds. Altogether, the whole sentence has a value, then, of five pounds, five ounces. In this sentence, one of the important positions, the beginning of the sentence, is taken by the unimportant word *however,* suggesting that this transition word might be better buried in the middle of the sentence. The second has even less emphasis. *She* is in the beginning position for one pound, but *cook,* the other key word, is lost in the middle position and can be assigned an importance of only five ounces. The whole sentence, then, has a weight of only one pound, five ounces. In the third sentence, the position of the key words is reversed, and the value of the sentence remains the same as for the second sentence. The fourth sentence, however, has a different arrangement. *She* is in the beginning position and weighs one pound, whereas *cook* is in the end position and weighs five pounds. The whole sentence weighs six pounds, more than any other so far considered. The reason for this is that the two key words come in the two important sentence positions. Note that the transition word, *however,* is in the middle position where it does not detract from the impact of the sentence on the reader. The fifth sentence also puts the key words in the important positions, but the difference is that the positions have been switched. The sentence emphasis remains the same on the surface because it is assigned the same weight as the fourth sentence. But the two sentences differ considerably.

The fourth sentence is in normal English word order, which indicates that we ordinarily use this arrangement of sentence parts in writing. The fifth sentence reverses the arrangment, and the very oddness of this switch will make it more emphatic if it is mingled in a context of sentences arranged in the expected normal order. Only occasionally would you rely on a sentence like the fifth one—only when you want an unusual emphasis on the sentence. Although sentence variety is important, most of your sentences will have the same arrangement of sentence parts as that in the fourth sentence.

### The Periodic Sentence

In any writing, the most powerful position for an idea—the one that gives the idea most emphasis—is usually at the end. In this respect, a sentence is no different from any other piece of writing. *The power spot in the sentence is at the end.* The main idea in a sentence, then, should come logically in this power spot. A sentence withholding its main idea until the end is called *periodic.* Look at this sentence:

**Just as he bent over to tie his shoelace, a car hit him.**

Here, the main idea, *a car hit him,* is at the end of the sentence. Certainly the other idea in the sentence is of less significance.

### The Loose Sentence

More common in English, the *loose* sentence ends with a dependent sentence element—a subordinate element. Rearranging the sentence just used as an example produces a loose sentence:

A car hit him, *just as he bent over to tie his shoelace.*

The main clause (the independent clause) containing the main idea comes first in the sentence, whereas the subordinate element (the dependent clause) is at the end. Take care to keep the main idea in the main clause. If you do not, sentence emphasis goes askew. In this sentence, for instance, the insignificant idea is in the main clause, and the main idea is in a dependent clause:

He bent over to tie his shoelace, *just as a car hit him.*

The first of the sentence is in the main clause; the second part, the dependent clause. Such a sentence can have no logical emphasis.

Here are two more examples of a loose and a periodic sentence; the main idea is italicized in each.

(Periodic) Having passed his house every day and knowing that it had been unoccupied for years, *I was surprised to see smoke coming from the chimney.*

(Loose) *I was surprised to see smoke coming from the chimney,* because I had passed his house every day and knew that it had been empty for years.

Periodic sentences build suspense to gain emphasis for the main idea. If the main idea is held to the last in the sentence, and modifying elements are built up in the first part of the sentence, a marvelous suspense can be achieved that makes the main idea hit the reader with force. For instance, a simple sentence of this type makes little impact on the reader:

The old woman fainted.

But we can add a dependent element before this sentence, make it periodic in tone, and increase its impact:

*As confetti showered her head,* the old woman fainted.

We can increase its impact even more by adding another dependent clause:

*As the laughing crowd swirled around her* and as confetti showered her head, the old woman fainted.

To heighten the impact yet further, add another dependent element:

*As the band blared louder,* as the laughing crowd swirled around her, and as confetti showered her head, the old woman fainted.

This type of periodic sentence is not as natural to the English language as it is to the modern Germanic languages. Most English sentences are loose in structure. That is, they are likely to be "strung" along with dependent elements at their end. They do not build to their point as the illustrative sentence above does. In English, the best sentences, then, are *periodic in tone but loose in structure.* You can achieve a periodic tone in three ways:

1. Suspending the subject
2. Suspending the verb
3. Suspending the complement

To suspend an element, delay its appearance in the sentence.

1. *Suspending the subject.* Here is a sentence, simple in structure and English in word order:

The man hurried down the street.

Here the subject is *man.* To suspend this subject and give the sentence a periodic tone, delay the point where it appears in the sentence. Just add simple adjective modifiers before the subject:

The *gray-haired old* man hurried down the street.

Or you can add adjective phrases modifying *man*:

*Limping on his wounded foot,* the gray-haired old man hurried down the street.

You can suspend this subject even further by adding another phrase:

Limping on his wounded foot and *staggering from side to side,* the gray-haired old man hurried down the street.

The sentence now has become periodic in structure as well as in tone. You can change the structure by adding modifying elements at the end:

Limping on his wounded foot and staggering from side to side, the gray-haired old man hurried down the street that was littered with tin cans and shattered glass.

2. *Suspending the verb.* Using the same sentence and the same modifiers, you can delay the appearance of the verb in the sentence and create a periodic tone:

The man *hurried* down the street. (verb italicized)

The man, *old* and *gray-haired,* hurried down the street. (modifiers italicized)

The man, *limping on his wounded foot,* hurried down the street. (modifiers italicized)

The man, *limping and staggering,* hurried down the street. (modifiers italicized)

3. *Suspending the complement.* In this same sentence, you can also suspend the complement. The phrase *down the street* is not actually a complement in the strictest sense. It is not a noun construction but an adverbial prepositional phrase. The *complement* is used to mean a completer of the verb. *Down the street* fits this definition. Here it is suspended:

The old man hurried *down the street.* (complement italicized)

The old man hurried *limping and staggering* down the street. (modifiers suspending the complement italicized)

*Caution:* The process of suspending sentence elements can be overdone. If every element in the sentence is suspended, the subject, verb, and complement become too separated for the reader's quick comprehension of the thought. In the same way, take care not to separate any two elements enough to interfere with the flow of thought. The student who wrote this sentence, for instance, put too much space between the verb and the complement:

Chris attempted, even though his foot hurt him so much that he staggered as he ran, to reach the rifle.

In this sentence, the verb *attempted* and the complement (a verbal phrase), *to reach the rifle,* are separated by a long dependent clause. The result is a clumsy sentence so involved that the reader loses sight of the verb before he reaches the completer.

### The Periodic-Loose Sentence

Consider these two sentences:

The ball soared toward the goalposts, which were fifty yards away from the kicker's toe. It wobbled end-over-end, but arced high and true.

Both sentences are concerned with one action, so they can easily be combined into one sentence. The second sentence can be reduced to two modifying phrases and worked into the first sentence. The first sentence would be improved by deleting the *which.* As the basic independent clause in the sentence, take this one:

The ball soared toward the goalposts.

Now, suspend the subject *ball* and the verb *soared* by adding modifying elements:

Arcing high and true, the ball, wobbling end-over-end, soared toward the goalposts fifty yards away.

Or, you can suspend the verb and the complement with these same modifiers:

The ball, wobbling end-over-end, soared in a high and true arc toward the goalposts fifty yards away.

These last two sentences are periodic-loose sentences because they have a periodic tone through the suspension of two sentence elements in the basic independent clause. The structure is loose because of the modifier *fifty yards away* at the end of the sentence.

## EXERCISE

From each group of sentences, make one sentence by suspending two elements in the basic independent clause (italicized in each group).

1. *Bertha labored to secure bait to hook.* She winced as the worm tried to escape her uncertain grasp, and she hoped none of the other fishermen noticed her squeamishness.

2. *Ralph transported his aching jaws straight to the dentist's chair.* He held himself aloof with his shoulders erect as he marched through the reception room.

3. *The car coasted to a stop.* Its motor was dead. It bumped on one flat tire. It was long, shiny, and black.

4. *The legislature finally revoked the law.* The law had been impossible to enforce because the people held it in contempt. The legislature met in special session.

5. *The puppy barked at the cat.* He pranced and dodged back and forth. He was an excited puppy. The cat spat and hissed at him.

6. I hesitated for two weeks before making my choice, but I finally decided to attend Glory University. *I think I made the best choice.* I had to choose between Glory and Primitive University.

7. *Fleance broke up the rehearsal.* He entered from stage right. His wig was askew and his mascara was running. Lady Macbeth had just urged the assembly to "Take seats."

8. *The children giggled and cavorted.* They chanted "The one-eyed flea keeps bugging me." They marched out of step and ill-aligned.

9. The English teacher looked the Salutatorian straight in the eye. She was angry. *She said, "When you chose that topic for your research paper, I told you it wasn't worthy of you."* The Salutatorian was embarrassed and crestfallen.

10. *Grandfather inched up the stairs.* He grasped the handrail with one hand. He leaned on his cane with the other. He firmly planted both feet on each step.

# Secondary Sentence Patterns:
# Coordination and Subordination

So far in this chapter we have dealt mostly with one type of sentence—the simple sentence with normal order (subject—verb—complement) and phrase and single word modifiers for one or more of the elements. In effect, we have been dealing with this pattern:

**I see the puppy.**

The idea expressed is approximately on the first-grade level and is appropriate for a primer. But educated writers need to communicate more complicated ideas than this sentence pattern can express. For this purpose, English provides secondary sentence patterns. The two most useful types of secondary sentence patterns are: (1) coordination (the simplest) and (2) subordination.

### Coordination

Coordination is joining together similar grammatical constructions with a connecting word called a *conjunction*. In its simplest form, two nouns or two verbs or two adjectives, for instance, can be joined by the conjunction *and.*

> Chris and Jane
> bacon and eggs
> read and write
> happy and carefree

*Signal words for coordination* (conjunctions), Group 1:

> and
> but
> for
> nor
> or
> so
> yet

Conjunctions in this group can be used to join *equal* grammatical structures only. That is, they can join together two independent clauses, two noun clauses, two prepositional phrases, two participles, or two of anything, as long as they are the same grammatically. They cannot join together, however, an independent clause and a dependent clause.

*Caution:* Group 1 signal words, especially *and,* are sometimes inappropriately used to string sentences together. This relatively short sample uses *and* four times:

I asked Dad for the car *and* then I picked up the corsage *and* got my date, *and* we went to the dance *and* had a wonderful time.

Although this sentence does have coordination, it defeats the purpose of coordination. Certainly there are no complicated ideas here that could not be expressed in the simplest sentence pattern.

*Signal words for coordination,* Group 2:

| | |
|---|---|
| consequently | nevertheless |
| hence | nonetheless |
| however | then |
| in fact | therefore |
| moreover | thus |

These signal words are used as conjunctions *only* to join two independent clauses. They have no other use as conjunctions.

To illustrate the use of this group of conjunctions, here are two sentences:

Marriage and hanging go by destiny. Matches are made in heaven.

Because these two are connected in idea, they may be joined grammatically into one sentence by making them independent clauses and by using a conjunction:

Marriage and hanging go by destiny, *but* matches are made in heaven.

The Group 1 conjunction *but* is used here because a contrast is being drawn and this conjunction is the appropriate one. (Remember the section on transition words.) Or a Group 2 conjunction can be just as appropriately used:

Marriage and hanging go by destiny; *however,* matches are made in heaven.

Or, the two sentences can be joined without a conjunction, if their ideas are closely enough related and if emphasis is needed:

Marriage and hanging go by destiny; matches are made in heaven.

### Punctuation of Coordinate Elements

Perhaps as many as sixty percent of your punctuation problems can be solved by knowing the Group 1 and Group 2 conjunctions and by understanding how they work.

1. Group 1 conjunctions *(and, but, for, or, nor, so, yet)*, when they join two independent clauses, take a comma before them. See the diagram below.

(Independent clause)     but     (Independent clause)

. . . . . . . . . . . . . . . . . . . ,       . . . . . . . . . . . . . . . . . . . .

2. Group 2 conjunctions *(however, then, thus,* for instance) join two independent clauses together with a semicolon, in this way:

(Independent clause)     thus,     (Independent clause)

. . . . . . . . . . . . . . . . . . . ;       . . . . . . . . . . . . . . . . . . . .

3. Two independent clauses may be joined without a conjunction if a semicolon separates them:

(Independent clause)         (Independent clause)

. . . . . . . . . . . . . . . . . . . ;       . . . . . . . . . . . . . . . . . . . .

### EXERCISES

Supply the proper mark of punctuation in the blanks of these sentences.

1. Great-grandfather would not refrain from chewing his noontime wad of tobacco . . . . . nor would Great-grandmother give up dipping snuff, no matter how often we complained.
2. Santa brought Robin three dolls, a swing set, a Cinderella watch, and a plug-in refrigerator . . . . . but Bobby seemed satisfied with his new socks and corduroy jeans.
3. The veteran scholar took her first degree in the history and literature of Persia . . . . . the next step was to master the Arabic language.
4. From 6:00 to 10:00 in the evening he supplemented his income by teaching local teens to bowl . . . . . so for eighteen hours a day he was on somebody's payroll.
5. Just before school opened, Old Hat found her way to Rita's doorstep . . . . . and before Thanksgiving, Jet wandered in . . . . . then, on Easter Sunday morning, the cat they call Peeps made it a threesome.
6. Sandra seemed to sense that her partner held the trump ace . . . . . yet she deliberately underbid the hand.
7. No one claims that the red rambling roses are more attractive than the New York Pinks . . . . . I simply state that they are a showier flower.
8. Yupon and Poison Sumac grew on the upper ten acres . . . . . elsewhere over the ranch grew mesquite and huisache.

9. She tried first tape, then glue, and finally staples .... however, Frances' Man in the Moon shadow box fell apart before fifth period.

10. The young wife insisted that air conditioning in that two-room west-side apartment was essential .... her husband called her an extravagant simpleton.

11. If the student lives in Duncan Hall, or Dorms 11, 12, or 13, his laundry problems are solved ..... if he lives in Milton Square or close to the Quadrangle, he practices the do-it-yourself system.

12. Bill bought shares in two local banks and spent two weeks fishing in Mexico ..... therefore his parents assumed that he could scrape by without further loans from them.

13. Mrs. Anderson embroidered icon after saintly icon ..... but she would not part with one of her collection, although they lay yellowing in the trunk of heirlooms in the parlor.

14. Six, seven, and eight come first ..... eleven comes somewhat later.

### Coordinate Elements in Series

When more than two coordinate elements appear together, they are a series. Any three or more equal grammatical elements can appear in a series—nouns, verbs, participles, noun clauses, prepositional phrases, or any part of a sentence. For instance, this sentence shows verbs in a series:

Cathy *ran, skipped,* and *jumped.*

Or this one has three noun clauses in a series:

Herb never stopped to consider *that the weather was not favorable, that the boys did not want to go,* and *that the highways would be too crowded for comfortable travel.*

1. When coordinate elements are used in a series, a comma separates each element from the others. The two sentences just used as examples illustrate this punctuation. It may be diagrammed this way:

(First element)    (Second element)   and   (Third element)
. . . . . . . . . . . . . . . . . ,   . . . . . . . . . . . . . . . . . ,   . . . . . . . . . . . . . . . .

The comma before *and* between the second and third elements is commonly left out. This practice is acceptable as long as the reader has no chance of assuming that the last two elements are linked together to the exclusion of the first.

2. The coordinate elements in a series must be parallel (that is, the same grammatically). The elements here are italicized:

**Jo did the job *quickly, competently,* and *hardly working at all.***

In this sentence, three adverbs are supposedly in a series; but one element in the series is not an adverb. This can be seen in a diagram.

|                | (1) quickly     |
|----------------|-----------------|
| Jo did the job | (2) competently |
|                | and             |
|                | (3) hardly working. |

The third element will have to be changed to make it parallel with the other two, that is, it must be grammatically the same. This sentence makes that change.

|                | (1) quickly     |
|----------------|-----------------|
| Jo did the job | (2) competently |
|                | and             |
|                | (3) easily.     |

**Jo did the job quickly, competently, and easily.**

Or look at this sentence:

**The instructor told them *to study Chapter IV, to make notes on it,* and *that they would have a quiz next period.***

A diagram will expose the elements in this sentence that are not parallel.

|                          | (1) to study Chapter IV       |
|--------------------------|-------------------------------|
| The instructor told them | (2) to make notes on it       |
|                          | and                           |
|                          | (3) that they would have a quiz next period. |

The first two elements of the series here are infinitive phrases (that is, *to* plus a verb plus a noun), but the third element is a noun clause (with *that* as the subordinating conjunction, *they* as the subject, and *would have* as the verb). Because these elements are not the same grammatically, the third element must be changed to make it an infinitive phrase starting with *to* plus a verb.

<pre>
                              (1)  to study Chapter IV
     The instructor told them  (2)  to make notes on it
                                       and
                              (3)  *to prepare* for a quiz
                                    next period.
</pre>

**The instructor told them to study Chapter IV, to make notes on it, and to prepare for a quiz next period.**

Here is a different one:

**Although not many of the class went, those who did found the lecture heavy, dull, and the acoustics in the lecture hall adequate, although not everything could be heard.**

This sentence appears to have a series of three. In truth it does not, because it has two subjects—*lecture* and *acoustics*. Look at this sentence in diagram form.

<pre>
Although not many of the class went,
                              (1)  heavy
                              (2)  dull
     those who did found the lecture        and
                                            (a)  adequate
                              (3)  acoustics
                                            (b)  not everything
                                                 could be heard.
</pre>

*Acoustics* (a noun) is not parallel with *heavy* and *dull* (adjectives), nor can these three be changed to make them parallel. But the sentence can be improved by making *lecture* parallel with *acoustics* (both nouns).

<pre>
Although not many of the class went,
                                            (a)  heavy
                              (1)  the lecture
                                            (b)  dull
     those who did found              and
                                            (a)  poor
                              (2)  the  acoustics
                                            (b)  adequate.
</pre>

**Although not many of the class went, those who did found the lecture**

heavy and dull, and the acoustics in the lecture hall poor but barely adequate.

All coordinate elements in a sentence must be clearly parallel, whether there are more than two elements or only two. Sometimes a fuzzy parallelism will confuse the reader temporarily, as in this sentence:

The lawyer begged that the accused be judged insane and committed to a mental hospital.

Momentary confusion may result here because the reader may want to insert *be judged* before committed, because apparently *insane* and another adjective are being joined by *and.* A diagram illustrates the possible confusion.

|  |  |
|---|---|
| The lawyer begged that the accused | (1) be judged insane |
|  | and |
|  | (2) committed to a mental hospital. |

The solution is simple: The parallelism is made clear if *be* is put before *committed,* as well as before *judged.*

|  |  |
|---|---|
| The lawyer begged that the accused | (1) be judged insane |
|  | and |
|  | (2) be committed to a mental hospital. |

The lawyer begged that the accused be judged insane and be committed to a mental hospital.

This sentence is similarly confusing:

He said he had read the poetry of Thomas, Spender, and the novels of Updike.

Here the writer has attempted to create a series of three coordinate elements, but there are only two. Look at a diagram of this sentence as the author wrote it.

|  |  |
|---|---|
| He said he had read the poetry of | (1) Thomas |
|  | (2) Spender |
|  | and |
|  | (3) the novels of Updike. |

Obviously, *Thomas, Spender,* and *the novels* are not parallel. *Poetry* and *novels* are, however. Then there is a better construction for the sentence:

|                      |                    | (a) Thomas        |
| :---                 | :---:              | :---              |
|                      | (1) the poetry of  |                   |
|                      |                    | (b) Spender       |
| He said he had read  | and                |                   |
|                      | (2) the novels of Updike. |            |

**He said he had read the poetry of Thomas and Spender, and the novels of Updike.**

The comma is placed before the second *and* for clarity. Otherwise the reader might expect the material following Spender to be a third element in a series. The comma specifies that it is not.

Here is another example of faulty parallelism:

**His musical career, unlike most students who played in the band, continued after he left high school.**

The fault here is one of logic. Careers and students are being compared, but they cannot be compared. It is like attempting to make a comparison between apples and wood splinters; they have nothing in common. So they cannot be made parallel in this way. A diagram of this attempted parallelism looks like this:

His musical *career*  
     unlike           continued. . . .  
most students

This sentence can be made logical and parallel.

His *musical career*  
     unlike            continued. . . .  
the *musical careers* of most students

Now careers are compared to careers, and the sentence is logically parallel. But a substitute, a pronoun for *career,* is more suitable than repeating the noun so soon after it is first given. The sentence then looks like this:

**His musical career, unlike *those* of most students who played in the band, continued after he left high school.**

**EXERCISE**

Correct any nonparallel elements you find in these sentences.

1. He studied the grouping of the stars in their constellations and how close Saturn is to Pluto.
2. The desk had a scratched top, a sticky drawer, and one leg wobbled.
3. Slicing away at the Winesap and whistling as he pared, Eric knew that the first cucumbers were already spoiled on the vine, how he would have to rebuild the chicken roosts tomorrow, and his son had asked him twice to repair his toy truck.
4. She bought a pound each of nails, woodscrews, and a gallon of red paint.
5. Dr. Payne's tests, like all the other professors', were complex, detailed, and offered great difficulty.
6. Since he had already ruined his chances to recover the money and recouping his loss, Ronald shrugged, grinned, and, turning away, sauntered whistling down the hall.
7. Pete was quite slow in discovering that he had no singing voice, could not act, and his personality did not project well.
8. The gold plastic bracelet from the local dime store, added to Ruthie's talent on the dance floor and appreciating the excellent dance band, made the evening a mad memory.
9. Despite his aversion to seafood and liquor, he ate oysters, catfish, and drank beer.
10. Although the house was dark and because he knew the family was out of town, Greg went ahead with his plan to repair the television set in the living room and resetting the loose tiles on the kitchen floor.

## Subordination

In considering matters of sentence structure, *superior* constructions are independent clauses; they carry the main thought of the sentence and are complete in themselves. Words, phrases, and dependent clauses are *inferior*, or subordinate, because they do not consist of a complete thought; they are used most often as modifiers of some part of the independent clause. Sometimes they are used as the subject or verb or complement in an independent clause. The process of subordination, then, is changing what might be stated in an independent clause into an inferior or subordinate construction and attaching it to a part of another independent clause. Consider these two sentences:

**John completed his final examination. Two hours still remained in the examination period.**

One of these independent clauses (independent clauses and sentences are the same structurally) can be subordinated to the other and the two combined into one sentence. First, you must decide which idea in the two sentences is the more important one, because it must come in the independent clause. Because the writer put it last, he apparently considers the idea of the second sentence the more important of the two. Then subordinate the first independent clause to the second in one of these ways:

*When John completed his final examination,* two hours still remained in the period. (Independent clause reduced to a dependent clause. Note that the only difference between an independent and a dependent clause is the presence of a subordinating conjunction, *when* in this sentence, at the beginning of the dependent clause. Other subordinating conjunctions are *while, that, since, although, until, which, who, because, as if, if, when, before.*)

*Upon completing his final examination,* John discovered that two hours remained in the period. (Independent clause reduced to a prepositional phrase.)

*Completing his final examination,* John discovered that two hours remained in the period. (Participial phrase)

*His final examination completed,* John discovered that two hours remained in the period. (Absolute construction)

John discovered *upon completing his final examination* that two hours remained in the period. (Prepositional phrase)

John discovered that two hours remained in the period, *although he had already completed the final examination.* (A dependent clause with the subordinating conjunction *although.* The addition of the dependent clause makes the sentence loose in structure.)

Here is a more complicated example:

[1]Our best quarterback was caught stealing Primitive University's mascot. [2]This happened at the beginning of the football season, and so [3]he was not allowed to play after the first game, [4]thus causing us to lose the championship.

This sentence is written in a primer style; it is a string of independent clauses, except that the main point—we lost the championship—is in a phrase at the close of the sentence. Because it is the most important idea in these sentences, this point should be in an independent clause to give it the most emphasis, whereas the other inferior material should be sub-ordinated. *This* (at 2) and *thus* (at 4) should be deleted. In this sentence, *this* is a pronoun with vague reference. It does not refer the reader to a single noun, as it should, but to action expressed in the preceding sentence. *Thus* is used as a conjunction. As one of the Group 2 coordinating conjunctions, it joins two independent clauses. But here it is not serving this function; instead, it is joining an independent clause to a phrase. *Thus* can then be deleted without affecting the meaning of the sentence, and there is no structural problem. Here is a revision with the main idea in the independent clause and with other ideas subordinated to it. The ideas are numbered for comparison with the unrevised version.

[4]We lost the championship because our best quarterback, [1]caught [2]at the beginning of the season stealing Primitive University's mascot, [3]was not allowed to play after the first game of the year.

In revising, remember to select the main point in your sentences and subordinate all others to it by casting them in dependent clauses, phrases, or single-word modifiers.

## EXERCISE

Make one sentence from each of the following groups of sentences. Cast the main idea in an independent clause and subordinate all other material.

1. It was dark and the night was cold and rainy. Emily started cautiously down the path. It was slippery and clogged by roots and weeds.
2. The chair had one broken leg. It was old and its upholstery was tattered. It collapsed with Pete when he sat in it. A loud noise resulted.
3. The secretary ripped the paper from the typewriter roller. She gave a sharp exclamation and slammed her pencil on the desk.
4. The gringos crowded the Mexican streets. They all appeared overfed, and they were all underdressed.
5. The book lay by the window. The window was open. Wind flipped and tore the book's pages, and they had been soaked with rain.
6. The university rates high scholastically. It has a library of four million volumes. Its teachers are internationally recognized, and its students are the best from quality high schools.
7. The American elk is a relative of the red deer of other continents. Its scientific name is *Cervus canadensis* of the family *Cervidae*. It is occasionally attacked by cougars.
8. They had loved their home. It had three bedrooms, a sun parlor, and impeccably kept gardens. But now the West Church Street School had

been built across the street. It housed the first graders who could not be accommodated in the old elementary school.

9. Nancy waltzed proudly around the floor. The hem of her stylish, black-sequined dress had come loose in two places. A lock hung limply from the back of her unswept hairdo. People were tittering. She did not know all this, of course.

10. Jordan was only three and a half when it happened, but he can still remember Uncle Jake shooting the largest elk the state had recorded. The elk stood five feet, nine inches tall and weighed 1100 pounds.

## Style

Style is the last of the major subjects discussed in this book (the other two are organization and discovery). By now you are probably aware that nearly everything you have studied to this point is in some way related to style. The ideas you discover to write about, for example, may not be original; still, *how* you use them, what you decide to include or to omit, what illustrations you use as support—these may very well be original, and, because of this, have something to do with what we call style. Similarly, the organization you choose for these ideas is also probably your own, unlike the organization someone else might use for the same set of ideas. In revising diction and sentences, again the choices you make will probably distinguish your writing from that of others. *How* you decide to get your reader interested, *how* you create a tone or "voice" that will win your reader are probably your own too. For no two writers solve the same communication problem in the same way. The resulting differences in the works may be explained as a matter of style.

To discuss style means trying to separate *what* is said from *how* it is said. Strictly speaking that's not possible. But for purposes of discussion it's useful to think about *the message* and *how it is sent* as if they were separate. Look at the following sentences:

**1**

That such a life is likely to be ecstatically happy I will not claim. But that it can be lived in quiet content, accepting resignedly what cannot be helped, not expecting the impossible, and thankful for small mercies, this I would maintain. That it will be difficult for men in general to learn this lesson I do not deny. But that it will be impossible I will not admit since so many have learned it already.

Because this writer chose to use balance for his sentence patterns, he has given the passage a special effect (see page 63 for a discussion of parallelism, antithesis, and coherence in this passage). You notice it immediately because the word order is unusual; you know it's unusual because it departs from the "normal," expected pattern, *subject-verb-object.* You notice, too, that he uses no simple, loose sentences; all are periodic and complex. Another writer might have done it differently:

**2**

I will not claim that such a life is likely to be ecstatically happy. But I would maintain that it can be lived in quiet content, accepting resignedly what cannot be helped, not expecting the impossible, and being thankful for small mercies. I do not deny that it will be difficult for people in general to learn this lesson. But I will not admit that it will be impossible since so many have learned it already.

Version two carries exactly the same meaning as the first; yet the *effect* is different. The "expected" word order moves the reader quickly to each main point: "I will not claim . . . ," "I would maintain . . . ," "I do not deny . . . ," "I will not admit . . ." The effect is one of directness and strength. Version one suspends each main statement, making the reader wait for it until the end of each sentence. The effect on the reader is probably a "sense of expectation," but this would depend on the kind of ear that was listening. Still, though different readers might argue about the exact effects of the two versions, they could hardly fail to see that they were intentionally different. Expected (or unexpected) *word order, directness* of movement and meaning, heightened *reader expectation*—these are matters of style. But style is also a matter of *sound.* Read version one aloud and listen for the effects that parallel structure, antithesis, and inversion create. Some listeners would say the passage sounded "formal," "heightened," "elevated," perhaps too "contrived." Others might say, simply, that the passage was "hard to read." Their disagreement would be about the effects of writing styles. But if both readers had stored in their memories the same basic sentence patterns, the same vocabularies, the same sounds, they would disagree far less. For judging the effects of differing writing styles depends largely on what a reader has "inside" to use as a sounding board.

Suppose, further, that we altered version two by changing some of the words, still keeping the meaning of the passages the same. For example:

**3**

I won't say that such a life will lead to great happiness. However, I would say that it can lead to contentment and quiet, stoically accepting what can't be helped, not expecting the impossible, and being thankful for small mercies. I don't deny that people will generally have a hard time learning this lesson. But I will not admit that it will be impossible since many men have already learned it.

The addition of contractions to version three adds some *informality* to the *tone;* simpler balance adds to directness. Most of the word changes increase the informal tone *(say, great, happiness, contentment, hard time).* The use of *however* plus a comma slows down the movement (compare the sound of "However, I would say . . ." with the sound of "But I would say . . .). All these choices are also a matter of style. Considering the possibilities suggested by the three versions, the trained writer would choose patterns and sounds and words that he felt *his reader would like.* Style, then, also includes *audience consideration.* You can see that the writing style you decide to use in a particular situation involves many decisions, only a few of which have been suggested in this discussion. What matters most is that you see style as conscious choice and realize that there are many solutions to each problem in communication. If, for example, you chose to write all your sentences in the style of version one, you would probably lose your reader quickly. Similarly, extended passages in the style of the second or third versions, with all sentences marching forward in the "normal" *subject-verb-object* pattern, would tend to sound monotonous. One solution to this problem would be to vary sentence patterns and lengths, though variety for its own sake shouldn't be your only aim. A study of style will increase the number of choices available to you and greatly expand the "sounding board" you have "inside"; it should also add to your sense of "play" and discovery, for you should become increasingly aware of the power and richness of language. Some changes in style you can probably strive for in your rough drafts, but it is during the careful process of revision that you'll be able to discover the need for stylistic changes.

Style, then, is a matter of *personal choice*—of ideas, of words to carry the ideas, of sentences, of organization, of appropriate tone, of paragraphing. And because it is personal, it is limited by who the writer is, by what knowledge and vocabulary he has, and even by the subjects he habitually writes about (since they probably will appear repeatedly in his work). In this sense, style *is* the person; your style is *you.* In fact, you already have many writing styles of your own which reflect the limits just described. But just because style reflects a person does not mean he's stuck with one way of writing.

Style is also the result of conscious *choice,* something you can therefore improve and change. If you let habit dictate your choice, as many beginning writers do, you'll find yourself tied to the diction and sentence patterns of your earliest training. (Remember the exercise on pre-school words? See page 162.) To change your writing habits, however, you will first have to recognize what they are. That means putting to work everything you have learned in this book—as you discover and plan, as you organize and write, and, most important, as you revise. It also means studying the ways in which other writers (students and professionals) use words and sentences to solve their communication problems. That is the basic approach: *Know your own style,* and *study the styles of other writers.*

To summarize. *Style can be defined as the individual, personal way in which you use your own knowledge and language to present your chosen subject to a specific audience in an appropriate "voice."* The full implications of this definition are seen in the following check sheet on style; its questions will help you look for qualities in your own style and in the styles of other writers.

You should now be able to put this check sheet to work. First, use

## CHECK SHEET FOR BASIC ELEMENTS OF STYLE

| A. USE OF TONE (The Writer's "Voice") | ✔ |
|---|---|
| 1. Does the tone fit the subject? | |
| 2. Does the tone fit the reader? | |
| 3. Does the paper create reader interest? | |
| 4. Does the paper try to get reader acceptance? | |
| 5. Is there unity of tone throughout the paper? | |
| **B. KIND OF DICTION (Word Choice)** | |
| 6. Is active voice used? | |
| 7. Are the verbs strong, meaningful? | |
| 8. Has wordiness ("deadwood") been eliminated? | |
| 9. Have trite, worn-out words been eliminated? | |
| 10. Are the words specific, concrete? | |
| 11. Are the words suitably formal or informal? | |
| 12. Are the words suitably denotative or connotative? | |
| 13. Are there any effective figures of speech? | |
| **C. SENTENCE LENGTH, KIND, VARIETY** | |
| 14. Is sentence length varied? | |
| 15. Is there variety in kinds of sentences? | |
| 16. Is there variety in sentence patterns? | |
| 17. Are coordination and subordination effective? | |
| **D. PARAGRAPHS** | |
| 18. Does the introductory paragraph succeed? | |
| 19. Are paragraph lengths suitably varied? | |
| 20. Are transitions effective and successful? | |

it to analyze the two student selections below; take notes on each of the twenty questions on the check sheet and be prepared to support and illustrate your impression of the style. Both selections are by the same student writing on the same subject; the difference between them is that in the first the tone is supposed to be "confident," while in the second it's supposed to be "angry and disgusted."

### A. The First Day
### (Tone: Confident)

Tackling the closed door with her foot, she conquered the hallway. It was the noncommittal green used in military installations. But most of this color was obliterated by the thundering herd of students. The width of the hall was equal to six students, shoulder-to-shoulder. The length, about thirty students. And the hall held its capcity at this time. But she made room. Among the masses, she stood out. Marching down the hall, heel first, she carried herself with confidence and authority.

Similar to Moses, she parted the sea of students, enabling her to go from the left side of the hall to the right. She grabbed for the door. The doorknob was cold and uninviting. She tried to force the locked doorknob to turn, then finally forced the slightly ajar door all the way open.

### B. The First Day
### (Tone: Angry)

Ramming the glass door with her foot, she stormed the hallway. It was the repulsive light-green used in military installations. But this color was obliterated by the screeching mob of students. The width of the hall could only be measured in terms of students—six students, shoulder-to-shoulder. The length, about thirty students. And the hall was bursting at the seams at this time. Forced to make room, she was caught up in the sweating, flowing current of bodies.

Only through struggling and pushing and griping did she manage to get across the hall. She grabbed for the door, only to find the doorknob shockingly cold and uninviting. She struggled with the doorknob, only to find the lock frozen and the door already slightly ajar. Infuriated by the wasted effort, she swung the door completely open.

Do you think this student has succeeded in creating the two tones? Are there any differences in detail? Compare the verbs in the two versions; are they consistently different? Make a list of the words in each selection that seem to you most appropriate to the tone the student tried to create. Are the sentence patterns similar in both selections? Do you think they should be similar? If you didn't know that both versions were written by the same student, what evidence could be presented to show that they probably were, that they are stylistically similar, despite some difference in tone? Do you think the two passages are aimed at different audiences? Point to specific words or phrases that support your conclusion. How would you change the passages to make them appeal more clearly to different audiences?

## EXERCISES ON STYLE

A. One way to become conscious of sentence patterns unlike your own is to imitate sentences written by others. Here, for example, is a very famous sentence from Henry David Thoreau's *Walden:*

> I went to the woods because I wished to live deliberately, to front only the essential facts of life, and see if I could learn what it had to teach, and not, when I came to die, discover that I had not lived.

Although you should try to match the model in its major parts (phrases, clauses, balance, inversions), you may depart in minor ways, as a student has done in this imitation:

> I questioned the system because I wanted to see how it worked, to determine its bad points, and see how effective it was, and then after thorough analysis, propose a system that would work better.

Here are some additional models with student imitations:

*Model:* The cat shivered in the barnyard, wet from nosing her way through the dew-filled grass and covered with damp cockle-spurs.

*Imitation:* The man ran in the race, wet from perspiring at every step and panting with laboring lungs.

*Model:* Disobedience, the rarest and most courageous of the virtues, is seldom distinguished from neglect, the laziest and commonest of the vices.

*Imitation:* Friendship, a rare and marvelous gift, is sometimes killed by hypocrisy, a shallow and worthless imitation.

*Model:* The human species, according to the best theory I can form of it, is composed of two distinct races, the men who borrow, and the men who lend.

*Imitation:* Friendship, as I see it, is based on two concepts, the idea of communication, and the idea of covenant.

*Model:* The apple tree never asks the beech how he shall grow; nor the lion, the horse, how he shall take his prey.

*Imitation:* The professor never asks the department head how he should teach; nor the gambler, the bookmaker, how he should place his bet.

## Exercise

1. Write imitations of the five models given above (include Thoreau). First write down the model; read it carefully and listen to the sound and the rhythm; then write your imitation of it.

2. Write imitations of the first two sentences in Paragraphs F and G on pages 160 and 161 (Faulkner and Frost).

3. The following three sentences come from the paragraph by E. B. White on page 113. Write a coherent, three-sentence imitation.

   New York should have destroyed itself long ago, from panic or fire or rioting or failure of some vital supply line in its circulatory system or from some deep labyrinthine short circuit. Long ago the city should have experienced an insoluble traffic snarl at some impossible bottleneck. It should have perished of hunger when food lines failed for a few days.

B. 1. Use the style check sheet to analyze one of your own papers written earlier in the course. Take notes and be prepared to write a one-paragraph commentary on your style.

   2. Using the style check sheet as your guide, analyze the style of the two paragraphs in the section "Sentences in General" (pages 165–66). Take notes. Be prepared to discuss and write about the four major subjects on the check sheet (tone, diction, sentences, paragraphs). If, for example, you think that the tone of these two paragraphs does *not* fit you (the reader), you should try to discover why. What can you discover about the length, kind, and variety of the sentences used?

C. Choose any five of the sentences you wrote for the exercise on page 187. Rewrite each sentence twice, changing the *kind* of sentence (see page 165 for kinds of sentences) or the sentence pattern; keep the mean- and details of your originals. (You may get some additional ideas by rereading pages 171–75.)

## Summary Exercises

### 1.

Monte Alban in period IIIb was a nearly incredible enterprise. It occupied not only the top of a large mountain, but also the tops and sides of a whole range of high hills adjoining, a total of some fifteen square miles of urban construction. Human labor may be characterized as cheap under some circumstances, but a man's time is never cheap in a pre-industrial economy, where what he eats has to be produced by hand labor. Except for the possibility of catching more or less rainwater during four or five months of the year, the population of Monte Alban had to drink water carried up the mountain—as much as 1,500 feet—in jars. This alone would be costly; but the quantities of water required in building construction make the location of a large city on this high ridge even more astonishing. In addition, the maintenance of a major religious capital such as Monte Alban would necessarily require the services of thousands of specialists: priests, artists, architects, the apprentices of all these, and many kinds of workmen, including servants for the dignitaries and their families.[2]

1. What is the pointer in the topic sentence (the first sentence)?
2. What method of paragraph development does the author use to support the topic sentence? Why might you have difficulty deciding which method is used?
3. Does this paragraph have coherence? Is there any point where the coherence might be improved? Why?
4. What is the purpose of *This alone would be costly* and *In addition?*
5. Explain the use of commas in the second sentence.
6. In the third sentence, why is *pre-industrial* hyphenated? Why not write *preindustrial?*
7. Why is a comma used after *circumstances* in the third sentence?
8. Why are dashes used in the fourth sentence?
9. In the fifth sentence, why would an author choose a semicolon rather than a comma?
10. Why is a comma used after *in addition* in the sixth sentence?
11. Explain the punctuation in the last sentence, particularly the use of the colon.
12. Comment on the length, kind, and variety of sentences used. How many kinds of balance can you find?
13. Are the verbs strong and meaningful? Are the words specific and concrete?
14. How does this writer try to gain and keep your interest? Do you think he succeeds?

2 John Paddock, "The Cloud People of Monte Alban," *Stanford Today,* October, 1966. Reprinted by permission of *Stanford Today,* Leland Stanford Junior University, Stanford, California.

## 2.

Spacecraft that produce immediate, tangible benefits are a fact of life. Weather satellites continually track weather over the entire earth, and communications satellites relay messages and pictures between continents. Soon there will be a third type of practical spacecraft, another tool to help man understand and control his environment—the natural resources satellite. In its effect on the billions of persons who inhabit this planet, it may be the most imporant space program yet undertaken.[3]

1. This introductory paragraph skillfully introduces a broad topic and narrows it to a specific thesis statement. What is the broad topic?
2. What means does the author use to narrow the broad topic to one of its parts?
3. What is the specific thesis statement introduced in this paragraph?
4. What would you expect the author to do in the remainder of the paper?

## 3.

More communications satellites are sure to be launched over Southeast Asia. Comsat is already planning for a second Pacific satellite to be placed in orbit this year. Later, there are plans for an even bigger satellite with a capacity for 1,200 two-way telephone circuits or four television channels—five times the capacity of Intelsat II and a lifetime that is two years longer. Nor is that all. Specifications have already been drawn by Comsat for an even more versatile, higher-capacity communications satellite that could accommodate 6,000 to 8,000 two-way telephone circuits, 12 to 20 television circuits, or perhaps a dozen circuits for communication between flying aircraft and ground stations. Even this huge, excess capacity over current needs is not expected to be too great, considering the future communications requirements of the area.[4]

1. What is the topic sentence?
2. What method has the author used to develop the topic sentence?
3. What coherence devices has he used?
4. One number, *five*, is spelled out. The others are not. What is the difference?
5. *Higher-capacity* and *two-way* are hyphenated. Why?

[3] Louis F. Slee, "Coming: A Natural Resources Satellite," *Electronic Age*, Autumn, 1966. Reprinted by permission of *Electronic Age*, Radio Corporation of America.

[4] Mitchell Levitas, "Communications Boom in Southeast Asia," *Electronic Age*, Autumn, 1966. Reprinted by permission of *Electronic Age*, Radio Corporation of America.

6. Account for the use of a dash before *five times.* Would a comma be as effective here? Why or why not?

## 4.

If Man has benefited immeasurably by his association with the dog, what, you may ask, has the dog got out of it? His scroll has, of course, been heavily charged with punishments: he has known the muzzle, the leash, and the tether; he has suffered the indignities of the show bench, the tin can on the tail, the ribbon in the hair; his love life with the other sex of his species has been regulated by the frigid hand of authority, his digestion ruined by the macaroons and marshmallows of doting women. The list of his woes could be continued indefinitely. But he has also had his fun, for he has been privileged to live with and study at close range the only creature with reason, the most unreasonable of creatures.

The dog has got more fun out of Man than Man has got out of the dog, for the clearly demonstrable reason that Man is the more laughable of the two animals. The dog has long been bemused by the singular activities and the curious practices of men, cocking his head inquiringly to one side, intently watching and listening to the strangest goings-on in the world. He has seen men sing together and fight one another in the same evening. He has watched them go to bed when it is time to get up, and get up when it is time to go to bed. He has observed them destroying the soil in vast areas, and nurturing it in small patches. He has stood by while men built strong and solid houses for rest and quiet, and then filled them with lights and bells and machinery. His sensitive nose, which can detect what's cooking in the next township, has caught at one and the same time the bewildering smells of the hospital and the munitions factory. He has seen men raise up great cities to heaven and then blow them to hell.[5]

1. These two paragraphs fit tightly together. Explain why by commenting on the first and last sentence of the first paragraph and the opening sentence of the second paragraph.
2. What is the major method of development used in both paragraphs?
3. What is the function of the second sentence in the first paragraph? What is its relation to the word *but* that introduces the last sentence of this paragraph?
4. Comment on the major effects of balance in these two paragraphs (include parallelism and antithesis).
5. What is the main function of the first paragraph? Does it contain a thesis statement where you would expect to find it?

6. What has been added to the thesis statement in the second paragraph?
7. How would you characterize the tone of these paragraphs? Point to specific words and phrases that illustrate this tone.
8. Is the main subject of these paragraphs presented in the thesis statements or in the last sentence of paragraph two? Explain.
9. Comment on the length and kinds of sentences. Can you explain the writer's strategy of development?

**5.**

The cultural fallout from television has been astounding. Critics may, of course, debate the level of musical discrimination shown by an audience that applauds on sight. Yet, the significant thing here is television's incredible ability to increase the awareness of a vast public. The opening of the Lincoln Center for the Performing Arts is a case in point. Some 25.6 million television viewers saw and heard some part of the two-hour concert; in contrast, 2,600 attended the concert that night in Philharmonic Hall. Television attracts the biggest and most heterogeneous audiences in the history of communications. It can attract 16 million people to a program like "Bonanza," and it can interest another 16 million in Leonard Bernstein's "Young People's Concert." Consider the social impact of a program such as Lou Hazam's NBC production, "The Louvre," which drew 15 million viewers when first shown in November, 1965. In 1966 it was run again before an estimated audience of 15 million people. That is a total of 30 million Americans—more Americans than visited the Louvre in Paris since George Washington was President.[6]

1. This paragraph is developed chiefly by reasons supported by illustrations. Outline it using this form:

Topic Sentence: ..........................................................
   *BECAUSE:*
     Reason 1: ..........................................................
     Supporting illustration ..........................................
   *BECAUSE:*
     Reason 2: ..........................................................
     Supporting illustrations:
       A. ..............................................................
       B. ..............................................................

[6] Desmond Smith, "The Social Impact of Television," *Electronic Age*, Summer, 1965. Reprinted by permission of *Electronic Age*, Radio Corporation of America.

2. What coherence devices are used in the paragraph? List examples of several methods.

3. Why has the writer inserted *of course* at the beginning of the second sentence? How does it affect the tone? How is it related to the argument presented? Why is the phrase set off by commas?

4. Comment on the relation between "astounding cultural fallout" and "increase in awareness" as "pointers" for this paragraph. To which of these is the support more closely related?

5. Find two examples of antithesis. How does the writer tag them?

6. Why is *yet* (third sentence) followed by a comma? What function does *yet* serve in the sentence? In the paragraph?

7. Why is a semicolon used after *concert* (fifth sentence)?

8. Why is a dash used in the last sentence?


### 6.

The uncanny ability of video to involve the viewer deeply is well known. For example: KQED, a San Francisco educational TV station, ran a half-hour program about Japanese brush painting. Since it was a "how to" program, a young woman producer bought 300 painting kits in anticipation of a moderate viewer response. The station eventually sold a staggering total of 14,000 sets at $3.00 each. And when the H. J. Heinz Company offered a salad recipe book on a single daytime commercial, more than 112,000 viewers wrote in for a copy. When Leonard Bernstein reported the reception the New York Philharmonic Symphony received on one of its recent tours, he said there was "an explanation other than musicianship to explain the extraordinary enthusiasm" of the audience. "You can't imagine," he said, "how we have been gathered in by audiences that obviously know about us through television." There were places where the audiences stood and cheered for minutes before the orchestra even played a note.[7]

1. What is the topic sentence of this paragraph?
2. What is the pointer in the topic sentence?
3. What basic method of development does the author use in this paragraph?
4. Is this paragraph unified? Does any sentence fail to support the pointer in the topic sentence?
5. What means of achieving coherence are used in this paragraph?
6. Why does the author place a colon after *For example?*
7. Why does he quote *how to?*

[7] Smith, "The Social Impact of Television."

8. Why is *half-hour* hyphenated?

9. Why does the author start the quotation, *an explanation other than* . . . , without capitalizing *an?*

10. At the end of the Bernstein quotation, the period is put inside the final quotation mark. Is this practice correct? Which marks are put inside the quotation marks and which outside?

**7.**

Though they are not produced in wide-screen Cinemascope, have never won an Oscar, and cannot be viewed on "Saturday Night at the Movies," electronic films are already smash hits in many important sectors of modern electronics technology. Increasingly, they are being "booked" into television equipment, computer logic and memory circuits, two-way communications systems, missile and spacecraft controls, and of course, pocket radios. In fact, if present trends continue, they may yet make the electronics industry the new "film capital" of the world.

As distinguished from photographic film, electronic films are delicate tattoos of electronically active material condensed, for the most part, from hot vapors onto cold, hard, insulating surfaces such as glass. Depending on the materials used and the manner in which they are deposited, such films— many of them 10 times thinner than the shimmering coat of an ordinary soap bubble—may act singly or in combination as whole electronic circuits or simply as components thereof from transistors, diodes, and oscillators to resistors, capacitors, and interconnection paths.[8]

These are beginning paragraphs from a long article. The first is an introductory paragraph, and the second is a paragraph of definition. Together they form the necessary introduction to the article.

1. What point is to be established in the article? What is the specific thesis statement for the article?

2. Is the introductory paragraph a good one? Why or why not?

3. In the second paragraph, is definition by classification used? If so, where is this definition found?

4. The author uses two other methods to make his definition clear. What are they?

5. In the first paragraph, why does the author use quotation marks around *Saturday Night at the Movies?* Why around *booked?* Why *film capital?* Would any of these be just as effective without the quotation marks?

[8] Bruce Shore, "Electronic Films," *Electronic Age,* Summer, 1966. Reprinted by permission of *Electronic Age,* Radio Corporation of America.

6. In the first paragraph, why are commas placed after *Cinemascope, Oscar,* and *Movies?* Is the comma inside the quotation mark after *Movies* properly placed?

7. In the second paragraph, explain the comma after *film;* after *condensed* and *part;* after *cold* and *hard.*

8. Why are dashes used after *films* and *bubble?* Would commas serve just as well here?

9. What coherence devices are employed in these paragraphs?

10. Analyze sentences for suspension of the subject, verb, or complement.


**8.**

The different international attitudes toward action and violence in children's programs were pointed out when NBC Enterprises co-produced an animated series with Mushi Productions in Japan. It seems the Japanese can comfortably separate reality from fantasy and do not object to a children's program in which death is presented. In one of the co-produced "Astro-Boy" episodes, the story included a highway accident in which a hot-rod driver kills a pedestrian. For syndication in the United States, the plot of the program was softened by skilled translators. Instead of being killed by a hot-rod driver, the pedestrian was slightly hurt in an unavoidable accident. The audience could then identify with the young driver of the automobile and sympathize with both the driver and the pedestrian.[9]

1. What is the topic sentence?

2. What is the pointer in the topic sentence?

3. What is the chief method of developing the topic sentence? What other method is used in combination with it?

4. Can you see any objection to beginning the second sentence with *It seems . . .* ? If so, what might you substitute?

5. Explain the use of a comma after *episodes* in the third sentence, after *United States* in the fourth, and after *driver* in the fifth.

6. Why is *hot-rod* hyphenated?

7. Why is a comma not used before the first *and* in the last sentence?


The next selection is excerpted from an article of about 2500 words. It is, in effect, a five-hundred-word paper within the longer paper, and it establishes one point in support of the thesis of the longer article. Here, in other words, the five-hundred-word paper serves the same function in a 2500-word article as the paragraph does in the shorter paper.

[9] Al Husted, "American Television Abroad," *Electronic Age,* Autumn, 1966. Reprinted by permission of *Electronic Age,* Radio Corporation of America.

**9.**

All of this is by way of saying that the computer will eventually have no less impact on engineers and engineering than gunpowder had on archery. It will be registered in several ways.

For one, the computer is going to intellectualize the practice of engineering to a degree inconceivable until now. In the past, the engineer has resorted to pencil, slide rule, and T-square to fashion his new designs; a machine shop and mechanical skills to develop his prototypes; and a pilot line to evolve their manufacture. Now, in theory, all but the conception of the idea can be accomplished by computer in tandem with automatic tools. Thus, instead of plotting his design on paper, the engineer will reduce it to a mathematical program. Instead of developing a physical prototype, he will construct a mathematical analogue and let it stand for his prototype. In addition, this analogue will take into account not only engineering matters but technological, operational, economic, and environmental factors that may be pertinent. The computer will then be asked to decide, in effect, whether the design is worth building. Waste and inefficiency in the design process will shrink to a minimum, hopefully, and ill-conceived products will never emerge from the computer.

There will be more to it than this, however. The computer will also make it possible for the engineer to consider the whole context in which his new design is to function. It will compel him consciously or unconsciously to think in systems rather than component terms. A greater emphasis on systems design will be in the inevitable result. More and more, the engineer will conceive the system and let the computer work out the components.

Finally, there is the somewhat imponderable but intriguing matter of the modifications and innovations in design which will stem directly from the man-machine interaction that results when he works with a computer. There is a modern anthropological theory that progress is the result of man's interaction with his own tools. It holds that the evolution of civilization has been and is a great boot-strap operation that has seen man invent tools, which experience then causes him to modify and differentiate until ultimately they inspire the invention of still more tools, which then are modified by experience and lead to yet newer tools, and so on.[10]

1. What is the thesis statement of this selection?
2. What is the topic sentence of the second paragraph?
3. What methods of paragraph development are used in the second paragraph?

[10] Bruce Shore, "Computers and Engineers," *Electronic Age,* Winter, 1966/67. Reprinted by permission of *Electronic Age,* Radio Corporation of America.

4. What point is made in the third paragraph? Do you consider this paragraph to be well-developed? Why or why not?
5. What point is made in the fourth paragraph? How is it established?
6. Note that this selection has no concluding statement because it is part of a longer article. Add a concluding statement.
7. How does the author achieve coherence between paragraphs?
8. What coherence devices does he use within paragraphs?
9. In the second sentence of the second paragraph, the author uses two semicolons. Why has he not used commas here?
10. Wherever commas have been used in this selection, explain their use.

The next selection is about twice the length of a five-hundred-word paper and is more argumentative than most expository essays. Read it carefully once to get the main thought; then reread it for tone and other elements of style. After you are through, use the two check sheets (for the whole paper, for basic elements of style) to analyze the selection more closely.

## 10.

### On Whose Side Are the Universities? [11]

**(1)** Ten years ago college kids resented being called kids. Today they call one another kids with pride and solidarity. Today students have power; they do not need to play pretend.

**(2)** What happens in the colleges today may be decisive for the next 30 years. Small but articulate groups of students have attained an astute political consciousness and are promising disruption and rebellion. The Congress—that band of old men two generations removed from reality—is threatening reprisal. A nation founded by an armed revolution and still pledging allegiance to unfulfilled revolutionary principles—like liberty and justice for all—does not wish to educate rebellious students.

**(3)** What, then, is an education for? In the minds of many, a kid who "turns out right" moves into the social network of American industry with an affable smile, an easygoing manner and the reliable, efficient, pragmatic style on which our technological society depends. Hardheaded, realistic and committed to the demands of the present order of things, such a promising young man is encouraged to indulge in sentimentalities about defending freedom.

**(4)** One sees his friends in combat: crew-cut, clear-eyed, soft-spoken, de-

[11] Michael Novak, "On Whose Side Are the Universities?" Reprinted from *Christianity and Crisis*, October 14, 1968. Copyright 1968 by Christianity and Crisis, Inc.

termined. One sees them everywhere in the universities: clean-shaven, hard-working, bright, smooth. These are the "silent students," not represented by the radicals who dominate the news; for there is nothing new about them. The American educational system has been geared to turning out millions of them.

**(5)** What is an education for? To keep the clocks ticking, the factories humming and the planes flying? To keep American democracy strong? To keep the young loyal? To teach them to be happy with bread and circuses?

**(6)** The liberal answer to that question during the past 30 years has been to use the schools as agencies of progressive political and social enlightenment. And, indeed, public opinion polls regularly show a marked correlation between length of education and progressive views. But the liberal solution was a compromise with the ongoing system. Against utopianism and apocalypse, liberalism under Franklin D. Roosevelt chose pragmatic adjustment from within the system. The fruits have been many. But the compromise appears, now, to have broken down. The evidence is the malaise felt almost everywhere.

**(7)** The public schools are supported by public money and the private schools are supported by industry and government. How can such schools prepare students to be revolutionaries? How can any system prepare young people to transcend itself? The problem is even more vexing than the problem the institutional church must face: how to catechize prophets. For in the society at large, all the wealth, power and force of arms of the social system are preserving the system on its present course.

**(8)** Where revolutionary criticism is neither promoted nor heeded, moreover, those who strike the revolutionary pose for its own sake—desiring neither power nor its responsibilities but inner exaltation—are difficult to distinguish from genuine men of power. Without the hot-blooded, the romantic and the profoundly confused, on the other hand, no revolution can proceed. A revolution is not an act of reflection but of passion. Tom Paine's instability is not an argument against the validity of 1776, and it is unfair to discredit the present revolution merely by denouncing its tactics or the personalities of some of its leaders.

**(9)** Do we want a political revolution in the United States, a serious rearrangement of the bases of power, wealth and prestige? That is the fundamental educational question. If we do not want a serious revolution, then we should allow our various educational systems to function as they are. The logic of such a political choice would lead us to: (a) squash the student revolutionaries forcibly, or (b) co-opt their energies in pseudo-revolutionary programs (place them on committees). Generally, it is the liberal administrator who is the slowest to grasp the force and the origin of such logic. That is why he is the most hateful in the students' eyes.

**(10)** There has not been much serious revolutionary passion in the U.S. since the days of Reinhold Niebuhr's *The End of an Era*. But the doors of the Pandora's box closed by World War II have again flown open. Can a capitalistic democracy possibly serve the ideals of "freedom and justice for all"? Or is the whole system inherently contradictory?

**(11)** When young radicals close down one or another university during this school year or next, it would be a mistake to imagine that merely procedural issues are at stake. A streamlining of the administrative process or functional adjustments that relieve the pressure at concrete points of protest will not meet the issue. (In liberal pragmatic theory, issues are swiftly reduced to functional, operational terms.) The revolution that has begun on the campuses is not raising a procedural issue; it is substantive.

**(12)** That revolutionary issue has two parts. In the first place, the crew-cut, affable American is not an attractive human type. He is repressed, empty, quietly and blindly savage, without an interior life, boring and bored. The first substantive issue has to do with inhibitions, repressions and diminished imaginative and affective capacities.

**(13)** In the second place, the revolutionary issue is concerned with economics, technology, the mass media and political machinery. What is good for Texas money does not, clearly, promote "freedom and justice for all." The "law and order" that police forces now defend does cruel and arrogant violence to too huge a number of human beings; it is not tolerable. The interests that dominate social and political decision-making in the U.S. are unfaithful to the revolutionary ideals on which this country is founded.

**(14)** Faced with such a revolution, on whose side are the universities? And do they dare to say so? There is no other basic educational issue.

1. This paper should be compared with the "Law and Order" paper at the end of Chapter 1 (page 21). Their methods of arrangement and development are quite different. Make a list of similarities and differences. (Check the rest of the questions in this exercise for ideas.)

2. In what ways is the first paragraph designed to gain reader attention and agreement? Does it succeed for you? Why or why not? (See also question 10.)

3. What is the purpose of the last sentence in the second paragraph? What is the purpose of paragraphs twelve, thirteen, and fourteen at the end?

4. Make a list of modifiers and judgment words (for example, *disruption, soft-spoken, loyal, hot-blooded*) that give away the basic tone of the paper. How would you describe this tone? (List at least three or four descriptive words and be prepared to support your list.)

5. How could you combine the first two paragraphs into one strong unit? Would it be possible to combine the third, fourth, and fifth paragraphs? What, if anything, would you omit?

6. According to paragraph three, on what kind of young man does "our technological society depend"? Do you agree with the statement? Why or why not? Can you find a similar problem in the fourth paragraph?

7. Does the paper contain any unsupported generalizations? List five, together with suggestions for making each more specific. (Be sure to consider stereotypes.)

8. Is the topic sentence in paragraph nine an accurate restatement of the thesis statement of paragraph one? How are these two sentences similar? Different?

9. This writer places the "system" on one side in a fight for change. Whom does he place on the opposing side? Do you agree with this two-part division? Why or why not? (Be sure to consider the paper's title and last paragraph.)

10. List some of the psychological and ethical appeals used by the writer. (Refresh your memory by rereading pages 76 and 77.) Do these appeals work for you? Why or why not?

11. Using the check sheet for style as a guide, comment on the diction and sentences in this paper. List your observations and be prepared to support them.

12. Use the simplified check sheet for the whole paper (page 122) to evaluate the thought, organization, tone, and mechanics of this paper. Does this evaluation fit your first impression of this paper? Why or why not? List your observations and be prepared to support them.

Also about twice the length of a five-hundred-word paper, this next essay presents special problems in meaning and tone. Even a quick reading should tell you that the "writer's voice" in the essay does not directly present the author's meaning. Read it carefully to decide what its main points are; then reread for tone and other elements of style using the two check sheets as a guide (for the whole paper, for basic elements of style).

## 11.

### Unsolicited Opening Day Address by Prexy [12]

(1) Ladies and gentlemen, welcome—and welcome back—to Diehard University. I shall start the academic year by describing the contract you have entered into by the act of enrolling in this university. That contract is clearly

---

[12] John Ciardi, "Unsolicited Opening Day Address by Prexy." First appeared in *Saturday Review,* September 28, 1968. Copyright 1968 by Saturday Review, Inc. Reprinted with permission of author and publication.

set forth in the university catalogue, but since literacy is no longer prerequisite to admission, let me lip-read the essential points of our agreement. As you emerge from this convocation you will be handed a digest of these remarks in attractively prepared comic-book form with all dialogue limited to basic English and with the drawings carefully designed to help you over any grammatical difficulties. Those of you, moreover, for whom the requirements of Sub-Literacy One have been waived, may dial AV for Audio Visual, followed by 0016, and a dramatized explication will appear on your TV sets.

**(2)** Diehard, as you know, is no longer dedicated to excellence. The trustees, the administration, the faculty, and the federal government—not necessarily in that order—have concurred that excellence has been outnumbered. The restated policy of Diehard University is simply to salvage what it can from what little it gets from the too much being thrust upon it.

**(3)** We recognize that the achievement of any given intellectual standard is no longer prerequisite to a bachelor's degree. The insistence of any educational institution is defined by its minimum standards, and Diehard no longer has any. As a contractual agreement, the faculty undertake to confer a bachelor's degree upon you in acknowledgment of four years of attendance.

**(4)** If you are willing to settle for that degree, I suggest you do not waste money on textbooks. The presence of a textbook may tempt you to open it. The psychological consequences are obvious: if you must actually open a textbook in order to meet nonexistent minimum standards, how will you ever be sure you are not a moron? Your whole future career could be warped, in such a case, by guilt and uncertainty. Our educational activities, let me say, are so organized that any member of the in- or out-group of the affluent society can stroll through them in the intervals between political rallies, draft-card burnings, love-ins, water fights, sit-ins, sit-outs, sympathy marches, student elections, anti-raids and generalized adolescent glandular upheavals. These programs have been carefully constructed to assist your social development as students. I urge them upon you as the social duty of every minimalist. Diehard would serve no purpose were it to allow an intemperate emphasis on learning to deflect its minimalists from the fullness of their undergraduate social development and thus, indirectly, from future computerization.

**(5)** To further that social development, Diehard imposes no rules of extracurricular behavior. We shall not act *in loco parentis*. With a mild shudder of revulsion, we return that function to your legal parents. We have problems enough with our own failures and cannot accept as ours the genetic failures of others.

**(6)** This university has eliminated dormitories. Where you live, with whom you live, and what you do off campus are matters between you and your parents, or between you and the police, as the case may be.

**(7)** You are free to demonstrate on all matters of conviction, or, simply, on all matters. For your convenience we have set aside a fireproof, waterproof, open-occupancy convention center called Hyde Park Hall. You are free to occupy it and to harangue in or from it at your pleasure. You have full license for all noncriminal acts that occur in Hyde Park Hall. Any criminal actions you may engage in there will be, of course, between you and the police.

**(8)** Should you choose to act unlawfully in any of the otherwise assigned buildings of the university, you will be warned once that your actions are unlawful, and the police will then be summoned to take normal action against a breach of the peace.

**(9)** The university will seek your advice on all matters of student organization, social development of the university, and community relations. We shall seek that advice temperately and with as much open-mindedness as we can achieve in our senility. In seeking it, however, we do not pledge ourselves to be bound by it. Where your views seem to be reasoned, they will be honored in reason; where they seem intemperate or shortsighted, they will be rejected in reason. A faculty-student board will be elected to study all grievances.

**(10)** In no case, however, will that board, or any body of this university, consider a general amnesty as a condition for ending a demonstration that violates lawful procedure.

**(11)** Diehard will not consider any request made by a minimalist for changes in the curriculum, faculty, or academic qualification. On these matters we ask nothing from you and we will hear nothing.

**(12)** We do confess to a vestigial nostalgia for the long-honored and now outmoded idea of the university as a bookish community of learning. While most of you are pursuing your social development, therefore, the faculty will direct such students as are inclined to volunteer for it, in a course of study leading to the degree of Laureate in Arts or in Science. We shall continue to grant the Bachelor's degree in Arts or in Science without requirement, though to assist your social development we do invite you to attend various discussion groups to be held at carefully spaced intervals.

**(13)** With those who elect the Laureate program, the university insists on a different contract. It insists that in the act of electing such a program, the student will have submitted himself to the faculty as candidate for a degree to be conferred at the discretion of the faculty. The faculty, having already thrown away minimums, must insist on reserving to itself the right to formulate maximums for those who are willing to reach for them. It is the student's business to qualify, or to revert (without prejudice), to the social development program leading to the degree of Bachelor.

**(14)** I ask all those who are interested in a course of study to return tomorrow to start our further discussions. The rest of you may now return to your pads to drop out, turn on, and tune in. If you are arrested between now and your graduation, the university will credit the time up to your conviction toward your attendance and will do its best to readmit you upon completion of your sentence. By decision of the board of trustees, days of attendance completed while out on bail pending an appeal will be counted toward a degree.

**(15)** If the police, that is, are willing to let you out of jail, and if you are willing to check in on the roster, we are willing to keep the attendance records and to grant appropriate degrees upon satisfaction of the requirement.

**(16)** We are not willing to have our reading and discussion time interrupted by protest, no matter how passionate, that breaks the law. Nor are we willing to police the law. Criminality is the proper concern of the police; ours, we believe, is reasoned discussion. When the discussion goes beyond reason and to the point of interfering with the curriculum of those who have chosen one, we reserve the right to suspend or to expel you from the hazy premises of our failing venture into education for those few who are interested in the unlikely.

**(17)** Hello. Goodbye. And may your standardization be your fulfillment.

1. What "role" has the poet-critic John Ciardi assumed as he writes this essay? If you didn't have the essay title, how could you tell?
2. List a number of reasons for Ciardi's use of the name "Diehard University." Is the "speaker" within the essay "for" or "against" Diehard U.? How can you tell? Is Ciardi "for" or "against" Diehard U.? How can you tell? (See question 4.)
3. What is the effect of the *I-you* relationship established at the beginning and carried throughout? List other words and phrases that add to the conversational tone. (Consider the shift from *I* to *we*.)
4. Irony is a device used by writers who want to say one thing but mean another. How can you tell that Ciardi is using irony? (Consider such things as overstatement, understatement, and departure from the reader's expectations.) If the writer is being ironical, how can you tell what he means? Is it possible that the president of Diehard U. (the "speaker") is also being ironical? Explain your views.
5. List as many words and phrases as you can that seem to be overstatements (for example, *comic-book form, four years of attendance, moron, minimalist, diehard, full license, senility, without requirement*).
6. What is the function of the first three paragraphs? (Consider problems of introduction, tone, and thesis statement.)

7. What are the main points made in paragraphs four through thirteen? Could you justify the use of so many short paragraphs? Could some of them be combined?

8. How do paragraphs fourteen through seventeen tie the paper together? Are they a conclusion?

9. List a number of reasons why the last sentence in the essay may be considered its most important one.

10. Does Ciardi depend on stereotypes to make his exaggerations clear? List some examples.

11. When you are through reading this essay, do you "identify with" the speaker ("I"), the students addressed ("you"), or the writer (Ciardi)? Or none of these? Explain your views.

12. Using the check sheet for style as a guide, comment on the diction and sentences in this paper. List your observations and be prepared to support them.

13. Use the simplified check sheet for the whole paper (page 122) to evaluate the thought, organization, tone, and mechanics of this essay. Does this evaluation fit your first impression of this paper? Why or why not? List your observations and be prepared to support them.

14. This selection is neither expository nor purely argumentative. The irony makes it *satire*. Check the word *satire* in a good dictionary and be prepared to write an extended definition of this kind of writing.

# Index